Previous praise for David Block's *Baseball before We Knew It: A Search for the Roots of the Game*

"A joyfully discursive romp through the history of ball sports and a compelling new theory of the game's origins."—*New York Times Book Review*

"A deliciously researched feast. . . . Block has assembled such a rich pile of evidence for the game's European origins that one might wonder why there ever was a controversy. . . . Once an American reader gets past the disappointment of discovering baseball's deep European roots, Block's book is a perfect delight. He has unearthed magnificent medieval manuscripts . . . that show that baseball is just the latest in a very long line of stick-and-ball games."—**Charles Hirshberg,** *Sports Illustrated*

"*Baseball before We Knew It* is a rare piece of historical research that transforms the historical landscape. It is also elegantly written and lightened with a subtle humor. No one who makes any claim to being a baseball historian or a student of the game can go forward without Block's stunning work."—*Sports Literature Association*

"An amusing and comprehensive look at the surprisingly long and complex lineage of our national pastime. The book is dizzyingly detailed in spots, with exhaustive descriptions of dozens of old English ballgames, but as the author plumbs the murky depths of the game's origins, he turns up bizarre footnotes and conspiracies and unravels the agendas of earlier baseball historians."—*American Heritage*

"This is without question the book for anyone at all interested in the history of the world's greatest game or, for that matter, in the manufacture of history."—*Boston Globe*

"Block is so thorough in his research, so meticulous in documenting his sources, and so generous in acknowledging his predecessors that it's hard to imagine anyone having done more impressive work on this subject—ever."—**David Shiner,** *Elysian Fields Quarterly*

"Block's book obviates the need for any other analysis of baseball's origins and roots. Including the illustrations that go back to the fourteenth-century manuscripts in the Bodleian Library emphasizing pre–Civil War sources, this one volume contains everything regarding the history of the origin of the American national pastime. Myths are debunked, fables are demystified, and in the end one is left with a comprehensive and convincing historical record."—*Choice*

"*Baseball before We Knew It* is an important book, erudite, entertaining, and truly groundbreaking. David Block goes beyond debunking the game's creation myths to creating a knowledge base upon which all future research will rely. This brilliant book takes a place on my shelf alongside Seymour, Voigt, and Henderson."—**John Thorn, editor of** *Total Baseball*

"*Baseball before We Knew It* is a magnificent piece of work that puts an end to the myths and errors that have clouded our understanding of where and how our national game began and developed. With this definitely settled, we are now also clear about the source and cause of the previous notions—altogether a masterpiece of research agreeably presented."—**Jacques Barzun, author of** *From Dawn to Decadence: 500 Years of Western Cultural Life—1500 to the Present*

"Masterfully researched and extraordinarily well-documented."
—*College and Research Libraries News*

Pastime Lost

◆

Pastime Lost

The Humble, Original, and
Now Completely Forgotten
Game of English Baseball

◆

DAVID BLOCK

University of Nebraska Press
Lincoln

Parts of chap. 1 were first published in "A Peek into the *Pocket-book*," in *Base Ball: A Journal of the Early Game* 2, no. 1 (Spring 2008): 17–28; parts of chap. 3 were first published in "The Story of William Bray's Diary" *in Base Ball: A Journal of the Early Game* 1, no. 2 (Fall 2007): 5–11; parts of chap. 7 were first published in the article "Batting Next . . . Jane Austen," in *This Diamond Isle* 1 (2014): 12–19.

Library of Congress Cataloging-in-Publication Data
Names: Block, David, 1944–, author.
Title: Pastime lost: the humble, original, and now completely forgotten game of English baseball / David Block.
Description: Lincoln: University of Nebraska Press, 2019.
| Includes bibliographical references and index.
Identifiers: LCCN 2018040942
ISBN 9781496208514 (hardback)
ISBN 9781496214140 (epub)
ISBN 9781496214157 (mobi)
Subjects: LCSH: Baseball—England—History. | England—Social life and customs—18th century. | England—Social life and customs—19th century.
BISAC: Sports & Recreation / Baseball / History. | History / Europe / Great Britain.
Classification: LCC GV863.44.A1 B56 2019 | DDC 796.3570941—dc23 LC record available at https://lccn.loc.gov/2018040942.

Set in Garamond Premier Pro by Mikala R. Kolander

To my parents' memory, and to Ori's future

Contents

Illustrations

Preface

My first (and only) previous book, *Baseball before We Knew It*, rolled off the presses in 2005 and quickly began arriving in the hands of friends, family members, fellow historians, and the general public. Shortly thereafter I found myself on the receiving end of several persistent questions, such as: "What will your next book be?" And "When's your next book coming out?" This hasn't stopped. Well over a decade later I'm still asked the same questions. My reaction to them is complicated. Partly I'm annoyed and a little defensive—why should I have to write another book? Can't the first one stand on its own? Then my more rational self wades in to acknowledge that inquiring about a second book is not an unreasonable question to ask an author. Moreover, it's somewhat flattering, suggesting that my inquisitors liked my first book and are looking forward to a second. To be honest, the real reason these questions about a second book began to bug me is that they stirred up feelings of guilt. For years my continuing research efforts had been turning up scads of new data, and I knew that I needed to devise a way to make those findings accessible to others. I had it in mind to package them in a new book, and yet I never quite managed to get around to writing it. Getting tweaked by questions about it only reminded me of my procrastination. In fairness to me, the reasons for delaying the project were more than simple laziness or writer's block, although those certainly played a part. More consequential was that I found myself struggling over how to organize the book, never quite able to settle on a clear way forward.

One problem was my subject—English baseball. Let's face it, the game has not been among the topics that you, my readers, have been clamoring to learn about. This reality led me into endless discussions with myself for how best to introduce it to you. Complicating matters was that, despite discovering numerous mentions of English baseball in books, newspapers, and other media spanning more than 150 years, few of those findings provided much descriptive content about the game. I was confronting a situation where my desire to write a book highlighting a trove of new discoveries about a little-known pastime was imperiled by a shortage of material to fill it with. In hopes of circumventing this problem, I tested out a couple of alternate strategies. One was to make the book less about English baseball and more about me. It would describe my voyage of discovery—how I set off to uncover the mysteries of English baseball while experiencing many exciting adventures along the way. This seemed promising—very Bill Bryson–like. But after toying with the idea for a while I decided it really wasn't for me. For one, I never kept a journal of my various travels in Britain and my memories of people, places, and dates have become somewhat muddled. Besides, my first priority was to illuminate English baseball, and I worried that this goal would be short-changed inside a glorified travelogue.

Another approach I considered was to organize the book around various themes and subtopics about English baseball. This might include chapters on the game's relationship to social class, gender, and geography, how it was treated by churches, schools, and civic organizations, where it fit within the hierarchy of other sports and pastimes, and so on. This seemed feasible because the new references to English baseball I had uncovered often provided greater insight into those sorts of things than into details of the game itself. Ultimately, though, I rejected this strategy because I couldn't figure out how to shoehorn some of my more important discoveries into it.

And then there's the brainstorm of my dear wife, Barbara, who proposed scrapping the constraints of nonfiction altogether to write a novel populated by some of the real-life characters who were known to be associated with English baseball, such as Frederick, Prince of

Wales, and Jane Austen. This was a tempting avenue given that I could take more liberties with a fictional approach while trying to stay faithful to the underlying history. But I also know my capabilities, and writing fiction and having it ring authentic are almost certainly not among them. I felt obliged to decline this suggestion, notwithstanding the risk of spousal disappointment.

Okay, what was I left with? Apparently the most conventional approach possible, a chronological history of English baseball. This was destined from the start to be a little lopsided, since much of the juicier stuff with the best backstories happened to fall in the eighteenth and early nineteenth centuries, while the references to English baseball I could document from later years, though far more plentiful, were not necessarily as compelling. (I hope I'm not deluding myself into thinking any of it is compelling.) Anyway, for better or worse, that's the strategy I chose. But don't despair. Littered throughout this chronology are many aspects of the various discarded approaches described above (minus the fictional one—sorry, Barbara!). All in all, I hope the end results fulfill the minimum goals I set out for myself: to gather my research on the hidden history of English baseball, make it available in an accessible format, and to do so in a way that readers might find instructive and entertaining. Time will tell whether I've succeeded.

Acknowledgments

A project like this could never have come to fruition without the encouragement and contributions of many colleagues, friends, family, and even the occasional stranger. To all of them I offer my utmost thanks. I am especially indebted to Brian Turner, John Bowman, Rick Huhn, Lawrence Hourahane, Andy Weltch, and Rob Garratt, who took the time to pore over various drafts of this work and offer their observations and suggestions, all of which led to a more cohesive and coherent final product. In Brian's case, his editorial acumen is exceeded only by his attention to historical nuance, and I benefited greatly from his expertise in both of those realms.

Thanks to Rob Taylor, Courtney Ochsner, Ann Baker, other staff members at the University of Nebraska Press, and copyeditor Elaine Otto, for making the entire process of moving this book through to the finish line as smooth and painless as possible.

My appreciation also extends to the following individuals whose words or efforts, great or small, helped propel my project in myriad ways: Elizabeth Johnston and Jonah Gabry for their research assistance; Fiona Karet and Mike Frankl for being my away-from-home London family by generously hosting me in their Camden Town flat conveniently located near the British Library; Sam Marchiano for inviting me to join and participate in her MLB video project that led to the William Bray diary adventure and the wonderful film *Base Ball Discovered*; Tricia St. John Barry for uncovering the diary and bringing it to our attention; Julian Pooley for lending his expertise and the resources of the Surrey History Centre to help validate and illuminate the two early Surrey baseball discoveries, the Bray diary and the 1749 game at Lord Middlesex's estate; Joe Gray, Martin Hoerchner, and John and Kay Price for benefiting me with their knowledge and encouragement during my travels to the UK; Jan Jones and Diana Edgecombe, the strangers on a train who introduced me to British baseball; Dale Melcher and Bill Newman for teasing me through my writer's block; the members of my baseball writing group for their suggestions and counsel; the many archivists and librarians in the UK who cheerfully aided this eccentric American who, for some reason, was researching baseball in their country; and Larry McCray, John Thorn, Monica Nucciarone, Peter Mancuso, Rob Fitts, Tom Shieber, Duke Goldman, Jean Ardell, Marlene Volgelsang, Bill Humber, and many other SABR colleagues and friends too numerous to name, for their friendship, advice, and support over the years.

Throughout the many years that I spent researching and writing this book, I was the beneficiary of a loving and patient family that tolerated my curious obsession with such an arcane topic. To Maggie, Jamie, Kelly, Frankie, and Linda, to my brothers Philip, Joel, and Mike, and to the rest of my Southern California and Northern California families, as well as all my non-SABR friends, I am immeasurably grateful for your never ending support and cheer. Finally and preeminently, I am forever indebted to my cheerful, intelligent, and truly virtuous wife, Barbara, without whose love and encouragement this project would never have happened.

Introduction

One day in 1908, Alice West, a thirteen-year-old English schoolgirl living near the town of Lewes in East Sussex, noticed that her local newspaper was sponsoring a children's essay contest. Alice liked to write, and since the topic for the contest—outdoor sports—appealed to her, she sat down and composed a piece entitled "The Value of Open-Air Games" and posted it to the paper. Happily for her, the entry won first prize, and the paper published it in its following issue. Alice wrote: "Most people, especially children, like to play games, such as football, hockey, cricket and tennis, which are all healthy games. The most favourite game among boys at our school is the game of hockey or soldiers. Our governess and teacher tell us how important health is, for there is nothing more dearer than our lives. Skipping, baseball, hoops, rounders, fox and hounds, and rings are the usual games for the girls."[1]

These thoughts of young Alice's may have charmed the contest judges but would be unremarkable today save for one curious inclusion: her naming baseball as one of the "usual games" played by girls at her school. That Britons were playing some form of baseball in 1908 is not, in itself, the unexpected element in Alice's statement. The game by then was far from unknown in the country. As early as 1870, a Scotsman who became enamored of baseball while living in the United States returned to his Highlands home near Inverness and formed a club with some of his neighbors to practice the sport. Then, in 1890, following the widely publicized tour of American ball players to Britain a year earlier, a small league of professional baseball clubs began play in the English Midlands. These and other efforts to implant the American game, however, remained sporadic and only marginally successful. Many of the players making up the rosters of the new clubs were borrowed footballers or athletes from other sports who were recruited and drafted into the baseball scene, but their loyalty to the newly introduced pastime was never very solid. Britons, on the whole, seemed reluctant to embrace the national sport of their former colonists across the Atlantic. American baseball, as observed by British sport historians who have studied the late Victorian era, failed to make any significant inroads into that nation's popular culture. It was rarely if ever seen in the schoolyards, village greens, and weekend picnic grounds where ordinary British citizens pursued their recreations.

American-style baseball was not, however, the only form of the game to be found in Great Britain at the turn of the twentieth century. There were at least two others. One was a unique pastime that had taken hold in the second half of the nineteenth century among working men in major seaports along the west coast of the island, including Cardiff, Liverpool, Bristol, and Glasgow. This sport was originally known as rounders and had derived from the children's bat and ball game of the same name. In 1892, however, all the major associations that governed the play of this working men's version of rounders abruptly changed its name to baseball, apparently to distinguish it from its juvenile namesake. Newly anointed as baseball, the sport retained a loyal following in its home territory on the west coast of Britain, but was virtually unknown in the counties of southern England such as Sussex where Alice West lived. It would not have been one of the "usual games" she and her classmates played at school. Because the clubs playing this formerly rounders version were located in Wales and Scotland, as well as in England, I've labeled it "British baseball" so as not to confuse it with other forms of the pastime.

That leaves one remaining candidate, one that up until the past decade I never would have dreamed to find alive and well in a 1908 East Sussex schoolyard. I call this version "English baseball" to differentiate it from the other variations named above. It was the oldest baseball of all, dating at least as far back as the 1740s. I wrote about this game in my 2005 book, *Baseball before We Knew It,* where I concluded it was almost certainly the ancestor of America's National Pastime. Back then, my research into English baseball was only just beginning, and I had yet to gain more than a very limited understanding of its elusive history. Indeed, some of my assumptions about it later proved to be just plain wrong. One of those was my estimate that the original game of English baseball had vanished by the middle of the nineteenth century. That calculation turns out to be spectacularly mistaken. English baseball, I've discovered to my amazement, not only prospered beyond the midpoint of the nineteenth century but continued to be played to the end of that century and beyond. Almost certainly the "usual game" of baseball that Alice West wrote about in her 1908 essay was this very same pastime. From beginning to end, English baseball had survived—completely under the radar—for at least 165 years. Despite this, and notwithstanding the slowly emerging historical record it left in its wake, almost no one in Britain today, or anywhere else for that matter, knows anything about the game or that it even existed.

By choosing the title *Pastime Lost* for this work I intend to highlight this most mystifying aspect of English baseball: that a game which by all indications was popular and widely played in parts of England for many generations, and which died out relatively recently by historical standards, could have so totally vanished from memory. Oh, I can understand why the average citizen of Britain today might not be familiar with it. After all, it was never anything close to being a major sport, nor is there any sign it was ever governed by formal organization or written rules. English baseball was mainly a country game, played casually in the towns and villages of the rural counties surrounding London. In the metropolis itself and in other sizable cities it was relatively unknown, even in its own time. In short, it's not the type of sport that might have made a heavy mark on history or spawned traditions and legends that might have carried down through the generations.

But what's puzzling is that it's not just the average Briton who has no recollection or awareness of English baseball. I've discovered that most scholars who study the history of folk games, sports, and leisure activities in the United Kingdom are equally unfamiliar with it. And it's not as if the game was so obscure that none of them could ever have come across it. In my own research I've found close to four hundred references to it. I suspect others could have encountered some of these same examples but not grasped what they were seeing. If you've never heard of English baseball, and then you come across the word *baseball* in some old document, you might naturally assume it to be a reference to the American version of the game.

My fascination with English baseball has multiplied over the past decade as I've uncovered more and more about its curiously shrouded history. Initially I was aware of only a handful of references to it, and I subordinated them to my broader mission of unravelling the origins of American baseball. Back then I considered the original English version of baseball to be essentially identical to the game of rounders. My theory was that the eighteenth-century name *baseball* gradually gave way in England to the name *rounders* in the early nineteenth century. In recent years, as ever more information about the pastime has come to my attention, I've realized that I was wrong. There is now no doubt in my mind that English baseball and rounders were distinct games.

What made it possible for me to gather scads of new information about English baseball was the revolutionary emergence in the past dozen years of searchable, full-text digital databases of historic books and newspapers. Almost none of these databases were available to me while researching my first book, for which I relied on the old methods of hopping from bookshelf to bookshelf and library to library, and spending endless, eye-straining hours bent over microfilm readers. As others who utilize these new databases will attest, the ability to scan in seconds what could never have been done previously in a lifetime has proved to be a windfall for research. As these new sources brought more and more evidence of English baseball to the fore, my whole picture of the game transformed. No longer could I view it simply as an obscure, eighteenth-century ancestor of American baseball. Instead I came to appreciate it as having a long and active life of its own.

In modern usage, the term *baseball* is spelled just as you see it, as a single word. Those familiar with the early history of the game will know that that wasn't always the case. In North America, up until the end of the nineteenth century, it typically appeared in print as two words (*base ball*). In England, editors often placed a hyphen between the words (*base-ball*), although *baseball* and *base ball* occasionally showed up there as well. And then there were the alternate spellings, the most common being *bass-ball*. This was an outgrowth of the perennial confusion among some spellers over the words *base* and *bass* (as in bass violin) because of their identical pronunciations. Another somewhat common spelling found in England was *baste-ball*. Its origin is unknown, but likely derived from sounding similar to baseball or from the verb *to baste* meaning "to strike or beat." Both alternate spellings appear with some regularity in English books and newspapers from the eighteenth century onward. In short, until the twentieth century, a Briton could expect no uniformity in how the word *baseball* might appear in one's reading material. To navigate this shifting playing field and to avoid confusion, I've settled on the spelling *baseball* as my standard in this work, to be used in all instances except where I am quoting directly from a historical source.

In this book I will tell the story of English baseball as I know it. Unfortunately, it is not a full picture, because there are still many aspects of the game that are unknown. For those who have read my first book and are looking for a sequel, you may be disappointed. Specifically, there is very little in this book about American baseball. Also, please be advised that in this new volume I have found the occasional need to repeat information from previous writings, but I have tried to keep such redundancies to a minimum. And for those of you looking for rich, descriptive accounts of English baseball, its rulebooks, or its rosters of players and teams, you may equally be let down. Virtually none of that sort of information can be found anywhere in the existing historical record. Instead, I will mete out my story of the game in the best way I am able, by identifying the places and contexts in which it was played, by entering the lives of some of the people who wrote about English baseball or are known to have enjoyed it, and by analyzing and drawing conclusions from the many references to the game I have documented over the years. By touching all of these points and by embellishing them with other digressions as my whims dictate, I hope to acquaint you with this long neglected original member of the baseball family.

Pastime Lost

◆

1

A Little Pretty Debut

This book is about English baseball. I realize that many of you have never heard of this game, and in that you're not alone. To most people, the terms *baseball* and *English* are an odd pairing, an oxymoron. You may be forgiven for thinking that somehow I've got it all backward, that Americans are the ones who practice baseball while the English are attached to their own traditional sports of cricket and rounders. This is true, of course, but once upon a time the English enjoyed playing baseball as well, albeit their own version of the game. In fact, theirs was the earliest form of baseball, the ancestor to both American baseball and rounders. For some strange reason, however, England's memory of its baseball experience has faded over the years to the point where knowledge of the game has now disappeared. Fear not. You're in the hands of the world's foremost expert on English baseball. I hope you're no less impressed when I acknowledge that I am also the world's *only* expert on English baseball; indeed, I am among a scant few who know anything about the game at all. What follows is the never-before-told history of this forgotten pastime. Any omissions or shortcomings you may come across while reading it, I regret to say, were unavoidable. They're the inevitable by-product of deciding that after fifteen years of research it was high time to put what I've learned into writing, well aware that unknowns about the game still abound. Nevertheless, English baseball has been crying out to have its story told, and this book should provide you with a good sense of what this lost pastime was all about.

In telling the story of English baseball it seems fitting to start at the beginning. My problem is that I don't know when that beginning actually began. I can't even narrow it to a range of several decades. Absent this, I have become accustomed to offering a hazy response to the question of when baseball began, usually accompanied by equally ambiguous answers to the questions of how and where this germination took place. English baseball evolved—or so I've said—from earlier games of ball, a process that played out somewhere in the south of England, sometime in the early eighteenth century or perhaps the late seventeenth. My theory has been that youthful ballplayers were forever tinkering with their games, trying to improve them, and at some unknown time, probably in the early 1700s, some small number of them settled on a method of play that became the ancestor of all baseball-like activity to follow. The fundamentals of this new entity, such as pitching, striking the ball, fielding, and baserunning, were borrowed willy-nilly from other games that were familiar to them at the time, or so I've always believed and advocated. At some point in this process they assigned the name *baseball* to the new pastime.

To me, this is all very plausible, but in all candidness, it is educated guesswork. I don't have any actual proof that the elements of baseball were adapted from earlier games. And I am only estimating when I say that the pastime originated in the early eighteenth century; for all I know it could have been a century earlier than that. My naming of southern England as baseball's home territory is also an assumption, based solely on where the earliest known signs of the game emerged. Who knows? Maybe baseball evolved somewhere else entirely, such as France or Germany, and then journeyed to England so stealthily that it went unnoticed by history. Coming right down to it, I have no real evidence that baseball evolved at all. Who's to say it wasn't invented? Sure, Abner Doubleday lived a century too late and was otherwise incapable of having done it.[1] But why couldn't some clever English youngster have been the one to conceive and sketch out a plan for baseball? Improbable, perhaps, but we really have no way of proving it didn't happen that way.

Apart from all this guessing and second-guessing, we do know one thing for certain: a game called baseball existed in England in the middle of the eighteenth century. For this we have solid proof. My conjectural theories of what came before—of how, where, and when the game first evolved—are extrapolated from this evidence, which consists of scattered mentions of a game identified as baseball that appear in English written sources of the 1740s, 1750s, and 1760s. The original media for these references are varied: handwritten documents, a novel, a children's book, a dictionary, and a newspaper squib. They all emerged from the south of England and reveal that, in those early years, adults and children, male and female, were playing the game. The diversity of these references suggests to me that English baseball at the midpoint of the eighteenth century had not just freshly arrived. My estimation of an earlier origin, sometime around the start of the 1700s, rests on the notion that it would have taken several decades for a new game to achieve even the modest level of acceptance it appears to have gained by midcentury. It's possible, of course, that I'm wrong about that. Baseball could have started up suddenly around 1740 and become an instant sensation. Then again, its origin may go back decades or centuries earlier than any of us have imagined but left no evidence behind to clue us in.

My assumption that baseball took shape over time through young English experimenters mixing and matching elements of earlier games is a reasonable one and certainly more likely than the alternative— that baseball was the inspired invention of some unknown genius. I never considered the latter possibility while writing *Baseball before We Knew It*, probably because I was occupied with rooting out American baseball's stubborn and numerous origins myths, including loose ends of the Doubleday story. In the book I thumbed through a roster of possible predecessor games to baseball, highlighting some of their individual features that might have contributed to its evolution. I observed that some forms of a popular early British pastime named stool-ball involved baserunning around a circuit. I also noted that players of another widely played game called trap-ball utilized a bat similar to American baseball's. Of all the possible ancestors, I speculated that a little-known pastime called tut-ball may have been the most influential. As for cricket, its resemblance to baseball leads to the obvious assumption that the two occupy proximate branches on the same family tree, although neither then nor since have I found any direct evidence that either sport influenced the development of the other. Now, fourteen years since my first book was published, and notwithstanding the several new discoveries of English baseball in the eighteenth century I've made in the interim, my basic guesstimate—that English baseball came into being through trial and error—has advanced very little. It will continue to remain an unproven hypothesis until I, or someone else, can produce solid, contemporary evidence showing that such a process actually transpired.

While we're at it, I should address another unproven hypothesis about English baseball, albeit one so robustly self-evident that I doubt anyone would challenge it barring the emergence of some stunning new proof. By this I am referring to the presumption that English baseball is, if not the immediate ancestor, then certainly a direct ancestor of American baseball. It is obvious and natural to assume a familial connection between the two, notwithstanding the lack of direct documentary evidence to support such a link. There are no records from 250 years ago that attribute the emergence of baseball in America to a like-named English game. There are no diary entries, memoirs, or letters from British colonists in the New World describing how they brought the pastime from the mother country and introduced it to their new neighbors. Any evidence in that vein would be sensational, and the thrill of making a discovery of such magnitude remains in the fantasies of those few of us who research in the realm of baseball's origins, but thus far it eludes us.

What we have instead is a powerful circumstantial case. This starts with the name itself: baseball. While it is within reason to imagine that the identical name could pop up independently on two continents, it is also unlikely. Even more doubtful are the chances that two namesake games could just happen to share similar features yet be unrelated. Both versions adhere to a common formula of pitching, striking, fielding, and baserunning. Taking these similarities into account, even lacking the types of direct evidence I discussed above, the case becomes very solid. Indeed, if English baseball wasn't a forerunner of America's pastime, what would be the alternative? That American baseball was the older of the two, and somehow, through reverse migration, it spawned the English game? All the evidence we have denies this and dates English baseball at least several decades earlier than its American namesake. What about the possibility that indigenous peoples in North America devised the game originally, and then when English settlers arrived, the newcomers appropriated it and labeled it as baseball? Not too likely. My extensive review of sources describing the many ball games played by the original occupants of the Americas convinces me that none of their pastimes resembled baseball. Ultimately, there can really be no debate. While technically unproven by anything other than circumstantial factors, the hypothesis that English baseball is the genetic forebear—and likely the immediate direct ancestor—of America's National Pastime must be viewed as a near certainty.

Because I am unable to pin down English baseball's definite beginnings, my story, by necessity, must start where it can, with those first detectable signs of the game in the mid-1700s. For giving us the earliest of these, and for offering up the first hints of what baseball was all about, we must credit the pioneering English publisher John Newbery and his iconic 1744 children's work, *A Little Pretty Pocketbook*. Both Newbery and *Pocket-book* are, of course, well known. He is considered the first publisher to bring respectability to the juvenile literature genre, and his contributions are memorialized in North America through the Newbery Medal, which since 1922 has honored the best children's book of the year. *Pocket-book* itself is often hailed as "the first true children's book" or "the first book intended primarily for children's enjoyment." These claims overstate the case, as several other entertaining children's works preceded Newbery's effort. Nevertheless, *A Little Pretty Pocket-book* remains enduringly charming and, for its time, highly innovative.

John Newbery was born in 1713 on a farm in the county of Berkshire. Lacking a formal education, but motivated by curiosity and ambition, he left home at the age of sixteen to become apprenticed to a printer in the town of Reading, about fifty miles west of London. When his master died a few years later, Newbery took over the business and married the widow (not an unusual arrangement for the times).[2] By the late 1730s he was publishing a newspaper in Reading and beginning to produce occasional books for an adult readership. This is when he began experimenting with other commercial ventures, including the one that was to become his most profitable lifelong source of wealth, the sale of patent medicines. In 1746 he signed a contract to be the exclusive marketer of the newly patented Dr. James's Fever Powder, a concoction of questionable, and possibly toxic, ingredients that was to become widely popular in Britain. It continued to generate sales well into the twentieth century. Meanwhile, Newbery had come to realize that his expanding enterprises were outgrowing the limited market opportunities available in Reading, and in the late summer of 1743 he began shifting his base of operations to London.[3]

It was also in the 1740s that the constrained and stuffy world of children's book publishing was beginning to undergo a major change. The influences of the age of reason and, in particular, the progressive educational ideas of the philosopher John Locke began seeping into juvenile literature, and a trickle of new titles appeared that were founded on the radical premise that books might entertain as well as educate. Moral instruction itself, though still an essential component of the genre, no longer threatened children with the throes of hellfire as the penalty for naughtiness. Newbery was always on the lookout for a good business opportunity, and he quickly recognized the potential of this new type of juvenile literature. *A Little Pretty*

BASE-BALL.

T H E *Ball* once ftruck off,
Away flies the *Boy*
To the next deftin'd Poft,
And then Home with Joy.

Fig. 1. From *A Little Pretty Pocket-book,* 1760. Credit: British Library.

Pocket-book was his first entrant in the field, and its great success led him to produce many more children's titles before his death in 1767.

As many times as I've looked at his baseball page in *Pocket-book,* it never ceases to amaze me. The young publisher could not have imagined what a precious gem he was leaving behind for future baseball researchers to marvel over. The first such marveler was the New York librarian and sports historian Robert W. Henderson, who in 1937 brought the contents of *A Little Pretty Pocket-book* to the attention of the baseball-reading public in his essay "How Baseball Began." Two years later, Henderson published a follow-up piece entitled "Baseball and Rounders" that completed his demolition of the Doubleday myth. In making his case he cited *Pocket-book* as proof of baseball's presence in 1744 England, a century prior to Doubleday's supposed invention of the game in Cooperstown, New York.[4]

Why am I so gaga about Newbery's baseball page? Not only does it contain the first known mention of the word *baseball* (spelled as *base-ball*), but the publisher masterly captured the essence of the game through his now-familiar four-line verse:

The *Ball* once struck off,
Away flies the *Boy*
To the next destin'd Post,
And then Home with Joy.[5]

This simple but vivid rhyme tells it all: a boy strikes a ball, flies to the "next destined post," and then returns to "home." Here, in its 1744 debut appearance, baseball was already recognizable. On the same page as the poem, Newbery printed an image of three boys—a striker, a pitcher, and a fielder—standing amid three posts or bases. You'll note that no bat is shown. While this could have been an oversight of the engraver, I believe it more likely was an early clue that use of a bat was not a requirement of English baseball. The Newbery image remains one of only two illustrations of English baseball I've ever been able to locate. The other is an 1854 painting about which I'll have more to say in chapter 16.

To the kiddies of mid-eighteenth-century England, *Pocket-book* must have seemed like a sneak preview of paradise. Never before had any of them encountered a book that illuminated such a cornucopia of pastimes and amusements. Everything was there, thirty-two games and activities in all: from kite flying to hopscotch, from leapfrog to blindman's buff. And besides baseball itself, the book devoted separate pages to the related games of cricket, stool-ball, trap-ball, and tip-cat. To top everything off, Newbery's promotion of the book promised special rewards to the children who purchased it. His newspaper ads informed readers that not only was *A Little Pretty Pocket-book* "intended for the Instruction and Amusement of little Master Tommy and pretty Miss Polly," but that it included "an agreeable Letter to each from Jack the Giant-Killer; as also a Ball and Pincushion, the

Use of which will infallibly make Tommy a good Boy, and Polly a good Girl." The catch in this was that these "letters" to Tommy and Polly provided instructions for how boys and girls were to use the ball and pincushion, although to follow these instructions Newbery obliged the children's parents to purchase the toys at an additional cost. This speaks to his skill as a marketer, and his revolutionary tactic of attaching a toy anticipates by 250 years the Klutz Book series of recent times.

Scholars who have written about Newbery's work have assumed the ball and pincushion were separate items, the former intended for boys and the latter for girls. A careful reading of the book, however, reveals the objects were one and the same: a soft, red-and-black ball that allowed for the insertion of pins. The "letters" from Jack the Giant-Killer published in *Pocket-book* and addressed to Tommy and Polly prescribed a common purpose for the ball/pincushion whether its recipient was a boy or girl. The child was directed to hang the toy up by an attached string. Then, putting to use ten pins that were also supplied, the child was instructed to stick a pin in the red half of the ball/pincushion whenever he/she did something good and a pin in the black half for every bad action. If the child managed to accumulate all ten pins in the red side, Jack the Giant-Killer pledged, ostensibly, to send the child a penny. Conversely, ten pins in the black side would result in Jack sending a rod with which the child was to be "whipt." The publishers of Klutz Books had the good sense not to adopt this darker aspect of Newbery's innovation.

No one knows how many individual ball/pincushion premiums were sold in tandem with copies of *A Little Pretty Pocket-book*. One thing that is certain, however, is that few, if any, of the toys have survived. The only institution to claim ownership of an original specimen is the Morgan Library in New York. Still, its example of the ball/pincushion is white on one side with an embroidered design on the other, not at all like the red-and-black object described in known editions of the *Pocket-book*. Moreover, the library's records cannot document the provenance of its copy, having no information predating 1991 when the toy was received as a gift.

Pocket-book proved to be wildly popular with its intended audience of English children and their parents. Newbery and subsequent publishers produced numerous editions over the course of the eighteenth century. Several appeared in North America as well, including a well-known 1787 edition printed in Worcester, Massachusetts, by the celebrated publisher Isaiah Thomas. Newbery appears to have printed significant quantities of his earliest English editions. Documents from a 1752 court case show he currently held a thousand copies of *Pocket-book* in his warehouse.[6] Yet, despite such abundance, copies of the book are quite rare today, with as few as ten of the London editions having survived. Apparently children who were fortunate enough to snare copies of the book loved them to death or passed them along to their younger siblings who completed the demolition. Moreover, parents in the eighteenth century would not have regarded a small children's book as a treasure to be preserved for future generations. Not a single known copy remains of any of the first nine editions of *Pocket-book*, with the earliest survivor being a lone incomplete copy of the 1760 tenth edition that rests in the collection of the British Library. In comparison, the American 1787 edition has fared better, with dozens of copies still to be found on the shelves of libraries and private collections.

That said, a couple of questions must be addressed: How do we know that Newbery produced the first edition of *A Little Pretty Pocket-book* in 1744 if no copies survive? And assuming he did, why are we confident that it or any of those other now extinct editions of the book contained the famous baseball page? The answer to the first of these is straightforward: Newbery inserted a series of display advertisements for the book in several London newspapers, with the first appearing on May 18, 1744. It began: "*This Day is publish'd, According to Act of Parliament (Neatly bound and gilt.) A Little pritty Pocket-book.*"[7] The typo "pritty" was corrected by the following day's editions. The words *this day is published* were not quite literal, seeing as they introduced every ad for the book that would appear until 1757, but they do identify the approximate time when *Pocket-book* was first printed and released.[8] Moreover, in the weeks following the advertisements, letters hailing the virtues of *A Little Pretty Pocket-book* began showing up on the pages of these same papers, seeming to confirm that this was indeed the initial rollout of the book.

These testimonials are curious in their own right. One of them was dated June 14, 1744, and was addressed "to the unknown author of the *Little Pretty Pocket-book.*" It rambled on and on with flowery praises such as "Here the paths of virtue are painted so as to please and engage, the child is captivated and led into a habit of doing well and made imperceptibly, as it were, both wise and virtuous."[9] The author of this accolade, identified only as "your unknown humble servant, A.Z.," also appended a thirty-four-line poem, purportedly written by his/her eldest son ("in behalf of his little brothers and sisters"), that added even more gushing praise. A.Z. concluded the testimonial with "P.S. Pray send me two dozen neatly bound with calf and gilt."

Two similar letters appeared in Newbery's own paper, the *Reading Mercury*. One accurately describes how the book presents "brief descriptions in verse . . . of the several plays or games with which children usually divert themselves, each game being represented by a small copper plate print, with a suitable moral or rule of life subjoined."[10] The writer noted that although "the author has modestly concealed himself . . . his performance . . . will undoubtedly meet with the approbation of all who would rather make learning a pleasure to those under their care, than weary themselves and their children with fruitless severities and correction." At least one modern scholar has raised the cynical hypothesis that Newbery himself may have written the newspaper testimonials praising his book, doing so as part of his campaign to puff it to the public. This type of promotion would not have been unusual for him, as he was adroit at using newspapers not only to sell books but to hype and peddle the products of his patent medicine business.

While *A Little Pretty Pocket-book*'s original publication window of May 1744 is all but certain, the matter of whether its baseball page actually appeared in that first edition is not quite as assured. The lone 1760 tenth edition does indeed include the baseball page, as do all subsequent editions. But there is no way to know whether, or how much, Newbery may have modified *Pocket-book*'s contents during the sixteen years between its first and tenth editions. The 1760 copy is ninety pages in length; a later edition in 1770 expanded to ninety-seven pages, and an even later 1790 copy was chopped back to eighty pages, suggesting Newbery and his successors regularly tinkered with the book's makeup. In all likelihood, *Pocket-book*'s first edition of 1744 did include the iconic baseball page, but without proof positive, a slight element of doubt must remain, and so in celebrating that year as the beginning of the pastime's recorded history we must do so with a small asterisk.

Pocket-book's baseball page raises another small intriguing question. Even assuming that the game itself was not newly born in the 1740s, baseball would not yet have been widely known except, perhaps, within the handful of southern English counties where it seems to have originated. Why then did Newbery choose to include the pastime in his book, a work he obviously intended for a national readership? My best guess is that the choice was a personal one. I suspect he had an intimate attachment to baseball from his own childhood and opted to include the game in his first children's book because of a desire to share its pleasures with other English youth. I base this conjecture almost totally on geography. Newbery was born and raised on a farm near the small village of Waltham St. Lawrence in northeastern Berkshire. In my study of the known locales where English baseball was played in the eighteenth and nineteenth centuries, I've discovered that Waltham St. Lawrence falls almost exactly in their geographic center. Of course, that doesn't prove that baseball originated in the immediate vicinity of his hometown, but it does suggest the possibility that Newbery was exposed to the game at a young age and might explain more than anything else why he selected it for his book.

All in all, we owe a great debt to John Newbery. Without him we would not be able to gaze back in time at the first tentative steps taken by that toddler, English baseball, the ancestor of America's National Pastime.

2

The Sporting Prince

As copies of John Newbery's *A Little Pretty Pocket-book* began appearing in English homes in the 1740s, one of them may have found its way into a particularly celebrated household. Situated upriver from Windsor Castle on the banks of the Thames, and located only eight miles northeast of John Newbery's boyhood home in the village of Waltham St. Lawrence, stood Cliveden, the stately country estate of Frederick, Prince of Wales. It is intriguing to imagine the prince's children getting their hands on a copy of the Newbery book and having that be their introduction to baseball (although I admit there is no evidence of such a thing actually happening). But whether *Pocket-book* launched their interest in the game or not, one fact about Frederick and his children is indisputable: theirs was the first known baseball family.

It's hard to imagine anyone's background making them more unsuited for the role of baseball pioneer than Frederick's. He was born in Germany in 1707 and lived in Hanover until the age of twenty-one when he was brought over to England and invested as Prince of Wales.[1] His grandfather, George I, had been first in the line of Hanoverian British monarchs, and upon his death Frederick's father, George II, assumed the throne. Frederick's biography is well known: he was the unloved child whose parents favored his younger brother William. As an adult, Frederick's estrangement from his parents became almost total, and he looked for any opportunity to oppose them. Defiantly, he set up his own court and allied himself with the political forces in Parliament opposing the government of Robert Walpole. In contrast to his brother William, the Duke of Cumberland, who embarked upon a military career, Frederick pursued a more domestic and artistic lifestyle, moving in literary circles, sponsoring operas, and collecting paintings.[2] His parents loathed him and harbored schemes to pass over him as successor to the throne in favor of William.

Frederick was very conscious of how his German-speaking parents and grandparents remained aloof from their British subjects. He determined to surmount this barrier for himself by embracing the culture and habits of a modern English aristocrat, hoping to gain popular acceptance for the day he would eventually assume the crown. This enthusiasm for establishing his patriotic credentials sometimes bordered on the extreme, such as the time he barred his courtiers from wearing any clothes made from fabrics not manufactured in England.[3] Frederick also embraced the gentlemanly sporting life by becoming an avid huntsman and a patron of horse racing. As early as 1731, he began experimenting with cricket, both as a sponsor of matches and as a player. He was active in the sport for years.[4]

One of Frederick's earliest English friends was John, Lord Hervey, who was a protégé of his mother, Queen Caroline. Hervey was a colorful and controversial aristocrat whose notoriety amused and scandalized the literary and political circles of English society. He was also instrumental in helping the young immigrant prince become acclimated to life at the Court of St. James's. Their friendship came to an end in the 1730s as the result of a love triangle—possibly a bisexual *ménage à trois*—gone bad. Hervey was married to Mary Lepel, a witty and charming courtier who earlier had been a maid of honor to Caroline. He was also known to be carrying on an affair with Stephen Fox, the son of an earl.[5] Lord Hervey is said to have craved intimacy with Frederick as well, and such a liaison may have happened. What is not in dispute is that both Hervey and Frederick were bedding the same mistress, Anne Vane, another of Queen Caroline's maids of honor. When Miss Vane bore a son, Frederick claimed the child as his own and settled mother and son in a fashionable townhouse.[6] Hervey, however, disputed the parentage and felt Frederick had betrayed their friendship, resulting in a permanent falling out between the two.

Lady Hervey seems to have been unperturbed by her husband's bisexuality, even maintaining close ties with his former lover, Stephen Fox.[7] She had eight children with Hervey and stayed on good terms with him up until his death in 1743. As a widow, Lady Hervey renewed a social relationship with Prince Frederick. On November 14, 1748, while paying a visit to the prince and his family at their London abode, Leicester House, she composed a chatty letter to her longtime correspondent, the Reverend Edmund Morris, a former tutor of her sons. In the letter she breezed through various topics including the recent distemper outbreak among cattle, how sickly London was, and how gaming had become excessively popular. Then she added:

> 'Tis really prodigious to see how deep the ladies play: but, in spite of all these irregularities, the Prince's family is an example of innocent and cheerful amusements. All this last summer they played abroad; and now, in the winter, in a large room, they divert themselves at base-ball, a play all who are, or have been, schoolboys are well acquainted with. The ladies, as well as gentlemen, join in this amusement; and the latter return the compliment in the evening, by playing for an hour at the old and amusing game of push-pin, at which *they* chiefly excel.[8]

These sentences offer important insights into the character and status of English baseball at the dawn of its recorded history. By sharing her observation that baseball was a game well known to all schoolboys, Lady Hervey documented that by 1748 it was not a newcomer and had already gained some traction as a pastime, at least within the social world she occupied. Her children, including her four sons, could well have played it while growing up in the 1730s and 1740s. Her daughters may have played as well, as suggested by her revelation that the "ladies" in Prince Frederick's household had joined the game in Leicester House. The participation of girls and women on this occasion, and in other early references to English baseball, established a pattern of gender neutrality that would last throughout the pastime's lifespan. And for at least a couple of decades in the early nineteenth century it seemed as if females had become the sport's dominant practitioners.

Lady Hervey's letter presaged another trait of English baseball that would endure: the game appeared to be a social activity rather than a rigorous physical sport. Her description of it being engaged by a mixed party of males and females, including children, is partly suggestive of this, as is the fact that on this occasion it was played not on an athletic field but in a large room within a city residence. Unsaid in the letter are the salient distinctions that English baseball was typically played without the use of a bat and with a soft ball, differentiating it from its cousins: American baseball, cricket, and rounders. Such characteristics suited the pastime for casual settings, allowing it to be played on lawns, in churchyards, or, as in this case, indoors. Never in its history would English baseball acquire the sophisticated hallmarks of related games, such as organized clubs and leagues, nor, to the best of my knowledge, would players of the pastime ever adopt a standardized set of rules. It entered its recorded history in the 1740s as a folk game unhampered by the strictures of more "serious" sports, and so it remained until its ultimate demise more than 150 years later.

In her letter, Lady Hervey identified the grouping who engaged in this early game of baseball as simply "the Prince's family." It is not known if these players included any relatives other than Frederick, his wife, Princess Augusta of Saxe-Gotha, whom he married in 1736, and six of their nine children (their other three children had yet to be born at the time of Lady Hervey's visit in November 1748). The four boys and two girls ranged in age from Princess Augusta, age eleven, to Prince Henry, about to turn three. In retrospect, the most interesting of the ballplayers was Frederick's eldest son, George, aged ten. He, of course, would be thrust into national attention less than three years following this innocent game as a result of his father's early death. George subsequently succeeded Frederick as Prince of Wales, and nine years later, following the death of his grandfather George

II, ascended the throne as George III. There is something deliciously ironic about George III, the iconic villain of the American Revolution, ranking as one of the first named individuals to have played a game called baseball, a pastime that would become inseparably associated with American patriotism. Years later, at the beginning of the twentieth century, baseball magnate Albert Spalding and other jingoists in the United States campaigned zealously against the notion that baseball's origins were English. One can only imagine their horror and consternation if they had known that Mad King George played the game before anyone in America.

Just as the early editions of *A Little Pretty Pocket-book* have not survived the centuries, so too the original copy of Lady Hervey's letter may be lost to posterity. I have searched far and wide for it, but its present whereabouts remain unknown to me. (I am not aware of anyone else having bothered to look for it.) Fortunately, a nineteenth-century publisher named John Murray looked upon Lady Hervey as a marketable commodity, and in 1821 he elected to publish a book containing her complete correspondence with pen-pal Morris. It includes the pivotal letter of November 14, 1748, and it was from this printing that future readers learned of her reference to baseball. I experienced a brief frisson some years ago when I came across an obviously old handwritten copy of this same letter in a collection of Hervey family papers in a record office in Bury St. Edmunds, Suffolk. My excitement was short-lived, however, as a quick comparison with samples of Lady Hervey's handwriting made it obvious, even to my untrained eye, that the letter I found was not the original. Still, the writer's use of the "long s" in her cursive script suggests an eighteenth-century origin, and it is thus likely to be the oldest surviving copy of the baseball missive.

Several years ago I got it into my head that the Hervey family may have played an even bigger role in baseball history than simply documenting the game played by the prince's family. Lady Hervey's youngest son, William, was still a schoolboy at the time she penned her letter, and thereby someone "well acquainted" with the game, if we are to take his mother's words literally. In due course, William finished school and took a commission in the army. In 1755 he received orders to proceed to North America as a replacement officer for British forces engaged in the Seven Years' War, the bitter contest between Britain and France over colonial control in the New World. This struggle is known as the French and Indian War in the United States because both sides brought Native American allies into the fighting. William Hervey landed in Boston, traveled by a circuitous route to the Hudson River, and then up the river beyond Albany where he became engaged in the fighting. He remained in North America for seven years, and during that time he kept detailed records of his experiences.

In my mind, he fit the bill. He was a perfect candidate. Here was someone who knew the original game of baseball in England and then traveled around North America during the very period of years when the game most likely migrated to its new home territory. Forget Alexander Cartwright. Surely William Hervey was baseball's Johnny Appleseed![9] All I had to do was read his diaries and find the evidence. My first step was scanning a lengthy work entitled *Journals of the Hon. William Hervey,* first published in Suffolk in 1906. No luck. The book held no references to baseball. All was not lost, however, for I discovered the published journals were excerpts from a much larger trove of original documents. On my next research trip to England, I traveled back to the same record office in Bury St. Edmunds I had visited earlier, this time to wade through every last page of William Hervey's journals. It wasn't easy; his eighteenth-century handwriting was hard to follow. And, in the end, it was a big disappointment. Virtually all of his writing was devoted to military concerns: troop movements, construction of camps and fortifications, descriptions of battles, and the like. There was almost nothing about his personal life or how he spent his leisure time, not that he had very much of that in a war zone. Still, even without the proof, it almost certainly had to have been someone, or several someones, like William Hervey who carried knowledge of the game with him (or her) to North American shores. The pastime of baseball didn't cross the ocean in a bottle or by floating on the wind.

Not finding any proof of baseball in William Hervey's papers was a letdown. But I didn't come away empty-handed. Among his papers was a notebook he used in his schooling. Pages and pages were filled with math problems and Greek lessons and other writings. But amid all these, I came across a poem written in his hand that was clearly about his mother. At first, I assumed the verse to be his own work, and I was shocked by it because it was conspicuously bawdy, even by the rather forgiving standards of the day. I later learned the poem originated in the 1720s, was cowritten by the Earls of Bath and Chesterfield, and was meant to make fun of Mary Lepel's alluring charms in the wake of her marriage to Lord Hervey. But still I find it a bit creepy for a son to copy a smutty poem about his mother into his workbook. The poem was entitled "The Ballad of Molly Lepel," and it had such memorable stanzas as this:

> So powerful her charms and so moving
> They could warm an old monk in his cell,
> Should the Pope himself ever go roving,
> He would follow dear Molly Lepel.

And this:

> Or were I the king of Great Britain,
> To govern my good people well,
> Instead of the throne which I sit on,
> I'd have under me Molly Lepel.[10]

Back to the business at hand. I was always a little curious about a couple of points having to do with Lady Hervey's letter. One was a brief note appended to the 1821 published version of the letter by an unidentified editor, who wrote: "I suspect a little irony here. Lady

Hervey never frequented Leicester House."[11] Am I wrong, or was this guy impugning the character of Lady Hervey by implying that she never visited the prince and fabricated the whole story, including her observation of baseball? He offered no evidence for this aspersion. My own reading of the letter set me wondering about a different ambiguity. Lady Hervey identified the group of ballplayers as "the Prince's family," and I wondered whether this descriptor included the prince himself or was limited to his youthful offspring. The latter always seemed to me to be the more likely alternative because John Newbery's portrayal of baseball in *A Little Pretty Pocket-book* implied it was a game for children. I tended to question whether a middle-aged aristocrat like Frederick, a serious cricket fancier, would deign to participate in such a juvenile endeavor.

But then the earth shifted. In early 2012, while searching through various digital databases of historic English newspapers, I came across a brief story from 1749 carrying astonishing content. It involved our old friend the Prince of Wales, but this time, instead of being in the bosom of his family, he was reported to be in the company of a fellow nobleman, one Charles Sackville, the Earl of Middlesex. Sackville was son of the Duke of Dorset, a close ally of Frederick's father and grandfather (George II and George I). Prince Frederick and Lord Middlesex met in the early 1730s and quickly formed a bond. They had much in common. Both were bitterly estranged from their parents and, as a logical extension of this perhaps, both also became supporters of the political opposition. The two shared a keen interest in the sporting life as well and often hunted together. As young men they both discovered the sport of cricket and embraced it with unusual ardor, and according to multiple newspaper reports, they maintained a friendly rivalry by captaining opposing sides. As was the norm, such matches did not proceed without a sporting wager. In July 1735 Frederick led a team of eleven men from London in two successive contests against Sackville's Kent squad.[12] The stakes were £1,000 per match, not an inconsequential sum in that year; in fact, it was a small fortune. Sackville's side trounced the prince's in both bouts. Notwithstanding their friendship, Frederick seems to have taken the second loss hard, and many in the crowd in attendance appear to have been stirred up as well. When the match concluded, "his Royal Highness immediately left the field," a newspaper reporter observed, and then added: "There was a surprizing Multitude of People present, and a great deal of Mischief was done, some falling from their Horses, others being rode over, &c. and one Man was carried off for dead as his Royal Highness pass'd by."[13]

As they progressed toward middle age, the two men grew even closer. Frederick named Sackville to be Master of the Horse in the alternate court he organized in the 1740s in defiance of his parents. They socialized regularly. On September 14, 1749, a brief announcement appeared in the a London paper: "Thursday, the Right Hon. The Earl of Middlesex, and his Lady, went to Cliefden [Cliveden], and on Tuesday next their Royal Highnesses the Prince and Princess of Wales go from Cliefden to Ashley, near Walton in Surry, Lord Middlesex's seat."[14] The second leg of these reciprocal visits found the two friends at Ashley Park, the grand estate at Walton-on-Thames in Surrey that Middlesex's wife had inherited from her parents. While there, the two sporting buddies engaged in an activity that might have seemed quite normal to them at the time but apparently was curious enough that on September 19, it was reported in the *Whitehall Evening Post*. This was the astonishing item I alluded to earlier. It reads: "On Tuesday last, his Royal Highness the Prince of Wales, and Lord Middlesex, played Bass-ball, at Walton in Surry; notwithstanding the Weather was extreme bad, they continued playing several Hours."[15]

Clearly, baseball in mid-eighteenth-century England was not only for children. Here two men in the prime of life (Frederick was forty-two, Middlesex thirty-eight) were so committed to the match that they endured terrible conditions for hours in order to complete it. This, too, says a great deal about the depth of the long-standing competition between the two friends. The brief news report, unfortunately,

On Tuefday laft his Royal Highnefs the Prince of Wales, and Lord Middlefex, played at Bafs-Ball, at Walton in Surry ; and notwithftanding the Weather was extreme bad, they continued playing feveral Hours.

Fig. 2. Report of "bass-ball" game that appeared in the *Whitehall Evening Post*, September 19–21, 1749. Credit: British Library.

makes no mention of how they actually played the game, who else may have participated, or which side wound up victorious. Nevertheless, even in its brevity the report contributes valuably to our knowledge of English baseball, not only letting us know that adults were enjoying the pastime in those early years, but also that it could, on occasion, be pursued with serious intensity. Finding this little news squib also eased my doubts over whether Frederick might have participated in the family baseball game that Lady Hervey wrote about ten months earlier and relieved any uncertainty about whether she made up the events described in the letter.

On a visit to England in the year following this discovery, I stopped by the Surrey History Centre in Woking, where Julian Pooley, the head of Public Services, helped me study a detailed historical map showing Lord Middlesex's Ashley Park estate. We were able to locate the likely plot of ground where the two aristocrats played more than 250 years earlier.[16] Even though much of Ashley Park has since been carved up and developed into subdivision housing for London commuters, we were both pleased to realize that the likely location of that long-ago game is still in dedicated use as a cricket pitch.

Julian Pooley and I staged a small press event about my discovery of the 1749 game, and some of the British media took interest. The BBC's headline read, "Baseball: Prince of Wales Played 'First' Game in Surrey," while the *Daily Mail* reported, "The birthplace of baseball was in Britain! US expert proves his country's national sport was first played in England by royalty on this village green."[17] While both of these news organizations slightly overstated the case, their enthusi-

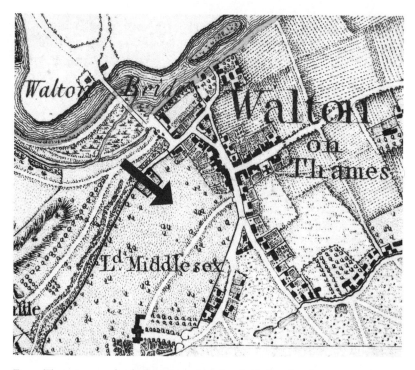

Fig. 3. The arrow marks the location where baseball was played in 1749 on Lord Middlesex's Ashley Park estate. Today, the Walton-on-Thames Cricket Club's pavilion and cricket pitch stand on the same spot. From John Rocque's 1762 map of Surrey, reproduced by permission of the Surrey History Centre.

asm for claiming British paternity of America's National Pastime is understandable.

Perhaps Frederick would have continued to play baseball with his children or with his friend Middlesex, but eighteen months following the game in the rain, Frederick died in London at Leicester House. His illness and death have been subjects of controversy ever since. He was known to be suffering from a malady, but the London newspapers were vague about its precise nature and prognosis. On March 18, the *London Advertiser and Literary Gazette* reported, "There was no Court Yesterday at Leicester House on account of his Royal Highness the Prince of Wales's late Indisposition: but we can

The birthplace of baseball was in Britain! US expert proves his country's national sport was first played in England by royalty on this village green

- Newspaper cutting reveals match involving Prince of Wales in 1749 in Surrey
- First mention of baseball in America was in 1791 in Pittsfield, Massachusetts
- U.S. expert on the sport discovers evidence in the British Library

Baseball: Prince of Wales played 'first' game in Surrey

Fig. 4. Headlines in the English news media reporting on the author's discovery of the 1749 "bass-ball" game.

with Pleasure assure the Public, that his Royal Highness is perfectly recovered."[18] That bright outlook was a tad optimistic, as the *London Evening Post* on the following day reported, "Last Night, about Eleven o'Clock, died, after a few Days Illness, at Leicester-House, his Royal Highness Frederick Lewis, Prince of Wales; to the greatest Grief of all his Royal Family and Household, and utmost Concern to the whole Nation."[19]

The cause of death was variously reported in the newspapers that week as a burst abscess, pleurisy, or some general "distemper." Two days after the sad news was first reported, the *London Advertiser* was still congratulating Frederick on his recovery![20] But by March 26, having finally acknowledged his death, the paper reported the following: "It's generally said his late Royal Highness the Prince of Wales got a Blow on his Side with a Ball about two Years ago, playing at Cricket, which Diversion he was fond of, and 'tis thought was the Occasion of his Death, having a Bag, near six Inches long, down his Side, full of Corruption."[21]

Whether Frederick's death was the consequence of a lingering cricket injury has been the subject of debate ever since, with most modern observers other than, perhaps, a few cricket advocates expressing skepticism. That the above explanation appeared in a newspaper only a week following his demise might appear to give the claim some credence. Then again, given that the publication carrying the story was the same one that reported him alive and well two days after he died, one might reasonably question its credibility.

Frederick's oft-quoted, anonymous epitaph was adapted from an elegy written decades earlier for someone else, but in the typically scathing manner of the times it captured the public's indifference to Frederick and the entire royal family:

Here lies Fred,
Who was alive and is dead.
Had it been his father,
I had much rather.
Had it been his brother,
Still better than another.
Had it been his sister,
No one would have missed her.
Had it been the whole generation,
Still better for the nation.

But since 'tis only Fred,
Who was alive and is dead,
There's no more to be said.[22]

He may never be elected to the Hall of Fame, but by my reckoning Frederick, Prince of Wales, was unquestionably a baseball pioneer.

3

Two Weeks, Two Discoveries

The eighteenth-century clergyman John Kidgell appears to have lacked the nobler graces of his calling. His moral character, or lack thereof, was best summarized by Horace Walpole, the prominent politician and man of letters, who referred to Kidgell as "that dirty dog."[1] Newspaper columnists of the 1760s routinely lashed him with derision. Yet, despite the unsavory manner in which he conducted his affairs, we can credit Reverend Kidgell with one salutary achievement: he was the first author to employ the word *baseball* in a literary novel.

His formal education and subsequent ordination in 1747 as a priest in the Church of England followed the usual road taken by the son of a churchman. But upon gaining his collar, Kidgell's interest in religion seems to have taken second seat to his zeal for writing satirical takedowns of various public figures. He accepted several minor clerical appointments in London during the 1750s, including one as chaplain to a titled former school chum, William Douglas, the Earl of March, whose "dissoluteness matched his own," according to the *Oxford Dictionary of National Biography*. Walpole described Kidgell in those days as being a "dainty, priggish parson, much in vogue among the old ladies for his gossiping and quaint sermons."

Kidgell achieved his greatest notoriety in the Wilkes affair of 1763. John Wilkes was a radical English journalist and politician who was a constant thorn in the side of the establishment. He later would stir up more consternation by supporting the American rebels in their war for independence. Wilkes was the accused coauthor of an obscene manuscript entitled "Essay on Woman" that was a parody of Alexander Pope's "Essay on Man." Its subject was the mistress of the Earl of Sandwich, one of Wilkes's political enemies. The piece was never intended for public consumption, but John Kidgell's bene-factor, Lord March, on behalf of Lord Sandwich, enlisted Kidgell to procure, secretly, a copy of the essay for use in building a libel case against Wilkes. The corrupt clergyman accomplished his task through bribery, but when the truth came out that Kidgell was a paid agent of powerful pro-government interests trying to dredge up dirt on a popular critic, he rushed to assemble a cover story.[2] Affecting an air of righteous indignation, he published his own essay, "A Genuine and Succinct Narrative of a Scandalous, Obscene, and Exceedingly Profane Libel, Entitled 'An Essay on Woman,' etc.," that everyone saw as a desperate ploy to justify his actions. His clumsy attempt at damage control made matters measurably worse for Kidgell, leading his aristocratic patrons to disown him, the Church to defrock him, and the press to ridicule him mercilessly. According to *Oxford DNB,* he was "damned as a sordid informer on all sides."

Shortly before the Wilkes affair, Kidgell had been appointed rector of the Godstone parish in Surrey. But in 1764, in scandal and disgrace, he absconded with the parish's highway funds and fled all the way to France and thereafter to Holland.[3] In the next few years he tried various means of resuscitating his reputation and financial health, including a failed attempt to blackmail Lord March.[4] Ultimately all this failed, and he died impoverished in exile in 1780.

Mr. Kidgell's transgressions may have been hot fodder for news-hounds in the 1760s, but his sordid adventures are all but forgotten today. I had never heard of him, nor would I have paid his story any heed had I not spent some extra time in the British Library one day in June 2007. I was sitting at a computer terminal in one of the library's reading rooms searching through ECCO, a full-text digital database of early English literature (its full name is Eighteenth Cen-tury Collections Online). I had utilized ECCO previously in my hunt for early references to baseball, but on those occasions I had searched for the terms *base ball,* *base-ball,* or *bass-ball,* the common forms in use in eighteenth-century England. This time I entered the word as *baseball*, the way we spell it today. Bingo! Up popped a citation for an anonymously authored novel entitled *The Card*, published in 1755 under the imprint of John Newbery, he of *A Little Pretty Pocket-book* fame. ECCO directed me to page 9 of *The Card*, to a scene where some adults were holding a hushed conversation about an absent family member. Realizing the presence of their children, they quieted, and: "The Silence became for some short space of Time universal; and the younger Part of the Family, perceiving Papa not inclined to *enlarge* upon the Matter, retired to an *interrupted Party* at *Base-ball*, (an *infant* Game, which as it advances into its *Teens*, improves into *Fives*, and in its State of *Manhood,* is called *Tennis*)."

The first thing I wondered about this discovery was why I made it in the first place. I had searched for *baseball* as one word, but its author would have written it—and Newbery printed it—as the compound *base-ball*. ECCO's image of the original printed page reveals the first half of the compound word (*base-*) falling at the end of one line of type, with the second half (*ball*) wrapping around to become the first word of the following line. Because ECCO's character recognition algorithm was still a work in progress in 2007, the software interpreted the term *baseball* in the novel as one whole word split between the two lines. The same searches conducted today show that ECCO has smartened up over the ensuing decade, and now entering either *base-ball* or *baseball* as search terms will direct users to *The Card*.

Naturally, I was very excited to find this reference. Any new discovery of baseball in the eighteenth century is unusual and at least by me, highly treasured. But beyond registering the presence of the term *baseball*, decoding the context of its use was not straightforward. What did the author mean by "an infant game"? Was he disparaging it? Was he categorizing it as the nethermost entry in a hierarchy of ball sports? As a baseball historian, how literally should I take this statement as evidence of the game's status in 1755?

While pondering these questions, I looked into who the author might be, and as you have gathered, it was none other than our dear

Reverend Kidgell. I knew nothing yet of his notoriety, but while perusing *The Card*, even as someone not remotely qualified as a literary critic, I could tell the author possessed an unusual, if not bizarre, writing style. Researching what others had written about the novel, I learned that Kidgell had parodied the techniques of several of his contemporaries and bitingly satirized others, including the poet Edward Young and the novelist Samuel Richardson. Some modern critics have cited Kidgell's unusual literary approach to writing *The Card* as being highly innovative. Perhaps the scoundrel contributed something positive after all.

Learning about Kidgell's history and writing style helped guide me in trying to interpret *The Card*'s reference to baseball. The author's language was satirical throughout, suggesting to me that almost nothing in the work could be taken literally. I tend to doubt that his classification of baseball as "an infant game" was meant to imply it was simple in construct or that it was suitable only for young children. Kidgell's patrons, Lord March and Lord Sandwich, mingled in the same society of sports-minded, titled aristocrats that also numbered among its ranks Lord Middlesex and Frederick, Prince of Wales. From them, Kidgell may have learned that baseball was a game appropriate for gentlemen of high standing. If there was any literal intention in the clergyman's comment about baseball's infancy, I suspect it had more to do with it being the relative newcomer among the three ball games he mentioned. The second of those, the pastime "fives," was a form of handball whose beginnings trace back to the early seventeenth century, while the longevity of the third game, tennis, extends back even further, at least another two hundred years.

According to its title page, *The Card* was published in 1755, and we know its actual availability was no later than February of that year thanks to a book review appearing that month in a literary journal.[5] This places its arrival at least two months prior to that of another early use of the word *baseball*, one whose fortuitous discovery came to light during the same productive 2007 visit to England on which I discovered *The Card*.

During that trip I had the pleasure of tagging along for several days with a video production team from MLB Advanced Media, the internet arm of Major League Baseball. MLBAM at that time normally concerned itself with filming and reporting on current baseball matters, as well as streaming live games to its mlb.com subscribers. But on that occasion it had undertaken an out-of-the-ordinary project to produce a documentary film on the origins of baseball. I was serving as the project's historian-in-tow, traveling through southern England with the filmmakers as they captured footage of various traditional games played with a ball.

One morning, as the crew and I drove away from a village in Kent—where the previous evening, in a pub yard, we had recorded scenes of local men playing "bat and trap"–we abruptly smashed into a parked car.[6] Our driver, an American, had not quite gotten the hang of driving on what we disoriented Yanks consider the wrong side of the road. Fortunately, no one was hurt, but our rental van needed replacement, and there were insurance matters to be dealt with. Because these tasks required two of the MLBAM people to stay behind, one of them being the creative force behind the film, Sam Marchiano, I was deputized to be her substitute director and interviewer. Because our cameraman and soundman were driving in a separate vehicle, I was able to squeeze in with them and their equipment and proceed to our next stop, a girls' school in the town of Horsham in West Sussex. Our mission there was to obtain footage of a game of rounders and conduct interviews with players, school officials, and the director of the National Rounders Association.

As I was making my directorial debut, we had another unexpected development. A second video production crew—dispatched by BBC news—showed up at the school. Apparently the network considered it newsworthy that MLB filmmakers were touring the English countryside in search of baseball's origins. So the BBC crew began filming our MLB crew, who were in turn filming the schoolgirls playing rounders. The BBC reporter also conducted interviews with me, the rounders official, and several others at the scene.

That evening, the story of the MLBAM film project appeared on BBC South's 6:00 p.m. news program. It included a clip of an interview with me where I mentioned that Jane Austen referred to baseball in her novel *Northanger Abbey*. By the time of the broadcast, the two crew members we had left behind in Kent had secured a replacement van and rejoined us in Horsham. As we were driving to cover a youth league baseball game that evening (yes, American-style baseball is alive and well in modern-day Sussex), Sam Marchiano's cell phone rang. It was BBC South. It seems that immediately following their airing of the piece about us, they had received a telephone call. A woman in the adjacent county of Surrey happened to catch the news show while visiting a friend's house, and she rang the studio to report that she knew of a reference to baseball far earlier than Jane Austen's. The caller claimed she had an old diary in her possession, the work of a young man named William Bray, who wrote an entry about playing baseball in the year 1755. As you might imagine, this news sent a charge through all of us. Eighteenth-century references to baseball don't just pop up every day, and for the MLBAM film project to be the catalyst for the discovery of a new one would be an unexpected coup. We immediately phoned the woman, Tricia St. John Barry, and arranged to visit her home the following morning.

Her home, it turned out, was an ancient cottage down a country lane near the Surrey-Sussex border. At 11:00 a.m., we approached her door in force, our group consisting of me, the four-person mlb.com crew, Larry McCray, a baseball history colleague of mine, and John Price, an official with the Sussex stool-ball association who was our local host in Horsham. Tricia answered the door, but instead of the smiling welcome we were expecting, she was in a state of great agitation. She was mortified! She couldn't find the diary! It had been in a Marks & Spencer bag next to her filing cabinet, she was certain of it, but it simply wasn't there. She had been searching her house high and low all morning, but to no avail.

One look at her cottage and you could tell it would be easy to misplace something there. It was all a jumble; its small, ancient rooms filled with piles of books and papers. Tricia is a delightfully charming lady, but a tad disorganized, and it turned out she hadn't actually seen the diary for quite some time. She had obtained it about twenty years earlier and was transcribing it, albeit very slowly. She had made photocopies of the whole thing, but, alas, she believed they were in the same bag as the diary. Still, she had no doubts whatsoever about its mention of baseball. She had first noticed the entry about fifteen years earlier, and knowing it to be an American game, she had taken it down the road to show to some American neighbors.

So there we were with a great story but no diary. Tricia may be a little eccentric, but there was no reason to question her credibility, and we were all convinced that the diary was buried somewhere in her house. She insisted that it would come to light; it just might take a little time. So the MLBAM team proceeded to interview her and shoot video footage of her house and garden. We trusted that it was just a matter of time before the diary would appear.

Shortly thereafter the film crew returned to New York, and I resumed my family vacation in England, hoping that Tricia would find the missing diary before I returned to the States myself. About a week later, while traveling in Northumberland, I received an email from Tricia. "Eureka! I found it!" This was great news. I called Sam Marchiano in New York to report the find, and she said she would try to line up a freelance cameraman to accompany me to film the precious document. The next day I called Tricia to tell her I had received her message and to arrange my next visit to her cottage. In the course of our conversation, one small detail became apparent. It seems Tricia hadn't actually found the diary itself, only the photocopies! True, this was better than nothing, but I had to bite my tongue to hide my disappointment. I consoled myself by knowing that at least I'd be able to return home with a copy of the 1755 diary page; that is, if upon my return to Tricia's house the photocopies hadn't disappeared again.

Two days later, at a library in Cornwall (a crazy itinerary, I know, but northern England was suffering an epic drenching so we cut short our stay there and headed south) I had another chance to check my email. A new message from Tricia: "Eureka again! I really found it this time!" And she really had. So five days later, on our final day in the UK, my wife, Barbara, and I returned to Tricia's cottage along with a cameraman arranged by Sam Marchiano. Also there for the big show was John Price of the stool-ball association, a BBC crew (by now they, too, had a stake in this discovery and came to tape another spot for the evening news), and Julian Pooley, the Surrey archivist who happens to be an expert on William Bray, the author of the diary.

As it turns out, William Bray was a notable historical figure of his time, a prominent eighteenth-century lawyer and antiquarian who cowrote a three-volume history of Surrey that remains the authoritative work on the subject. More important, Bray had a vast range of interests that spanned science, politics, literature, and the arts and a lively curiosity about all of the new developments of his age. And he wrote about them diligently in the diaries and journals he kept. He lived to the age of ninety-six and maintained his journals for nearly the entirety of his adult years. The bulk of these, dating from 1756 when he was twenty, are located in the Surrey History Centre and have been studied extensively because of their unusual insights into the goings-on of that era.

At some time in the past, however, a single volume of William Bray's diary, the one spanning the years 1754 and 1755, was separated from the others. Until recently, its existence was unknown to scholars. It first surfaced twenty years earlier when a neighbor of Tricia's, knowing that she liked "old things," gave her a call to see if she was interested in a stack of old papers. It seems this neighbor's deceased ex-husband, who had once worked on the Bray estate, had stored a collection of documents in a tea chest in a shed on their property. She was threatening to "dump them on the bonfire" unless Tricia took them off her hands. The William Bray diary was among this lot, and Tricia immediately recognized it as a treasure. It just took her a bit of time to let the rest of the world know about it.

What did he have to say about baseball? Young William's words don't reveal anything about how the game was played, only that he played it and whom he played it with. His entry for Easter Monday, March 31, 1755, reads as follows: "Went to Stoke Ch[urch] this Morn.–After Dinner Went to Miss Jeale's to play at Base Ball, with her, the 3 Miss Whiteheads, Miss Billinghurst, Miss Molly Fluttor, Mr. Chandler, Mr. Ford, H. Parsons & Jelly. Drank tea and stayed till 8."[7]

Despite its brevity, this casual notation helps shape our understanding of English baseball in its early years. Bray was eighteen or nineteen at the time he wrote the entry (his birth year, 1736, is known, but not his precise birth date). From other writings in his diaries, we know that his fellow participants in the baseball game were all young adults living in the Surrey town of Guildford. This was the first certain indicator that baseball in mid-eighteenth-century England provided recreation for age groups other than children, a finding supported by my later discovery of the 1749 Surrey game involving the Prince of Wales and Lord Middlesex. William Bray's revelation that the gathering involved both males and females confirmed an important aspect of Lady Hervey's letter of 1748, that the pastime in those years was gender neutral.

The gathering at Tricia's cottage after she found the misplaced diary was a festive one. We took new video images of her cottage, many shots of the diary, and even went down the road to film the shed where Tricia's friend unearthed the document twenty years earlier. After conducting interviews with Tricia and Julian Pooley, I switched sides of the camera and became the interviewee myself, with Barbara, always a good sport, agreeing to toss me some questions. After that, all of us sat down to enjoy the lasagna and salad that Tricia had prepared for us. The story of Bray's diary went on to become the centerpiece

Fig. 5. Tricia St. John Barry and the author celebrating her rediscovery of the William Bray diary in 2007. Inset shows the diary's "base ball" entry of March 31, 1755. Reproduced by permission of the Surrey History Centre.

of *Base Ball Discovered*, the name given the MLBAM documentary that debuted in 2008 to very positive reviews.

A sad footnote to this story is that the wayward diary has gone missing again. Several years after the celebratory gathering described above, Tricia returned the precious document to her neighbor in whose shed it was found. Shortly thereafter, the neighbor's health declined and she slipped into dementia. The diary, ostensibly, had been locked in a safe in her house along with other important personal papers. When her condition worsened to the point that her second husband felt it necessary to move her to a nursing home, he opened the safe and found it empty. By then, the neighbor was incapable of offering any information that might help locate the missing diary and other documents. A short time later, after putting their house up for sale, the husband conducted a thorough search before leaving, but to no avail. Barring some miracle, the diary may be lost forever, vanishing as dramatically as it was found.

It would be a tragedy if the precious artifact has, indeed, met the same unhappy fate as the early editions of *A Little Pretty Pocket-book* and the Lady Hervey's original letter. I never would have contemplated such an outcome when I held it in my hands in 2007. Still, we must celebrate the convergence of coincidences that led to William Bray's buried baseball entry coming to light in the first place. It was a happenstance of pure serendipity and illustrates that sometimes, out of the blue, it's the needle in the haystack that finds you.

4

Word Perfect

If serendipity was responsible for bringing forth the Bray diary, it was orneriness that led me to unearth another precious baseball specimen from the eighteenth century. It was late November 2011, and I was sitting at my computer plugging away at the same ECCO database of English literary sources that four years earlier had yielded my discovery of John Kidgell's novel, *The Card*. I never tire of going back to ECCO, always hoping I can create a clever new search argument that will miraculously dredge up some previously unknown early baseball find from its digital depths. Methodically I went through my standard list of search terms: *baseball, base-ball, bass-ball,* etc. Then I attempted various proximity searches: *cricket* within five words of *base*, or *play* within two words of *ball*, and so on. Most of these various combinations turn up nothing new no matter how many times I try them. Others return so many hits that it is impractical to look through them all. Usually I abandon this frustrating exercise after about an hour, but on that day I stayed with it longer, keying in one search after another.

Finally, getting nowhere, I entered a proximity combination that was certain to return a good number of responses but not so many that I wouldn't have time to review them all. I queried the database for all examples where the word *ball* appeared in a text passage within ten words of the term *game*. As with many of my searches it was the longest of long shots. ECCO came back with almost four hundred results, and one by one I started going through them. Midway in, I noticed that one of the hits was for a dictionary published in 1768. This, in itself, was nothing unusual. In the course of my research I had looked through many eighteenth-century dictionaries for entries on baseball and related pastimes. These efforts yielded little. Often I would find references to ball games particular to the times, such as bandy, pall mall, or stool-ball. Occasionally I might spot a definition for the word *base* that would read simply "a rural game," or "a rustic play," or some such. My assumption, when coming across one of these, was that *base* referred to the common game of "prisoner's base," the tag-like pastime played without a ball that had been popular in Britain for centuries.

Notwithstanding my limited success with dictionaries, I opened this one to examine its contents. Unsurprisingly, ECCO directed me to a page containing the word *bandy* that was defined as "a particular kind of game at ball."[1] This was rather unhelpful and, in any case, irrelevant to my search for baseball. But since I was inside the dictionary already, I decided to take a quick look to see if there was anything else of interest. Situated in the "B" section with *bandy*, it was short work to click a few pages ahead to check out what I might find for the word *base*. As I did, it became apparent that this was no ordinary dictionary. For *base*, the authors had provided thirteen separate definitions, a number comparable to Samuel Johnson's treatment of the word in his celebrated *Dictionary of the English Language* of a decade earlier. Moreover, the 1768 dictionary cited examples from literature for most of its definitions, a method Dr. Johnson had employed as well. Today we are accustomed to dictionaries providing examples of words used in context to illustrate their various meanings, but among eighteenth-century lexicographers such practice was cutting edge.

As I scanned through the entries for *base*, one of them jerked me to attention. I boggled. Could that be? Not quite believing what I was seeing, I blinked and read it again. There was no mistake. The words were clear as could be:

> Base: A rural play, called also *Baseball*; as,
> Lads more like to run,
> The country *base*.
> —Shakespeare.

This was truly remarkable. Only in my fondest fantasies would I have expected to find the word *baseball* in a dictionary from 1768. True, the entry is a brief one and lacks a description. But to me it felt momentous, as if the dictionary had extended an official welcome to the nascent pastime by admitting its name into the English lexicon. Adding to my incredulity was that, until then, I had not known of the term *baseball* appearing in any dictionary prior to 1847—nearly eighty years later!—when James Orchard Halliwell mentioned it in his *Dictionary of Archaic and Provincial Words.* But the best was yet to come. Idly my eyes began wandering further down the page, through the remainder of the *base* definitions, until reaching the bottom. There, jumping out at me as big as Babe Ruth was another entry, not for *base* but for the next word in alphabetical order: *baseball.* Now things were getting surreal. Here was a separate listing for the word *baseball,* bearing its own definition:

> Ba'seball: (from *base* and *ball*) A rural game in which the person striking the ball must run to his *base* or goal.

I could hardly contain myself. For someone who has spent untold hours researching the beginnings of baseball, this was a moment of great satisfaction. To be sure, it was not the most elaborate of definitions, but it was a step beyond calling baseball simply "a rural play." In its brevity the entry spelled out that the object was to hit a ball and then run to a base, complementing *A Little Pretty Pocket-book*'s primitive portrayal of the game from twenty-four years earlier.

The full name of the 1768 work in which I found these glorious nuggets is *A General Dictionary of the English Language, Compiled with the Greatest Care from the Best Authors and Dictionaries Now Extant.* It was printed in London by J. and R. Fuller, and its authors are identified only as "A Society of Gentlemen." Perhaps almost as surprising as its inclusion of baseball is the fact that this dictionary is extremely rare. I could locate only two extant copies in libraries, and I have no knowledge of any that may be in private hands. Its rarity is a

BA´SEBALL, *f.* (From *bafe* and *ball)* A rural game in which the perfon ſtriking the ball muſt run to his *bafe* or goal.

Fig. 6. Definition of baseball as it appeared in *A General Dictionary of the English Language*, 1768. Credit: British Library.

mystery to me because, even allowing for age, reference works such as dictionaries were the types of treasured volumes that families tended to keep on their shelves for generations. A great deal of research and writing went into its preparation. A year before its formal publication date, the dictionary's creators were already advertising that an initial section of the book would go on sale May 2, 1767. These ads were placed in many newspapers and made the following pledge: "In this Work the Derivation of Words will be properly pointed out; the Accents justly fixed; and their Appellations, either a Substantive, Adjective, Verb, &c. marked by proper Initials; barbarous Words will be stigmatized by proper Marks either as Obsolete, Wanting Authority, or being seldom used; the Spelling will be carefully attended to; and the Sense of each Word explained with Clearness, Conciseness, and Precision."[2]

Even a casual look at the resulting work confirms that the Society of Gentlemen achieved these forecasted standards. The advertisements also announced that the publishers would release further segments of the dictionary every succeeding Saturday for at least forty-five weeks, and that if the total number of segments exceeded fifty, "the overplus to be given gratis." Once all sections were printed and distributed, purchasers were responsible for having the completed dictionary bound through the services of an independent bookbinder, a common practice in the eighteenth century. The purpose of releasing the dictionary serially was both to spread out the costs and resources needed for its production and as a means of raising funds to underwrite the project. The hope was that booksellers could enlist interested buyers to subscribe in advance for the entire work. The subscription drive must have attained some level of success, or additional funds were obtained from other sources, because the dictionary's backers managed to complete the undertaking. We don't know how many copies of the book came off the presses, but the number must have exceeded a minimum baseline to justify the typesetting and production costs of such an ambitious work. I can't help wondering why virtually all of them disappeared.

Another mystery is the identity of its compilers, the augustly named Society of Gentlemen. It wasn't unusual for authors of published works in that era to choose anonymity, but typically it is a relatively easy matter to discover their names. Not so with these guys. I've made a sizable effort to unmask them, including appealing for help from dictionary societies in both the United States and United Kingdom, but no one seems to know anything about them, and I couldn't find any clues to their identities in the written record. My first thought was that they might be related to the Society of Gentlemen who released the first edition of the *Encyclopædia Britannica* that very same year of 1768, but that noble group operated out of Edinburgh, and it wasn't likely they would be issuing a second major work simultaneously in London.

Those aren't the only quirks about this dictionary that have me puzzled. Another has to do with its definition for the word *base*. Generally, whenever baseball historians, including myself, happen across a reference to a game called *base* in an eighteenth-century source, we assume that it denotes the widely played game of prisoner's base. But here, plain as day, a dictionary was defining *base* as "a rural play, called also baseball." This would seem to turn the assumption on its head. But then again, maybe not. Consider the literary example the dictionary's authors chose to illustrate their definition: "Lads more like to run, the country *base*." They lifted this fragment of dialogue from act 5, scene 3 of Shakespeare's *Cymbeline*:

Close by the battle, ditch'd, and wall'd with turf;
Which gave advantage to an ancient soldier,
An honest one, I warrant; who deserved
So long a breeding as his white beard came to,
In doing this for's country: athwart the lane,
He, with two striplings—lads more like to run
The country base than to commit such slaughter
With faces fit for masks, or rather fairer
Than those for preservation cased, or shame—

Even taking into account the Bard's status as the most innovative
of writers, it is too much of a stretch to give him credit for foreshadowing baseball. Nothing in these lines, in my opinion, even vaguely
suggests a ball game. The expression "to run the base," or "running the
base," appeared frequently in early modern English literature, with
examples dating as far back as the fifteenth century. In citing one such
usage, the editors of *A General Dictionary of the English Language*
seem to have suffered from the same congenital and enduring confusion between prisoner's base and baseball that persists to this day.

Another curious note about the dictionary is that its authors chose
to spell *baseball* as a single word. That's how we do it today, of course,
but in England in the eighteenth century, *base-ball* usually appeared as
two words connected by a hyphen, as it did in *A Little Pretty Pocket-
book*, Lady Hervey's letter of 1748, and the novel *The Card*. Spelling
baseball as a whole word would not be seen again until the 1820s in
England and even later in North America. Why the dictionary's editors chose that form is a mystery. It is also curious that they typeset
the word with an accent mark after the first two letters: *ba'seball*. This,
presumably, was to meet the pledge stated in their newspaper proposal
to provide "accents justly fixed," although why they chose to place
the accent where they did instead of at the end of the syllable *base* is
puzzling. But their unusual choice explains, in part, why it took me
so many visits to the ECCO database before I found it. As I explained

in chapter 3, my search of the database for *baseball* as a whole word turned up the *base-ball* reference from *The Card*, but failed to snare this 1768 dictionary entry. Even though I try to get creative with my search terms, it never occurred to me to attempt an odd formulation like *ba'seball*. Clearly, I still have a way to go before managing to anticipate all the idiosyncrasies of eighteenth-century lexicographers.

Bringing to light this 1768 reference to baseball was an important moment in the humble realm of early baseball research. True, I am the one who made the discovery, and it is therefore fair to question whether I am the best one to judge; but even taking my bias and immodesty into account, this was a big deal. Here's why. Prior to this, what we knew about English baseball in the mid-eighteenth century emanated from the handful of references to the pastime from the 1740s and 1750s. These suggested that practitioners of baseball in those years were not confined to any particular age or gender and hinted that the game may have enjoyed some tangible popularity. Still, the latter assumption was based solely upon a collection of inferences, ones I made by parsing the words of sources that mentioned the pastime, such as Lady Hervey's letter and William Bray's diary. But with the term *baseball* now meriting a definition within a sophisticated national dictionary, we are provided, in my opinion, a far more authoritative measure of the game's presence in the era's culture. Overall, the dictionary's editors chose to define relatively few games among its 750-odd pages, and those definitions were consistently spare. For example, the entry for *cricket* reads simply "a diversion or sport played with bats and balls." By comparison, their definition for baseball, arguably a lesser known game, was paid greater care. It is the only ball game included in the dictionary whose definition suggests even the slightest hint of how it was played: "a rural game in which the person striking the ball must run to his base or goal." Perhaps I'm reading too much into these subtleties, but I'm convinced that among our small pool of clues about early baseball, this 1768 dictionary entry offers the strongest indicator that the young pastime had gained acceptance into the established family of English games.

5

Wild Geese and Red Herrings

The seemingly eternal tendency to confuse the pastime of prisoner's base with the game of baseball is not the only semantical mix-up I've come across in my research. I described one prime example of this phenomenon in my first book. As with William Bray's diary entry of 1755, this one too looked to be a case of a man mentioning the term *baseball* in his personal journal. It was an especially early occurrence, predating William Bray's by more than fifty years. Unfortunately, it also turned out to be considerably less credible. I encountered it back in 2001, shortly after I first began researching the origins of baseball. At that time I was attempting to survey everything on the subject I could get my hands on, and one of the first documents coming to my attention was a baseball chronology prepared by two highly regarded historians. Among their entries was a quotation from the year 1700 purportedly from the memoirs of Reverend Thomas Wilson, a Puritan divine from Maidstone, England. It read: "I have seen Morris-dancing, cudgel-playing, baseball and cricketts, and many other sports on the Lord's Day."

Even as a novice historian I recognized that Reverend Wilson's observation, if verified, was of momentous significance. Indeed, it would stand as the earliest known documented reference to baseball. All that was needed to anoint it as such was to locate the original memoir. As it turned out, that was no easy task. Working backward, I quickly learned that the two historians who compiled the chronology, John Thorn and Thomas Heitz, had sourced the Wilson quotation from a 1947 book, *Ball, Bat and Bishop,* written by Robert W. Henderson, the respected researcher I credited previously as the first to tout the baseball page from *A Little Pretty Pocket-book.*[1] Henderson in turn had found the Wilson quote, worded identically, in a July 1901 article on the history of cricket from the British publication *Baily's Magazine of Sports and Pastimes*.[2] Unfortunately, that's where the trail ended because the author of the *Baily's* piece, C. H. Woodruff, failed to cite any earlier source. Foiled, I regrouped and shifted to a different tactic; I would seek out what I could about the mysterious Reverend Wilson and try to track down his memoirs. This proved to be a fruitless endeavor. I found that there were many men of the cloth named Thomas Wilson serving English parishes of all denominations, but none of them was a Puritan clergyman who could have been alive and writing his memoirs in the year 1700. At that point I dropped the matter and went on to other priorities.

I occasionally returned to my hunt for the elusive Reverend Wilson, but it wasn't until 2003 that I made a breakthrough. Combing through historical accounts of English Puritans in the seventeenth century, I found a reference to a preacher and parliamentarian named Thomas Wilson. But unless he was a zombie he couldn't have written a memoir in 1700, having departed for Puritan heaven nearly a half century earlier than that. Nevertheless, having gotten that far I skimmed through microfilms of Wilson's various speeches and sermons, all of which showed him to be a fiercely conservative anti-monarchist and anti-papal rabble-rouser. But other than his railing against the blasphemy of King James's controversial *Book of Sports,* a royal decree that approved the play of several innocuous games on Sundays, I found nothing in this Wilson's writings even remotely connected to baseball. Then, in a university library's catalog, I noticed a reference to a biography of Wilson written and published in 1672. That work was on microfilm as well, and after skimming through it I finally found a resolution to my nearly two-year pursuit. It was not the result I had hoped for, but at least I was now able to put the matter to bed. It turns out it was not our dear departed Reverend Wilson who penned the troublesome quotation; instead, it was his biographer, a certain George Swinnock, who wrote the statement about Maidstone, albeit in a slightly variant form. A great admirer of Wilson, Swinnock claimed to have witnessed the reverend's success in cleaning up the once sin-ridden town, commenting that "Maidstone was formerly a very prophane Town, insomuch that I have seen Morrice dancing, Cudgel playing, Stool-ball, Crickets, and many other sports openly and publickly on the Lords Day."[3]

What a difference a word makes. Stool-ball was a popular game played in Britain for centuries. Some of its elements were similar to baseball's, and it may well have been one of baseball's ancestors, but it was *not* baseball. Sometime prior to the quote's appearance in Woodruff's 1901 article in *Baily's Magazine*, someone replaced the one word with the other. Perhaps Woodruff himself was the culprit or someone else working at the magazine. But whoever made the switch, what was their point? Why would anyone bother tampering with an obscure, two-hundred-year-old statement? The act wouldn't seem to provide any benefit to Woodruff, since his purpose for including the Wilson quote in his article was to document a seventeenth-century reference to cricket. What difference could it have made to him if the quote mentioned baseball instead of stool-ball? The only thing that makes sense to me is that whoever made the substitution, whether Woodruff or some other actor, did it in the misguided belief he was being helpful to a contemporary audience. By 1901 the formerly ubiquitous English pastime of stool-ball had faded into obscurity. Most Britons had long forgotten about it, other than residents of a couple of rural southern counties where it was still being played in a modernized form. Conversely, at that time, most of the British public, including *Baily's* readers, would readily recognize the name *baseball*. Believing stool-ball to be related to baseball, the perpetrator might have considered it a harmless but helpful act to substitute the name of the known game for that of the unknown one. I prefer this explanation to that of another possibility, that the switch was made for insidious reasons; that some unknown mischief maker elected to insert the word *baseball* into the quote in order to make it appear as if that game was older than it really was. Such an action seems as improbable as it is silly, but we'll probably never really know.

Speaking of improbable and silly, I would never have guessed that by making the connection between the alleged Reverend Wilson's quote and his 1672 biography I would find myself unwittingly laying the groundwork for a weird and personal episode of "fake news." In May 2013, while viewing a webpage entitled "The History of Baseball" on the website baseballsquare.com, I was astonished to come across the following statement: "The history of baseball can be traced back to the year 1672, when David Block started the ancient version of base-ball, called stoolball."[4] I take pride in knowing that my research efforts have helped illuminate the early history of baseball, but never appreciated that my contributions were quite so profound. But just to set the record straight for those who believe anything they read on the internet, I did not live in the seventeenth century, no matter how ancient I might appear. Nor can I take credit for that lovely old game of stoolball. Still and all, one affirmative outcome of this flattering case of misdirection is that I can now claim to share something in common with the storied Reverend Wilson, not to mention Abner Doubleday.

You might think that after chasing down the source of the Wilson misquote and finally sending that particular red herring to wherever red herrings go to bed, I would be wary of any new, too-good-to-be-true intimations of seventeenth-century baseball that happened to cross my path. Apparently not, for I nearly got taken in by another tantalizing illusion. Thankfully, I got wise to this one in a matter of hours rather than the many months it took me to run down the Wilson story. This latest teaser struck me while camped at a computer terminal in a reading room of the British Library on an otherwise dreary November day in late 2009. I was searching databases of nineteenth-century books and newspapers for references to English baseball, an exercise I had gone through on many previous occasions. A query for the term *base-ball* produced innumerable hits, most of them referring to the more common American version of the game. To filter these out, I eliminated any responses that contained words such as *umpire*, *nine, diamond,* or *America* itself. This left me a far smaller pool of hits to comb through, and while doing so I came across one that seemed, on the face of it, totally preposterous. Logic told me that something had to be wrong with it and not to get my hopes up. Nonetheless, the enticing possibility of finding an absurdly early reference to baseball left me blind to reason, my pulse quickening with anticipation.

What I spotted was a mention of "base ball" in the April 21, 1876, issue of an English newspaper, the *Manchester Courier and Lancashire General Advertiser.* The word appeared in a column entitled "Local Gleanings" that was devoted to newsy events taking place in the rural areas surrounding Manchester. The columnist's subject that day was a two-hundred-year-old diary that had come to his attention, one that had been kept by a young man named Roger Lowe who had lived in the village of Ashton-in-Makerfield in nearby rural Lancashire. A prominent local mill owner had acquired the diary and passed a transcribed copy of it to the columnist. The diary was quite unusual in that, unlike most surviving journals from the seventeenth or eighteenth centuries that documented the affairs of aristocrats or churchmen, this one chronicled the daily life of a common villager, in this case an apprentice storekeeper. The column's author was fascinated by Roger Lowe's entries for the year 1663 and published summaries and excerpts. He praised the young man's detailed observations of the "manners and customs" of village society, such as how the local alehouse was the meeting place for business transactions involving the clergy. To this, he added: "Then too we have mention of the amusement and games of that day, the races at Warrington and Newton, hare hunting, 'foomert' catching, &c., a grand game at base ball, when each side had drums playing and other music to encourage them, (but which the diarist describes as all 'Vanity'), playing at bowls in the 'bowling alley,' Whitsun ales, funeral feasts, &c. &c."[5]

Reading this I did a double take. It couldn't be possible! What were the odds that a storekeeper in a remote corner of seventeenth-century England could have witnessed a "grand game of base ball"? Still, I had to consider the facts in front of me. The columnist was describing the diary's excerpts firsthand. I had no reason to doubt his veracity or the faithfulness of the transcription he received. There was no obvious reason why a provincial English journalist writing in 1876 would fabricate baseball's presence in a diary written in the 1660s. After all, it's doubtful the game meant anything more to him than hare hunting or foomert [polecat] catching. But unless the unimaginable was true, that Roger Lowe really had observed baseball 350 years ago in that rural Lancashire village, there had to be some other logical explanation for this absurdity.

There was, of course, but I didn't see it at the time. Instead, I resolved there was no other course for me but to get my hands on the diary itself. I had to see the word *baseball* written in Roger Lowe's handwriting with my very own eyes. My excitement was building. Was I really on the verge of making a big discovery? The first step was to locate the document. That was easy; I quickly determined it was housed in a small archive in Lancashire. Next up, check the train schedules, plan my departure from London, determine where I would stay up north, and so forth. My mind was whirling with energy. Then, out of my reverie the obvious dawned on me. Before galavanting all over the country, maybe I should first see whether a transcription of the diary was available. Maybe one was right there in the British Library. Maybe I'm an idiot. Check, check, and check.

The diary, it turns out, had been transcribed and published more than once, and, yes, all versions were in the collection of the British Library. No train journeys required. Had I been a little more patient and paid closer attention to the transcribed diary excerpts in the newspaper column, I would have had all I needed to figure out the mystery. Luckily for me, it took only two hours of additional time to realize what I had overlooked. In that interval I was able to request and collect everything the Library had on the subject of Roger Lowe's diary.

The two most recent works, one published in 1938 and the other in 1994, were of little help. Neither mentioned anything about baseball. Nor did the earliest of the transcriptions, a booklet dated 1876 and marked "for private circulation." That one was published by the *Manchester Courier* and contained the original column plus additional excerpts from the diary that had appeared in subsequent issues of the paper. It added nothing new to the baseball puzzle. One more book remained upon my reading room table. A second newspaper, one from the nearby town of Leigh, had also picked up the Roger Lowe story. The Leigh paper printed sections of the transcribed diary in serialized format over a period of weeks in 1876 and gathered them the following year into a little pamphlet entitled *The Diary of R. Lowe, 1663–1678, Re-printed from the Leigh Chronicle*. Prior to either newspaper getting possession of the transcription, someone had added clarifying notes to help nineteenth-century readers understand some of the unfamiliar seventeenth-century terms and concepts mentioned by Roger Lowe. Editors of the *Leigh Chronicle* incorporated these notes while publishing excerpts from the diary, and it didn't take me long while paging through their pamphlet before the answer to the baseball conundrum smacked me in the face. In his entry for July 18, 1663, Roger Lowe wrote the following: "I sat forward and upon Latchford Heath there was a great compeny of persons with 2 drums amongst the young men ware playing at prison barrs where I stayed awhile to see them but concluded it was but vanitie." Then the editors appended a helpful comment: "The game of prison bars or base ball is an old English game. The one witnessed on Latchford Heath by the diarist appears to have been somewhat of a match, much as friendly games of cricket are played now, with the similar attraction of music to encourage the players and entertain the spectators."[6]

In all likelihood, the chain of events went something like this: 1. The diary was transcribed. 2. Someone added clarifying notes. 3. The enhanced transcription came into the hands of the Manchester journalist. 4. The journalist summarized the diary in his 1876 column. 5. Rather than naming the game "prison barrs" as Roger Lowe did in 1663, the columnist instead chose to call it a "grand game of base ball," presumably in the belief the change would make it more recognizable to his readers. 6. I read the summary with its suggestion of seventeenth-century baseball and allowed my wishful thinking to blind me to a more rational appraisal.

As with the Reverend Wilson quote, here again was a case of a well-meaning Victorian editor transporting the term *baseball* back into a seventeenth-century context. By doing so he set loose another wild goose for this poor baseball historian to go chasing. Have these people no heart? As for prison bars, it may have been a delightful game, it may even have been accompanied by drums on occasion, but it most certainly wasn't baseball. Prison bars, in fact, is simply an alternate name for our old friend, prisoner's base. Whoever wrote that "helpful" note in the transcription fell victim to the same perennial confusion between the two unrelated games named "base" that a century earlier had tripped up the editors of the 1768 dictionary that I described in the previous chapter. And despite the passage of time, modern chroniclers of baseball history don't appear to have grown any wiser. It is not uncommon these days to find writers who cite a game called "base" described in the Revolutionary War diary of a soldier at Valley Forge, or point to another mention of "base" in the journals of the Lewis and Clark expedition, as primal examples of the National Pastime. In neither of those early American documents is there any suggestion that a ball was employed in the games described, and in both cases the writers were almost certainly alluding to prisoner's base.

The penchant to muddle and monkey with the names of baseball-related games, as we have seen, is a timeworn phenomenon. This temptation to tinker appears to reach all the way back to antiquity, affecting even the earliest of ball games, one attributed to the Greek poet Homer. There is a famous scene in the *Odyssey* where a princess named Nausicaa goes down to the river bank with her attending maidens to wash some clothes. As their garments are drying in the sun, and while Ulysses is sleeping nearby in the bushes, the young women engage in a game of ball. For eons, writers have cited this scene as the earliest literary reference to humans playing with a ball. It influenced a Greek scholar named Agallis living in Alexandria hundreds of years afterward to credit her countrywoman, Nausicaa, for actually being the inventor of ball games.[7] Aside from its foreshadowing of Doubledayism, and notwithstanding the fact that Nausicaa was probably a fictional character, Agallis's claim set the stage for many interpretations and reinterpretations of the pastime that Nausicaa and her companions played along the shoreline all those years ago.

We can't possibly know what words Homer used to describe that event. Historians believe he lived in the eighth or ninth century BCE, and no manuscripts from his era have survived. Even the question of whether Homer existed as a real person is a subject of debate. Some scholars believe his name was a collective label for a number of ancient Greek bards who turned traditional stories into verse that was shared orally at first and only later written down. In any case, the works credited to Homer have taken shape and evolved over the centuries, first in Greek and later translated into many other languages. The earliest and perhaps best-known English translation of the *Odyssey* is the one by George Chapman published in 1616. He left no doubt as to how he interpreted the ball game scene:

> Yet still watcht when the Sunne, their cloaths had dride,
> Till which time (having din'd) *Nausicae*
> With other virgins, did at stool-ball play;
> Their shoulder-reaching head-tyres laying by.
> *Nausicae* (with the wrists of Ivory)
> The liking stroke strooke; singing first a song.

Meanwhile, Ulysses is sleeping in the nearby bushes, and Minerva, planning to pair him with Nausicaa, hatches a plan to wake him:

Her meane was this, (though thought a stool-ball chance)
The Queene now (for the upstroke) strooke the ball
Quite wide off th' other maids; and made it fall
Amidst the whirlpooles. At which, out shriekt all;
And with the shrieke, did wise *Ulysses* wake.[8]

During Chapman's lifetime, Britons played stool-ball more widely than any other ball sport, with the possible exception of football. Poets loved to write about it because it often brought young men and women together in physical proximity, presenting delightful opportunities for romantic engagement. Stool-ball would have been the natural choice for Chapman, just as some later interpreters of the *Odyssey* would be influenced by the preferences of their own eras. The Greek texts upon which Chapman and others based their translations did not assign the ball game any particular name. Nor is it easy to determine the precise nature of the game from a literal reading of those texts. Jed Thorn, a classics scholar and son of the baseball historian John Thorn, offered me this translation of the pertinent passage: "And then, when they had enjoyed their food, both she and her servants, having thrown their veils aside, played a game of ball; and white-armed Nausicaa led them in their chant. . . . So then the princess threw the ball to one of her servants; but she missed her target, and threw it into a deep eddy."[9]

In the eighteenth century, several English intellectuals, including Alexander Pope, produced new translations of the *Odyssey*. These efforts followed the original Greek in opting not to assign any specific name to the ball game, although some editions included notes speculating on how the game might have been played. It was not until later that a young man writing about Homer in a literary journal departed from the more traditional approach. His untitled essay appeared in the December 13, 1788, issue of the *Trifler*, a short-lived weekly publication issued under the nom de plume of Timothy Touchstone. The anonymous author, presumably one of four students said to be the journal's creators, was a candid Homer fanboy.[10] His opening words were: "The works of Homer may be considered as a beautiful and spacious garden, in which thousands, in ages past, have walked with delight." He then proceeded to heap praise upon the poet and his characters, singling out the one who was his particular favorite: "There is, perhaps, no prettier character in the whole of his works than that of Nausicaa in the Odyssey."[11]

Her virtues were many, according to the young *Trifler* writer, and he chose to highlight a few: "She is the very pattern of excellence, to please the female *jarveys* she drives four in hand and manages her whip with utmost skill, to delight the domestic part of her sex, she sings most charmingly, and, in fine, is not above playing a game of baste ball with her attendants."[12] The game that was stool-ball to Chapman 150 years earlier had now transformed into "baste ball," at least in the mind of this eighteenth-century groupie. His new appraisal of the pastime was eminently sensible, reflecting what the young man observed in the world around him. Stool-ball by then was fading in popularity. Instead, girls and young women of the towns and villages of southern England were embracing the game of baseball.

The *Trifler* author may have been the first to offer this new slant on Homer's ball game, but others would follow. One such convert, writing almost a century later, was a columnist for the *Daily News* of London. Writing in the paper's June 25, 1878, issue, he expressed his take on the Nausicaa game in a piece otherwise devoted to a comparison of various theories on the origin of tennis. He noted:

Some theorists have set up a claim for Nausicaa, who plays a ball game in the "Odyssey." Old Chapman, in this passage, is all for stool-ball, which was the origin of cricket:

Nausicaa
With other virgins did at stool-ball play.

She struck the "liking stroke," answering to the "trial ball," which the bigots of the MCC no longer allow. Again:

The Queen now, for the upstroke, struck the ball,
Quite wide of th' other maids,

says Chapman, in his liberal way. What she really did was to throw the ball at one of her companions and miss her. The sober critic will admit that Nausicaa played neither tennis, nor stool-ball, but rounders, or base-ball, and that she threw at, and missed, an opponent who was running between the bases.[13]

The sober critic will admit that this fellow might have gotten a bit carried away. His examination of Homer's words revealed to him not only the genus of the ancient game but also the hidden message that all previous studies of the *Odyssey* had missed: that Nausicaa's act of throwing a ball at another player was an attempt to "soak" an opposing runner, a practice then still common in English baseball and rounders. Apparently this columnist's telepathic powers were so formidable that they had no difficulty traversing three millennia to divine Homer's true intentions.

Modern-day English translators of the *Odyssey*, for better or for worse (depending on your point of view), have veered away from the practice of embellishing the long-ago ball play of Nausicaa and her maidens with contemporary labels. In doing this they are following the original Greek more faithfully, though not nearly as delightfully. Chapman and those following him may have taken a few liberties by retrofitting stool-ball and baseball into an ancient setting, but they were only trying to make Homer's works more relevant to their readers. And while they were at it, they also gave us yet more examples of well-meaning writers corrupting the historical landscape by heedlessly swapping the names of baseball and other games in and out of their original contexts.

6

Ball, Bat, and Beyond

It was my first big discovery. The year was 2001, my rookie season as a baseball researcher. I had become fixated on uncovering the true story of baseball's origins and was eagerly surveying everything that others had written on the subject. One work that particularly caught my interest was Harold Peterson's 1973 book, *The Man Who Invented Baseball*. Peterson's thesis was that a New York banking clerk and volunteer fireman named Alexander Cartwright was almost solely responsible for organizing the first baseball club and drawing up its rules. I was aware other historians had begun to poke holes in Peterson's theories about Cartwright, but what drew me to his book was its opening chapters in which he meandered through his unique narrative of baseball's prehistory.[1] He enumerated myriad examples of ancient ball games played in countries around the world that he claimed were part of baseball's ancestry. Scandalously, Peterson committed the scholarly sin of failing to document most of his sources, leading me and others to treat his findings with skepticism. Nevertheless, the sheer volume of early games he served up presented me with many tempting leads to follow.

One of those leads was his reference to an old German ball game (literally, *das deutsche Ballspiel*) that he represented as a close cousin of baseball. Peterson learned about the pastime, or so he claimed, from a pioneering work on games published in 1796 by a progressive educator in Germany, J. C. F. Gutsmuths.[2] As an avid collector of early books on children's games and sports, I took an immediate interest in this Gutsmuths book and began searching for a copy to purchase. I soon discovered a bookseller in Germany who had one to offer, and I placed my order.

Several weeks passed. It was now August 2001, and my family and I were about to fly off for a long-planned vacation to Alaska. The day before our departure, the book from the German bookseller finally arrived. I opened the package and caressed the old volume in my hands. Turning to its table of contents, my eyes roamed down the list of games. Yes, there was *das deutsche Ballspiel,* just as Peterson had promised. But then my focus drifted down to the next game on the list. I looked at it, blinked, and looked again. Huh? I knew what I was seeing, but it seemed totally out of place. The name of the game, spelled out in full, was *Ball mit Freystäten (oder das englische Base-ball).*[3] I don't read German, but some words are universal. Baseball? This book has a section on baseball? It was published in 1796! In Germany! I was very confused. Excited, but confused.

Quickly turning to the promised chapter for *englische Base-ball,* I found seven pages of old German text. It might as well have been Martian for all that I was able to decipher it. My mind was burning with curiosity and fantasizing the possibilities. What untold mysteries about baseball could this eighteenth-century volume be harboring? I also couldn't help wondering what unlikely circumstances led Gutsmuths to include it in his book in the first place. I needed immediate answers but had no way to get them because we were about to disappear for three weeks into the land of eagles and glaciers, with no German translators along for the ride. My only recourse was to dash out to a copy store and photocopy the seven *englische Base-ball* pages, and then pack the copies together with my other belongings as we flew off to the north.

Several days later we were enjoying spectacular Alaskan scenery along the course of a four-and-a-half-hour ferry ride from Juneau to Haines. At one point I noticed that some tourists on the boat were speaking German. My wife, Barbara, urged me to approach them with the photocopies I was carrying in my backpack. I felt a little shy and stupid about doing that, but she prodded me (I mean, encouraged me) and so I walked up to the group and showed them the pages.

They were very obliging and began passing them around to each other, reading them and murmuring back and forth. They apologized for not knowing much about baseball, but also admitted that it was hard to make much sense out of what I had given them. What I've since learned is that the German language, unlike English and French, has transformed quite a bit in the past two hundred years. Germany wasn't even a unified country back then, only a hodgepodge of loosely allied city-states, dukedoms, and principalities. Dialects among them varied considerably, as did syntax, sentence structure, spelling, and the like. My new friends, the German tourists, gamely tried translating a few sentences from the photocopied pages. What they gave back to me, with some embarrassment, was a smattering of nearly nonsensical English phrases, but not so nonsensical that I couldn't discern among them a few recognizable signs. Standing there with the German tourists on the Alaskan ferry I was filled with the first real hope that the game Gutsmuths described in his book might actually be somewhat akin to what we now know as baseball, although at that point I was still mostly in the dark. The Germans handed the sheets back to me with regrets that they couldn't have been more helpful.

As we boarded a plane back to San Francisco a couple of weeks later, I was sad, of course, to bid fond farewell to glaciers and all that, but at least now I could get down to the business of finding someone to provide me a proper translation of the baseball chapter. A call to the German Department at UC Berkeley connected me with a graduate student specializing in early German literature who was willing to take on the job. A week later she delivered her finished translation, and much to my delight it revealed that the *englische Base-ball* described in the Gutsmuths book was eminently recognizable. Of course, there were some elements in its makeup that might appear a bit strange to current fans of the game, such as the number of bases in the infield varying by the number of players participating, or the bases themselves being positioned much closer together than they are today. Additionally, this 1796 description featured some quirky rules that would seem truly bizarre if anyone attempted them now, one being that, after all members had been put out, the batting team could retain its at-bats by running onto the field, retrieving the ball, and then striking one of the opposing players with it before they could scramble back to the sidelines. It became evident to me from reading the translation that this early version of baseball did not demand a great deal of athleticism of its participants and was clearly more suited for children than adults. Still, at its core, the game Gutsmuths described was unmistakably something that most people today would identify as baseball. It featured batting (with a short, one-handed bat), pitching, fielding, and baserunning around a circuit, and to this eager, novice baseball researcher it felt like I had just opened the door to King Tut's tomb.

Brimming with self-satisfaction for making this discovery, I couldn't wait to share it with others. After all, to the best of my knowledge, Gutsmuths's baseball chapter was the earliest attempt in any language to present a detailed account of the game's characteristics, antedating by almost forty years the earliest known description of the pastime in English. I proudly announced my find in an essay entitled "Baseball's Earliest Rules" that I circulated to other baseball historians. Their response was universally positive. My discovery of *Ball mit Freystäten (oder das englische Base-ball)* in Gutsmuths's work of 1796 would, in essence, become the centerpiece of my first book. Its significance, in my view, went beyond its status as the earliest description of baseball. To me it represented the missing link, the bridge of proof connecting the few tenuous English references to the word *baseball* from the eighteenth century to the iconic American national pastime that would follow. I believed Gutsmuths's portrait of the pastime, replete with its familiar features and use of a bat, established that all games called baseball, whether ancient or modern, were related to each other in substance as well as in name.

My dissection and analysis of *das englische Base-ball* occupied most of a chapter in *Baseball before We Knew It*. Not only did Gutsmuths's contribution anchor my theory of baseball's evolution, it also helped bolster a parallel focal point of the book, my rebuttal of the widely held notion that baseball descended from rounders. My case for baseball's primacy rested on the obvious, that baseball was the older name of the two, dating at least as far back as 1744 (as evidenced by *A Little Pretty Pocket-book*), while the name *rounders* would not show up in the historical record for another eighty-four years. When references to the word *rounders* began populating English books and newspapers in the mid-nineteenth century, they coincided with the disappearance of the name *baseball* from those same sources, or so I thought at the time. This I took as circumstantial proof that the two games were one and the same and that rounders was simply a new name that boys in England had begun attaching to the old game of baseball, a label that would eventually displace the original designation. Yes, there did seem to be at least one small discrepancy in this argument. Nearly all accounts of rounders indicated it was played with a bat, while none of the references to English baseball did—except Gutsmuths's, of course. His description of English baseball was more elaborate than any other, and it distinctly mentioned a bat. My missing link!

But as time passed, my lovely Gutsmuths discovery began to show some cracks. New findings suggested to me that I may have overstated the significance of *das englische Base-ball* in decoding the evolution of baseball and its relationship to rounders. This comedown was self-inflicted. Instead of leaving well enough alone and moving on to other topics, I couldn't resist the urge to uncover more evidence about English baseball. I was bewitched by this obscure game that was so important to the rise of America's National Pastime but about which so little was known. In more than a decade of follow-up research I identified hundreds of new references to it. And, to my amazement, I learned that English baseball did not, as I had long assumed, disappear from the written record by the mid-nineteenth century. My new findings proved the game had prospered to the end of that century and beyond. What's more, none of these many newly discovered references to English baseball followed Gutsmuths's example of mentioning a bat. I had to confront the humbling possibility that the German's description of *das englische Base-ball,* the one that had served as the cornerstone for all my theories, was not an accurate representation of the way English baseball was played on most occasions. For all its rarity and richness, the 1796 description appeared to be an outlier, one that now begged for further explanation.

Searching for an answer, I probed deeper into my research. Along with my new findings about English baseball, my digging had also uncovered occasional and seemingly innocuous mentions of a pastime known simply as "bat and ball." I had come across these in a scattering of English books and newspaper articles from the late eighteenth and early nineteenth centuries. One such reference appeared in a children's novel, published in 1790, that identified the protagonist's favorite amusements as "marbles, bat and ball [and] hop-step-and-jump."[4] At first I assumed this "bat and ball" was shorthand for cricket, but other examples quickly rebutted that notion. One surfaced in a 1797 newspaper piece praising the layout of a new school's playing ground, noting that "it affords ample space for cricket, for bat and ball, or any other school-boy exercise."[5] Another came within an 1801 English children's chapbook where the author cautioned that "bat and ball is an inferior kind of cricket, and more suitable for little children, who may safely play at it, if they will be careful not to break windows."[6] "Bat and ball" was still being tagged as a distinct game as late as 1824, when the writer of a journal article observed, "On Sunday, after afternoon service, the young people joined in football and hurling, bat and ball, or cricket."[7]

Then, in 1828, the following sentence appeared in a newly published book on juvenile games: "In the west of England this is one of the most favourite sports with the bat and ball."[8] The work was *The Boy's Own Book,* and the pastime being described was called rounders. This was the first known usage of that term. The book included instructions on how to play the game, and as with all subsequent accounts of rounders that would follow during the course of the nineteenth century, the description in *The Boy's Own Book* made clear that use of a bat was intrinsic to its play. It was inevitable, therefore, that I would connect rounders to my discoveries of the aforementioned game of "bat and ball." From the references I quoted above it was evident that "bat and ball" was something other than cricket. It was also unlikely to be a casual designation for the still-played, ancient sport of trap-ball, as writers for centuries had always referred to that game by its full name, and it was implausible that a cluster of unrelated authors would suddenly conspire to give it a shorthand label. I began to suspect that the game bat and ball was rounders-in-the-making, a generic placeholder that attached to the pastime until the name rounders came into use. Moreover, it did not escape me that the game Gutsmuths described as *das englische Base-ball* seemed to line up more closely with this emerging bat-and-ball/rounders form of play than with the apparently bat-less game of English baseball.

Saddled with this slew of new findings that upended some of my claims in my first book, I did what any responsible historian must do under such circumstances, which is to rejiggle my hypotheses to fit the facts. Taking into account what I now knew, I estimated the pastime later known as rounders began to coalesce sometime in the second half of the eighteenth century as an experimental offshoot of English baseball. Over a period of several decades it crystallized into a separate game, distinguished from its forebear, in part, by its adaptation of a bat. I strongly suspect it was this newly spun version, still bearing its legacy name of baseball, that came to Gutsmuths's attention when he was compiling his book. Ultimately, rounders and English baseball followed parallel developmental paths. Related by many commonalities, the two games coexisted in Britain during the nineteenth century, appealing to different populations and filling different recreational niches. I'll have more to say about the growth and spread of both pastimes in later chapters.

But before tying the bow on this tidy new package that reconciles the early history of English baseball with that of rounders, I have to concede that the package is, perhaps, a little too neat. My discoveries of a game bearing the simple label "bat and ball" offered a handy mechanism for explaining the disparity between the original English baseball, which didn't seem to employ a bat, and Gutsmuths's *englische Base-ball*, which did, while also allowing me to make the connection between the latter and rounders. It is possible, of course, that I was mistaken about these deductions, that I was reading too much into the scant body of evidence available, and that the respective evolutions of English baseball and rounders could have transpired in some other way. Furthermore, my "bat and ball" discoveries unintentionally introduced a new, confusing element into a related matter that was already puzzling me: how to understand the relationship between these English games and the parallel rise of baseball in America, the latter process still in its infancy in the late eighteenth century?

One aspect of this ambiguity is that usage of the term *bat and ball*, as a label for identifying a specific game, was not unique to England. The historian Brian Turner has uncovered numerous examples in North America from the mid-1700s to the early 1800s where diarists and newspaper writers applied the same appellation to games played in New England, particularly in eastern Massachusetts. Turner's research suggests that these mentions of "bat and ball" most likely pointed to localized baseball-like games rather than the game of cricket. This was prior to the years when the term *round-ball*, as well as the name *baseball* itself, would become standard usage in New England. One particular significance of these "bat and ball" sightings is that they may document what previously had been only a matter of assumption, that players of the earliest forms of baseball in North America utilized a bat in their game. It would not be until 1834 that a written source in North America, a children's book entitled *The Book of Sports*, unambiguously connected the word *bat* with the American game of baseball.[9]

It might only be a coincidence that "bat and ball" became attached to games in both England and North America at about the same time. The moniker "bat and ball" is hardly imaginative. It is simple and to the point and a handy and obvious choice for describing any activity that employed both pieces of equipment. Yet aside from their names, an essential question about these parallel, cross-ocean games remains unanswered. Whether called "bat and ball" or "baseball," how do we explain the fact that players on both continents began using a bat in these games nearly simultaneously, when evidence suggests that their root game, the original English baseball, made do without the use of one?

In attempting to tackle this question, I must acknowledge that the inconvenient shortage of evidence from the period hinders me from doing anything more than speculate. Still, it may be useful to at least try to frame a hypothetical answer. There has to be some logical reason for why early baseball activity in America appears to have incorporated a bat from its very beginning, while in England, use of the bat in rounders seems to have come about as a spinoff from an earlier bat-less form of play. One possibility is that the form of English baseball that first migrated to North America came with a bat already attached. This would have been the game known as "bat and ball" in England, the one that was later called *das englische Baseball* by Gutsmuths and that would even later morph into rounders. Had it happened like this, the near simultaneous appearance of bats on both sides of the ocean would not have been a coincidence. An alternate possibility is that the type of baseball that first crossed the Atlantic was the original form where players struck the ball using their bare hands. While there is no specific evidence that this version was ever played in colonial North America, it can't be ruled out. It is noteworthy that as early as 1750, advertisements for the juvenile works of John Newbery were appearing in newspapers on the Eastern Seaboard, and by 1862 an American publisher named Hugh Gaine was marketing a pirated edition of *A Little Pretty Pocket-book* under the abridged title of *A Little Pretty Book*.[10] While it's unlikely the simple act of reading this book would have prompted children in the colonies to go outdoors and begin practicing bat-less baseball, the notion is not completely out of the question, especially if it rekindled some family member's memory of the game from the mother country. Had these children done so, their game could have acquired a bat at some later time under the influence of subsequent arrivals of young people from England.

All this is conjecture, what we're reduced to when trying to explain historical developments without solid facts to draw upon. But, as it happens, there does exist one actual historical incident that might shed a ray of light on the question, one that was also brought to my attention by historian Brian Turner. In 1777 a colonel in the Continental army named David Henley was appointed commander of the city of Cambridge, Massachusetts, and put in charge of a large group of British prisoners whom American authorities had confined there after capturing them at the Battle of Saratoga. In the process of quashing a confrontation between his guards and the prisoners, Colonel Henley stabbed one of the Britons with his sword. The senior British officer among the captives, Gen. John Burgoyne, protested vigorously, and Henley was brought before a court-martial in 1778 to answer for his actions. The court transcript reveals details about the affair, including allegations that the prisoners had clubs in their possession, "clubs designed to play at bat and ball." One witness described these clubs as "hickery-sticks three or four feet long, and near as thick as my wrist."[11] From this description it seems unlikely that these implements were of the flat-faced variety appropriate for cricket, especially since hickory wood was used in their construction, a tree not native to Great Britain. What is significant about all this is that the transcript shows that both sides involved in the case, the British prisoners as well as Colonel Henley's American defense team, seemed to recognize and accept the concept of a distinct game called "bat and ball." One doesn't want to read too much into this, and it is only a single example, but it does suggest that Americans and Britons by the 1770s shared a common familiarity with a baseball-like activity that utilized a bat.

Even though the version of English baseball I discovered in Gutsmuths's writings may have varied from the pastime's typical mode of play, I still consider it among my niftiest finds. It remains the earliest detailed description of any game in the baseball-rounders family. Satisfied that I had analyzed it as well as I could, I was ready to move on to other challenges. But before doing so, there were a couple of loose ends about the German educator's book that still needed nailing down. One was a nagging mystery about how I chanced upon its existence in the first place. Earlier in this chapter I mentioned that the author Harold Peterson tipped me to Gutsmuths in his book about Alexander Cartwright, although Peterson only cited Gutsmuths's description of *das deutsche Ballspiel.* Indeed, he devoted the better part of three pages highlighting the German ball game and its importance to baseball's origins, even celebrating it as a "missing link."[12] Yet, inexplicably, he neglected to make any mention of *englische Base-ball,* a far more significant game historically and one that followed immediately after the German ball game in Gutsmuths's table of contents. How could Peterson have missed it? His chapter was all about premodern baseball and predecessor games. Discovering a description of baseball from 1796 would have been a major coup for him, just as it had been for me nearly forty years later. I tried to make sense out of his omission, but couldn't see any obvious explanations.

Peterson was a journalist and college instructor. He died more than thirty years ago, so the option of asking him directly why he overlooked Gutsmuths's description of English baseball would have made for a decidedly one-sided conversation. I tried tracking down his notes and papers, but to no avail, as his German-born wife was also deceased, they had no children, and the rest of his family was scattered about. Without anything else to go by, I narrowed it down to two speculative possibilities. One was that he never actually held the Gutsmuths book in his hands. Peterson was a Harvard educated scholar, someone who would have looked at the work and instantly spotted its baseball content. It is far more likely he never had possession of the entire volume, just the individual chapter describing the German game. Perhaps a colleague in Germany thought he might be interested in it and sent him a copy. Or, even less likely, his wife came across the book, and for some unknown reason translated only *das deutsche Ballspiel* chapter for her husband.

My other guess is that Peterson read the seven pages that Gutsmuths wrote about English baseball and made a decision to suppress them. Yes, scorn me as a conspiracy theorist if you will, but follow my reasoning. Peterson was in the midst of writing a book promoting Alexander Cartwright as the brilliant innovator who composed the first rules for baseball in 1845. He feared that disclosure of the rules and description published by Gutsmuths fifty years earlier would undercut his entire theory. His only alternative was to bury *das englische Base-ball* and hope nobody would ever be the wiser. Okay, okay, I concede this isn't very plausible, but that's what I've come to. Maybe I'm having a hard time accepting that I'll never solve the Peterson paradox. Only poor, dead Harold knows the answer, and wherever he's gone for his final rest, he's probably twisting with frustration over his failure to scoop me on *das englische Base-ball*.

My other loose thread was something that puzzled me even more than Peterson's disregard of Gutsmuths's baseball content. How did the German author learn about baseball in the first place? It was early in the 1790s, and the volatile French Revolution was unsettling the European continent. Baseball was unknown in the many small German principalities, nor was it a household word everywhere in Britain. Gutsmuths was living in the small town of Schnepfenthal and teaching at the progressive Salzmann School. He was an innovative young educator who advocated the importance of physical education as part of a well-rounded course of study. In support of this, he was compiling a comprehensive book of games and sports for his students to choose from. Collecting these pastimes, especially ones from foreign lands, would have been difficult, since Schnepfenthal was far removed from any major city. I tried to imagine the means through which Gutsmuths might have learned about baseball. Though he was well read, he traveled little, and according to the records of the Salzmann School he never journeyed to Britain. He kept an active correspondence, but a librarian at the Jena State Library where his papers are archived advised me that they had no record of him exchanging letters with anyone in England during the time in question.[13]

Trying to explore every possible avenue, I started thumbing through a book written by Christian Salzmann, the founder and headmaster of the Salzmann School who was Gutsmuths's boss. I was able to read the book because in 1790 it had been translated into English and published under the title *Elements of Morality for the Use of Children.* On the lookout for anything related to sports, my attention was rewarded by a lesson in the book that revolved around a group of boys playing a game of ball. Salzmann did not name the game or offer many details, but he did write that "some struck the ball in the air, and others received it as it fell."[14] While this greatly interested me, it wasn't until I learned who had translated the book into English that my enthusiasm went into overdrive. It was Mary Wollstonecraft, the pioneering English feminist and author of *A Vindication of the Rights of Women.* Wow! Moreover, I learned from a memoir written by Wollstonecraft's widower, William Godwin, that she and Salzmann maintained an ongoing correspondence and that the educator "repaid the obligation to her in kind by a German translation of the *Rights of Women.*"[15] My mind spun with ideas for tying this all together. Got it! Salzmann sends his book to Wollstonecraft for translation. While working on it she comes upon the ball-playing scene. Oh, she thinks, that reminds me of baseball. In her next communication with Salzmann she mentions this to him, describing how the game is played. Salzmann dutifully passes the information along to Gutsmuths, who he knows is working on a book about games. Voila![16]

I bet you can guess how this turned out. I tried out my theory on a couple of Gutsmuths experts from Germany. They politely shot it down, pointing out that there was no evidence to support such a link and that Salzmann's interactions with Wollstonecraft had nothing to do with Gutsmuths's special interest in the field of physical education.[17] Their rejection of my brilliant idea was disappointing, but my consultations with these experts wound up providing an unexpected bonus. I learned from one of them that during the course of Gutsmuths's lifelong tenure in Schnepfenthal, five students from England were in residence at the school at one time or another. One of those students, Samuel Glover, had been present during the period when Gutsmuths was collecting material for his book on games. The expert who provided this gem of information, the retired professor Herr Dr. Leonhard Friedrich, also informed me through an intermediary that it was Gutsmuths's practice to encourage the foreign students at the Salzmann School to provide him with details about athletic games played in their home countries.[18] It was highly likely, in Dr. Friedrich's view, that Glover was the source for Gutsmuths's description of baseball.

His opinion was not pure conjecture. Gutsmuths and his family seem to have been especially fond of Samuel Glover, welcoming him into their home during the young man's three-year stay in Schnepfenthal. Samuel reciprocated for this warm reception by helping his instructor improve his understanding of English ("together with my Glover, I have read a lot of English," wrote Gutsmuths on June 7, 1791, to a university friend).[19] Two weeks later the young Englishman ended his tenure at the Salzmann School and departed for home. Gutsmuths was quite emotional about losing his favorite student. In another letter to the same friend he wrote: "Oh, I lost a splendid young man yesterday, who was (from the year 1789 until 6 June 1791) my pupil, who clave with his entire soul to me, a young English 16-year-old, Sam Glover. Oh heavens, how his true heart trembled when I released him from my arms on his departure for England! Live well, good

Sam!"[20] In the best of all worlds, I'd like to find another note from Gutsmuths, one he wrote to Glover thanking his student ward for providing the details of baseball. What a pity that this document probably only exists in my imagination. Barring the faint possibility I'll yet discover such proof, I'll have to be satisfied with the strong circumstantial likelihood that Sam Glover was, indeed, Gutsmuths's baseball whisperer.

Once he returned to England, Glover's life did not turn out as gloriously as his old teacher might have hoped. The young man represented himself in society as heir to a large fortune, but in reality he had been cut off completely by his father. He met and married a young actress by the name of Julia Betterton. She had been on the stage since the age of six, and though quite successful in her decades-long professional career, she had the misfortune to be involved with a couple of very bad actors in her private life. One was her father, who exploited her financially from her childhood until his death at the age of eighty. The second was Samuel Glover, who proved every bit as despicable. He essentially bought Miss Betterton from her father for a promised payment of £1,000 that he never actually paid. According to the *Oxford Dictionary of National Biography,* "The marriage, which took place on 20 March, 1800, merely added to the burdens of the young actress: to her rapacious father's demands were added the extravagance of and persecution by a neglectful husband." Julia eventually bore eight children in the marriage, only four of whom survived to adulthood. She was almost solely responsible for their care while also serving as the family's breadwinner. In 1817 Samuel, from whom she was now estranged, "attempted to use the law to claim custody of their children, and to have her salary paid directly to himself so that he could use it to maintain another (illegitimate) family and his French mistress. In both these attempts he was unsuccessful," wrote the author of Julia's entry in *ODNB*. In the end, Samuel's bad behavior caught up with him, and he was sent to the Marshalsea prison for debtors. He died there in 1832.[21]

It is disappointing that the young man who may have helpfully alerted Gutsmuths to the eighteenth-century English game known to him as baseball would turn out to be such a jerk. However, there is one additional fact about his background that leaves us with a hint about the true identity of the pastime he delivered to his German mentor. Samuel Glover was born and raised in Falmouth, a seaport on the southern coast of Cornwall. You may recall that in *The Boy's Own Book*, the 1828 work that was the first to mention the term *rounders*, it specifies that the game was a favorite in the west of England. Falmouth is about as far west as it gets.

7

Austen's Aura

It was raining like crazy when I stepped off the bus from Basingstoke. I looked around and tried to orient myself. It wasn't much of a village. There weren't any shops in view, not even a pub where I might nurse a pint and cozy up before a warming fire. The steady downpour made it difficult to maneuver my wheelie bag along the muddy verge, so I looked for somewhere to park it. A kindly woman allowed me to tuck it under her porch in exchange for my promise not to forget I had left it there.

It was late February 2007, and I was wandering about southern England on my second research trip to the UK since *Baseball before We Knew It* went to press two years earlier. My book had examined the broad topic of American baseball's origins, but now I was on a narrower mission. I had become intrigued by the largely unknown original game of English baseball, and determined to learn everything I could about it. And on this rainy day, in between visits to archives and history centers, I had taken a detour to the place where the best-known reference to English baseball had first flowed from quill to paper. The venue was the village of Steventon in the county of Hampshire, and the author was Jane Austen.

Freed of my luggage, I wandered east out of the village toward a wide green field on the right side of the road. This was the site of the long vanished rectory where Jane was born in 1775. Nothing marked the hallowed ground save for remains of an old water pump that pushed up through the grass. Standing in the downpour and gazing out at the field, I wondered, not for the first time, why I had taken the trouble to be here, traveling well out of my way by train from the town of Reading to Basingstoke and onward to Steventon by bus.

No historical mystery demanded my presence, and the village certainly offered nothing in the way of archival records for me to pore over. Deep down I knew it was the pull of the Austen mystique that drew me, flavored by my own particular curiosity about her attachment to baseball.

In the first chapter of Jane's novel *Northanger Abbey* she offered a mild reproof of her heroine, Catherine Morland: "It was not very wonderful that Catherine . . . should prefer cricket, base-ball, riding on horseback, and running about the country at the age of fourteen, to books."[1] Those words are old news and have populated discussions of baseball's origins since the nineteenth century. Nevertheless, they always captivated me. The novel was not published until December 1817 in the wake of Jane's death earlier that year, although Austen scholars agree she composed its earliest draft between 1798 and 1799 while still living in the rectory whose aura hovered before me. Some have speculated that Jane herself may have played baseball, reasoning that only an intimate familiarity with the game would have led to its mention in *Northanger Abbey*. If these musings are accurate, she may well have taken part in long ago contests in the very green meadow I now gazed upon. It wasn't difficult standing there in the rain to imagine the shouts of the Austen boys and girls as they chased the ball and ran the bases.[2]

My daydream that day was not so far-fetched. Baseball could well have been among the regular amusements enjoyed by Jane, her siblings, and others of the Austens' social class in rural Hampshire. "A girl growing up in a boys' school is likely to take up boys' games," wrote the Austen biographer Claire Tomalin. "This is the best reason for believing Jane made Catherine Morland in *Northanger Abbey* partly in her own image, 'fond of all boys' plays,' and preferring cricket and baseball to playing with dolls or keeping a pet dormouse or canary."[3] This alludes to the fact that Jane's father, the Reverend George Austen, maintained a small school for boys at the rectory. Ms. Tomalin aptly describes how Jane and her siblings mixed freely in both work and play with the resident schoolboys, although the biographer makes the common but mistaken assumption that baseball was strictly a "boys' play."

I continued up the road and then turned right onto a narrow lane that rose into a wood. It was still showering steadily as I walked up the muddy incline, thankful that I hadn't needed to drag my luggage along with me. After a quarter of a mile or so I came to an old church on my left. This was St. Nicolas, the parish church where Reverend Austen had been rector and where Jane and her family went to worship. There was no one about except for me and a couple of women from Belgium who were wandering about the churchyard. I entered and explored the dimly lit interior, appreciating that the place looked much as it might have two hundred years earlier. I took notice of a plaque on the wall acknowledging its most famous former parishioner, as well as a monument to Jane's older brother, James, who had succeeded their father as rector.

Stepping outside, I meandered about the churchyard, noticing the graves of James and his wife, Mary. Jane herself had moved away from Steventon long before her death in 1817 and was buried in Winchester Cathedral. (Curiously, a brief obituary notice appearing in a local newspaper following her death identified her simply as "Miss Jane Austen, youngest daughter of the late Rev. George Austen," omitting any acknowledgment of her reputation as an author.)[4] In that setting I found myself so absorbed in soaking up all I could about the environment of Jane's upbringing that I became detached from such mundane considerations as transit schedules. A fortuitous glance at my watch, however, brought me abruptly back to reality. I realized with a jolt of panic that my return bus to Basingstoke was due to pass through the village barely ten minutes from then. It seemed inconceivable that I could retrace my steps down the lane and along the road, retrieve my wheelie bag from the kindly villager, and still be able to catch my ride. This was not a pleasant prospect, as there were no more scheduled buses for the day, and the idea of spending a rainy night in a village with no apparent accommodations for travelers was dismaying. Happily, the benevolent aura of our Miss Austen was looking out for me because as I hastened to the lane I noticed that the Belgian tourists were just about to enter their car. I quickly explained my situation, and they cheerfully agreed to shuttle me to the village. In a blink we were there, and moments afterward, with bag in hand, I jumped aboard the bus with an explosive sigh of relief.

In the years since, whenever I think of my sojourn to Steventon, it arouses nostalgic feelings for more than just my physical experiences there. The quiet beauty of the village and its surroundings had transported me back to a world that Jane inhabited, one distant in time but uniquely meaningful to me because of its baseball connection. It was those fond memories that heightened my anticipation when I learned a few months later I'd have another opportunity to visit a location associated with Jane's life. In June of that year, as part of the tour I took with the MLB Advanced Media team filming *Base Ball Discovered*, we traveled to the Hampshire town of Chawton where, beginning in 1809, Jane lived with her mother, sister Cassandra, and friend Martha Lloyd. Their modest home in Chawton has been turned into a small museum, and the film crew's cameras roamed about it, obtaining footage of house and grounds. I admit to being a little awed when I set my eyes upon Jane's original writing desk where she turned out the final manuscripts for most of her novels, including *Northanger Abbey*. The curator expressed surprise and amusement when informed that Jane had referenced baseball in the novel, and he pulled a first edition off the shelf to confirm it for himself.

Jane's renown as an author explains why her simple mention of baseball has drawn such notice over the years. She was not, however, the only English novelist of her era to allude to the game in her work, not even the only one within her own family. Another such mention appears in a novel entitled *Battleridge: An Historical Tale, Founded on Facts*, which was published in 1799. In the book, a lawyer recalls a conversation he had with a friend years earlier: "'Ah!' says he, 'no more cricket, no more base-ball, they are sending me to Geneva.'"[5]

What is remarkable about this little scrap of dialogue is that the novel was set in the 1650s in the aftermath of the English Civil War, and the quoted line was recalled by the character as something spoken to him by his friend twenty years earlier. So if we are to believe the author, it would be entirely reasonable for the word *baseball* to have appeared in a 1630s conversation.

But don't believe the author! The book's title page identifies her only as "A Lady of Quality," but in life she was Cassandra Leigh Cooke, a first cousin of Jane Austen's mother.[6] Jane seems to have enjoyed a fairly close relationship with this older cousin. Mrs. Cooke's husband, the Rev. Samuel Cooke, was Jane's godfather and, according to a book written by two of Jane's descendants, the Cooke and Austen families often socialized.[7] There was one occasion, however, when Jane may not have been so eager to see Mrs. Cooke. In 1799 Mrs. Austen proposed that the family visit the Cookes at their home in Surrey. According to biographer Tomalin, Jane was reluctant to make the trip because *Battleridge* had just come off the presses and any visiting family members would be expected to read it during their stay. Jane may have suspected that working her way through her cousin's two-volume novel would be a difficult ordeal. In *Battleridge*, Mrs. Cooke employed various tortured Gothic clichés such as tower imprisonments, moonlit grottos, and false-bottom chests, some of which Jane gleefully chose to spoof in the draft of *Northanger Abbey* she was working on at the very time of her visit to Cousin Cassandra.[8]

Another Austen biographer, Paula Byrne, speculated that Jane's nascent interest in writing was stimulated when Mrs. Cooke became a published author. However, Jane's reading of *Battleridge* would have been more likely to depress than arouse her, as it is obvious that the blood relationship between her and her cousin did not extend to the writing gene. *Battleridge* received only one contemporary review, in a journal called *Critical Review*, which opined, "The work is not very amusing; and in point of composition, it is despicable."[9] And as evidenced by Mrs. Cooke's implication that baseball was a subject for discussion in the 1630s, she appears to have been just as wanting as a historian as she was a writer. Even so, biographer Byrne suggests that Catherine Morland's "tomboyish taste for baseball and cricket" in *Northanger Abbey* was "a playful echo" of the "no more cricket, no more base-ball" line from *Battleridge*.[10] This is possible, I suppose, but I suspect the cousins' common mention of baseball had more to do with their family connection and mutual familiarity with the game. As authors, they could not have been less alike, although Cassandra Cooke at least had the good sense to know when to leave well enough alone. *Battleridge* was her one and only literary effort.

References to English baseball from the eighteenth century are extremely rare. I know of only ten such examples. Yet it is through these few precious examples that we know anything at all about English baseball in the eighteenth century. Moreover, I suspect they vastly underrepresent the game's actual presence and popularity during those years. Books and newspapers of the era largely ignored what children and young women were doing to entertain themselves, and it is only through random and occasional glimpses that we know anything at all about minor amusements such as baseball. With Jane and Cousin Cassandra we have two writers invoking a pastime that was likely part of their own personal experiences and one whose name they expected their respective readerships to be familiar with. In chapter 8 I will show how such brief mentions of baseball in the writings of other English women working in the early nineteenth century would again be among the few available sources for tracking the game's unheralded progression.

8

Science and Letters

I am a contented member of the Society for American Baseball Research (SABR), a group that attracts the loyalty of serious nerds like me who love digging up forgotten gems in the remote outlands of the pastime's history. Because SABR is a big tent that accommodates many interests, I have no fear of excommunication for researching the distinctly non-American game of English baseball. Indeed, my colleagues are generally tolerant of my propensity to look for baseball in all the wrong places. One day, well over a decade ago, one of those colleagues alerted me to a message that had been posted to an online discussion board administered by SABR. The message reported the discovery of an early use of the term *baseball* in an 1806 English science textbook.[1] This find, according to the SABR member who posted it, was made by a retired physics professor from Marquette University who located it in a book entitled *Conversations on Chymistry, in Which the Elements of That Science are Familiarly Explained and Illustrated by Experiments and Plates.*[2] The 1806 work was published anonymously, although later editions identified the author as Jane Haldimand Marcet.

The Marquette professor, according to the message, indicated that the baseball reference appeared within the textbook's explanation of *inertia*. The author, Mrs. Marcet, framed the inertia lesson—as she did with all of the lessons in the book—as a dialogue between a teacher and two students. In this instance, a girl named Emily was prompted by the teacher to offer an example of how the effects of inertia could be seen in an everyday activity. Emily replied: "In playing base-ball I am obliged to use all my strengths to give a rapid motion to the ball; and when I have to catch it, I am sure I feel the resistance it makes to being stopped. But if I do not catch it, it would soon fall to the ground and stop itself."[3]

In the little world of early baseball I dwell in, this was obviously an important find, and the historian in me was excited to see it. At the same time, and it's embarrassing to admit, I also felt a twinge of disappointment. *Baseball before We Knew It* at that moment was only months away from rolling off the presses, and I had long passed the deadline for making any changes or additions to the text. Now this cool discovery comes along and, darn it, it was too late to incorporate it into the book. I knew, of course, that something like this was inevitable, that researchers would keep digging up new evidence on the topic. And, as things turned out, I would become the chief culprit in this, as many of the subsequent discoveries of English baseball from the eighteenth and nineteenth centuries were ones I'd uncover myself. Yet for a couple of years following my book's release I couldn't easily shake off the tiny pangs of regret that tweaked me whenever some new find materialized, no matter how silly I knew I was being. Eventually I became so consumed by the hunt for fresh evidence of English baseball that I finally managed to get beyond my hang-up and started regarding every new clue as fodder for a second book rather than a loss to the previous one. I just didn't realize that it would take more than a decade before I got around to writing it.

Turning back to Mrs. Marcet's mention of baseball, one thing about it puzzled me almost from the start. Her book was about . . . chemistry. Even many decades removed from high school I had not forgotten that the principle of inertia belonged to a different branch of science: physics. This curious discrepancy accelerated my interest in seeking what I've always sought whenever a new claim of early baseball crosses my senses: validation of its authenticity by going back and confirming its original source. So I did—but I couldn't. It was easy to locate copies of *Conversations on Chymistry* in academic libraries close to my home in San Francisco. But when I got one in my hands, all I found inside were what you might expect: lessons about chemistry. Clearly, something didn't square. The post on the SABR discussion board about the Marquette professor's discovery stated definitely that *Conversations on Chymistry* was the title of the book containing the inertia lesson. The library copy I examined was an original London edition, dated 1806. A closer look at the SABR message board, however, revealed that the professor had found the baseball reference in an 1836 American edition, one that had been edited by a Reverend J. L. Blake, "who said," according to the posting, "he did not change the book." Hmmm. Maybe Reverend Blake tinkered with the text more than he let on. I went to a different library and found an 1833 American edition of the book, not precisely the one the professor had used but perhaps close enough. No luck. Just as with the English edition I examined earlier, there was no mention of inertia. Frustrated, I inquired as to whether there were any other editions of the book in the library's collection and was told, yes, one more. I submitted a request for it and awaited its retrieval, but when I got my hands on it I saw they had pulled the wrong title. The author was Mrs. Marcet, but the book was *Conversations on Natural Philosophy*. If the inertia lesson couldn't be found in a chemistry book, I certainly didn't expect it would show up in one on philosophy. But it did, and there on page 13 was Mrs. Marcet's inertia/baseball example that had eluded me. Science was never my strong suit in school, but had I been a bit more attentive I might have known that "natural philosophy" was what the study of the physical world had been called prior to the development of modern scientific classifications later in the nineteenth century.

One mystery solved, but that led to another. How could the professor have so totally flubbed identifying the correct title of the book? I considered pursuing this, but then decided the answer wasn't really that important. I wrote it off as just another of those innocent slip-ups that can send a fussy person like me reeling. In this case, the baseball reference was real and, to me, fairly momentous. *Conversations on Natural Philosophy* was first published in London in 1819 and, like its cousin the chemistry book, went through many editions. At the time I believed that its appearance, along with that of *Northanger Abbey* in 1817, were the first works to mention English baseball since the publication of *Battleridge* two decades earlier. I knew of no explanation for this drought other than random chance. I strongly suspect that baseball was played throughout this era, especially by girls and young women. In my view, the absence of evidence from the years 1799 to 1817 was no more indicative of it falling into temporary disfavor than an abundance of baseball evidence from another period might be considered proof of expanding popularity.

Jane Haldimand Marcet was a very unusual woman for her time. Lacking a formal education but receiving excellent tutoring at home alongside her brothers, she evinced a keen intellect and curiosity about many subjects. She read extensively in English and French, studied under the painter Joshua Reynolds, and served as her father's hostess when he entertained scientists, politicians, and intellectuals. In 1799 at the age of twenty she married a successful physician, and with him she attended lectures and developed friendships with many of the leading scientists and economists of the day, a circle that included such luminaries as Sir Humphry Davy, Thomas Malthus, David Ricardo, and Michael Faraday.[4] Almost from the start she felt a need to share her burgeoning knowledge of the latest scientific principles with other women whom she knew lacked her opportunities and advantages. Her first written effort was *Conversations on Natural Philosophy*, and although she completed the initial manuscript in 1805, it would not be published until 1819. *Conversations on Chymistry* followed in 1806. Her decision to communicate lessons by means of dialogues was intended to make the material as accessible as possible to her intended audience of young women, an approach that proved highly successful. Employing examples from everyday life to illustrate her lessons served the same goal and suggests that she selected baseball to demonstrate the principle of inertia because she believed her readership would be familiar with the game. This is an important indicator, given that many of the other references to baseball in the eighteenth and early nineteenth centuries offer limited insight into the pastime's reach or popularity. Mrs. Marcet's contribution alone doesn't settle the issue, but combined with a bevy of other clues about English baseball that would appear in writings of the 1820s, a stronger sense of the game's standing in popular culture begins to emerge.

As far as I can tell, Jane Marcet never came into direct contact with the other Jane in my story, our dear Miss Austen. Following the latter's death, however, and the publication of *Northanger Abbey* and *Persuasion* in late 1817, Mrs. Marcet inscribed a letter to her close friend Maria Edgeworth revealing surprisingly catty thoughts about the final Austen novels. Miss Edgeworth, the Anglo-Irish writer who, until Jane Austen came along, was the most admired and successful novelist of her day, responded: "We were reading Mrs. Austin's [*sic*] last novels when your letter came & your observation—'that one grows tired at last of milk and water even tho the water be pure and the milk sweet—so exactly and happily describes our own feelings."[5] Jane Austen, it should be noted, had been among Miss Edgeworth's biggest fans and paid homage to her in *Northanger Abbey* by mentioning her novel *Belinda* in glowing terms.[6] She also sent her a pre-publication copy of *Emma* in 1816. Maria Edgeworth never thanked Jane for the gift nor acknowledged it in any way. In a letter to a friend she dismissed *Emma* with the comment, "It has no story."[7] Perhaps these jibes were competitive reflexes. Edgeworth's literary output, according to her biographical entry in ODNB, "vied with that of Jane Austen in certain areas of critical esteem."[8] But if envy was at play here, it was strictly of the little league variety compared with that shown by another Austen contemporary, one whose connection to Jane was far closer to home.

During her early years in the village of Steventon, Jane Austen and her family were neighbors of another clerical family, the Russells, who were situated in the nearby Hampshire village of Ashe.

Dr. Richard Russell was rector of the Ashe parish, and in 1750 his wife, Mary, gave birth to a daughter, also named Mary, the only one of their children to survive childhood.[9] Because of the proximity of the two parishes, the families socialized on a regular basis, a fact confirmed by Jane's nephew, J. E. Austen-Leigh, who wrote that the Austens and Russells were "intimately acquainted."[10] Following Dr. Russell's death in 1783, widow and daughter moved away from Ashe and settled in Alresford, Hampshire, where daughter Mary married a man named George Mitford.[11] This turned out to be a rather poor choice, as he promptly squandered the massive £28,000 inheritance Mary came into upon the death of her mother. Mrs. Mitford gave birth to a daughter in 1787, also named Mary, as was the family custom. When this youngest Mary won the huge sum of £20,000 on a lottery ticket given her for her tenth birthday, her father took control of it and quickly went through those funds as well. His weaknesses, according to his daughter's entry in the ODNB, were "gambling, speculation, greyhounds, entertaining, and Whig electioneering." The third Mary would grow up to become well known in her day as the storyteller, poet, and playwright Mary Russell Mitford. She has the minor distinction of alluding to baseball in her published works more than any fiction writer in either Britain or the United States until at least the 1860s. All told, she mentioned the game in four stories spanning the years 1826 to 1835, a statistic for the record books in an era when the pastime's name rarely appeared in literature.

In 1811, after her father completed a sentence in debtor's prison, Miss Mitford moved with him to the village of Three Mile Cross, just south of the town of Reading in Berkshire. From there she launched her literary career in earnest, using the everyday experiences of her neighbors as subject matter for her popular series of village sketches. Many of these sketches were collected in her five-volume work *Our Village* published in the 1820s. In volume 2, issued in 1826, Miss Mitford mentioned baseball in two stories. As with all her references to the game, young girls were its principal devotees. In one tale, "Jack

Hatch," the author tracked the progress of a girl through different stages of childhood. As "a sun-burnt gipsy of six" the girl stood by the village green, she wrote, "her longing eyes fixed on a game of base-ball." Then, at the age of ten, "the little damsel gets admission to the charity-school and trips mincingly thither every morning, dressed in the old-fashioned blue gown, and white cap, and tippet, and bib and apron of that primitive institution, looking as demure as a Nun, and as tidy; her thoughts fixed on button-holes, and spelling books—those ensigns of promotion; despising dirt and baseball and all their joys."[12]

In a second story from the same volume, "The Tenants of Beech-grove," Miss Mitford describes the preferences of another girl in the village: "Better than playing with her doll, better even than base-ball, or sliding or romping, does she like to creep of an evening to her father's knee."[13] Similarly, in her introduction to the third volume of *Our Village*, the author again reinforces the theme that schoolgirls formed the village's baseball-playing demographic, only this time contrasting their activity with what the neighborhood boys were doing: "And yet they have light hearts too, poor urchins; witness Dame Wilson's three sun-burnt ragged boys who with Ben Kirby and a few comrades of lesser note, are bawling and squabbling at marbles on one side of the road; and Master Andrew's four fair-haired girls who are scrambling and squalling at baseball on the other!"[14]

Miss Mitford again counterposed the diversions of boys and girls of the village in "The Carpenter's Daughter," which was included in a new, three-volume collection of sketches, *Belford Regis*, published in 1835. She described a group of "ragged urchins at cricket on the common," including "the eight-year-old boy who would not leave his wicket; the seven and nine-year-old imps who are trying to force him from his post."[15] Continuing:

> What can be prettier than this, unless it be the fellow-group of girls—sisters, I presume, to the boys—who are laughing and screaming round the great oak; then darting to and fro, in a

game compounded of hide-and-seek and base-ball. Now tossing the ball high, high amidst the branches; now flinging it low
along the common, bowling as it were almost within reach of
the cricketers now pursuing, now retreating, running, jumping,
shouting, bawling—almost shrieking with ecstasy; whilst one
sunburnt black-eyed gipsy throws forth her laughing face from
behind the trunk of the old oak, and then flings a newer and
a gayer ball—fortunate purchase of some hoarded six-pence—
amongst her admiring playmates. Happy, happy children! that
one hour of innocent enjoyment is worth an age![16]

Besides mentioning baseball in her stories, Miss Mitford has also
been recognized for weaving cricket into them, with one authoritative encyclopedia of the sport citing her various descriptions in *Our
Village* as "the first major prose on the game."[17]

Although her tales were fictional, it is probable that Miss Mitford
witnessed the girls in Three Mile Cross playing baseball on a regular
basis. But she may also have known the game before she ever moved
there, perhaps playing it as a child with other girls in Alresford. Or
possibly she learned it from her mother, who in her own childhood
socialized with the Austen family in the Hampshire countryside.

Whatever the nature of those encounters, Miss Mitford's mother
apparently came away with a decidedly unfavorable opinion of the
young Jane Austen. She may have passed this sentiment on to her
daughter, who years later conveyed it in a letter to a friend:

À propos to novels, I have discovered that our great favourite,
Miss Austen, is my countrywoman; that mamma knew all her
family very intimately; and that she herself is an old maid (I beg
her pardon—I mean a young lady) with whom mamma before
her marriage was acquainted. Mamma says that she was then
the prettiest, silliest, most affected, husband-hunting butterfly
she ever remembers; A friend of mine, who visits her now, says
that she has stiffened into the most perpendicular, precise, taci-

turn piece of a "single blessedness" that ever existed, and that till "Pride and Prejudice" showed what a precious gem was hidden in the unbending case, she was no more regarded in society than a poker or a fire-screen, or any other thin upright piece of wood or iron that fills its corner in peace and quietness.[18]

Whether this was a big league case of envy or simply a matter of a daughter parroting her mother's prejudices, it didn't stop the younger Mary Russell Mitford from trying to emulate the style and success of Jane Austen nor of replicating her more heralded contemporary's placement of baseball in the text of her writings.

9

Ladies First

It's England in the 1820s, and baseball is in the air! One sentimental essayist writing in 1821 ruminated on the familiar presence of the pastime: "A village green, with its girls and boys playing at bass-ball, and its grown-up lads at cricket, is one of those English sights which I hope no false refinement will ever banish from among us."[1] These are touching words and undoubtedly heartfelt, though a departure in tone from the rest of the author's essay. In it he described a stroll he had taken "on a fine spring evening, in the suburbs of a country town." Along the way he came upon some open ground near a public house where young people were engaged in innocent rural sports, baseball among them. His pleasure at witnessing this scene soon turned to anger when he entered the pub and found a crowd of drunken men making wagers and arguing. The writer then spent the remainder of the piece railing against the evils of liquor and gambling. His moralistic diatribe, however, does not detract from his commentary on what he witnessed on the village green. Baseball, he implied, had become a routine recreational choice for English youth of both genders.

That same year, a thirty-one-year-old Englishwoman named Elizabeth Appleton also alluded to baseball's longtime acceptance. She was a writer of books advising parents on the proper ways to raise and educate their children, although her expertise came from employment as a governess and not from any personal experience with motherhood. She had just released her second work on the topic, one bearing the vaguely unctuous title of *Early Education; or, The Management of Children Considered with a View to Their Future Character.* Here Miss Appleton emphasized that the playing of games, including ball games, was important to a child's well-rounded upbringing. One page includes a footnote specifying several pastimes she felt were especially suited to young children: "A few others, old-fashioned, it is true, but ever interesting to childhood, may be added. Blind man's buff; Puss in the corner; Questions and Commands; Forfeits; My Lady's Toilette; Hunt the Slipper; Prison Bars; Base Ball; Hide and Seek; Cross Questions; and Riddles; but these last should be selected with great care for tender and innocent minds."[2]

By placing baseball in the "old-fashioned" category, Miss Appleton confirmed what the essayist above had suggested, that by the 1820s English youngsters had been playing the pastime for generations and that contemporary observers counted it among the country's traditional games. Further evidence of this kept cropping up in the literature of the decade.

In 1823 a man from the county of Suffolk named Edward Moor produced a glossary of the common words and phrases then in use by residents of the county, what he termed "lingual localisms." It was an ambitious undertaking—the book ran to 525 pages—but it may have seemed trifling to Moor in light of some of his previous projects and adventures. He was a retired imperialist, having spent much of his working life as a mercenary in the employ of the East India Company. In that role he participated in numerous military campaigns against local Indian rulers who resisted British efforts to subdue them. Along the way he developed an interest in the culture of the people he was subjugating and became fluent in India's languages. He studied Hinduism and learned its tenets so well that on retirement he published a major scholarly tome, *The Hindoo Pantheon,* that stood for fifty years as the only authoritative work on the subject in English.[3] After returning to England and settling in the county of his birth, his expertise in languages and culture fed naturally into his glossary project, *Suffolk Words and Phrases.* It was an impressive and detailed work, and among its pages Moor included a long list of pastimes practiced in the county: "We have . . . a great variety of games, active and sedentary," he wrote, "omitting games so universal as Cricket, Leap-frog, Marbles, etc., we have . . . Bandy, Bandy-wicket, Base-ball, Bandy-ball, Bubble-hole . . . Foot ball, Hocky," and so on.[4]

While Moor's observation of baseball's presence was lexicographic, fiction writers of the decade chronicled it in less formal ways. Compared with Jane Austen and Mary Russell Mitford, these authors were, perhaps, somewhat less accomplished at their craft. One such was a young woman who in 1826 published a four-volume novel entitled *Geraldine Murray, a Tale of Fashionable Life*. The book relates the dizzying comings, goings, and doings of various high-born society types. In one passage a married couple, who have been bickering while traveling in their coach, approach a stately mansion that had been the husband's boyhood home. The wife is sullen and grumpy, but her husband is excited because he has not been there in many years: "'Is this the house?' said she, determined not to be pleased with anything. 'Yes: look, Cary—there's where I have played trap-ball and bass-ball many a time.'"[5]

The title page of *Geraldine Murray* identities the author only as "E.H.P., late Miss M'Leod." A contemporary critic reviewing the novel in an 1826 literary journal poked some fun at "late Miss M'Leod's" manner of identifying herself as well as at the subject matter of the work itself:

> We have heard of ladies changing their names, but never before met with a lady who had given up her name for initial letters as Miss M'Leod seems to have done. She dates her preface, however, from a place which *sounds* extremely matrimonial, viz. Fing-ring-ho Hall, Essex; and we dare hope that E.H.P is as happy as the late Miss M'Leod could wish her to be. So much for the author; and we have little more to say about the book. As drudging critics, we cannot be expected to know aught of Fashionable Life; and we can only guess that the Lords, Ladies, Honourable Mr.'s, Mistresses and Misses, Counts, Baronets and other great folks who figure in these pages, are drawn to the *Life*.[6]

Regardless of its literary worthiness, the novel's brief mention of baseball ensures some enduring relevance. The same might be said of another work from the time, an insignificant short story called "The Gipsey Girl" published in 1828 as part of *The Amulet*, a volume of similar short sketches and poems. The tale revolves around an abandoned orphan girl named Ellen who has been sheltered and cared for by a kindly vicar's wife, but who has also come into conflict with the village's "most choleric of all school mistresses." The teacher has little tolerance or sympathy for what she perceives as Ellen's failure to comport herself properly, and she gives her a scolding: "She [the vicar's wife] clothed you, and fed you, and placed you under my care: you have been with me now nearly three years, and yet you have not half got through your sampler. You can't say three times three without missing; you'd rather play at bass-ball, or hunt the hedges for wild flowers, than mend your stockings."[7]

Mentions of baseball in that decade occasionally showed up in nonfiction as well. One example from 1828 appeared on the pages of the *London Magazine*. A regular feature of that monthly publication was a "diary" containing reviews and commentaries on news events that occurred on particular days of the preceding month. The "Diary for the Month of July" appeared in the August issue, and among its entries was one for July 23 concerning a report from the association of brewers that beer consumption had dropped considerably over the previous twelve months. The unsigned writer of the rambling piece then went on to rant against lowered duties on gin, public drunkenness, and the absence of healthy recreational options for the urban working man:

> He must, in most cases, walk three or four miles before he can get into fresh air; and it is utterly impossible that he can find any place where a manly game may be played, as in the old days. It is the same in all over-grown towns. At Manchester, many of the walls announce that any person playing at ball against

them will be prosecuted "according to law." The unhappy boys of the metropolis are sadly off in this particular. Where can they assemble for cricket, or trap-bat, or bass-ball? The beadle is after them if they attempt to profane a square; and thus they naturally resort to "chuck-farthing."[8]

Not much has changed in two hundred years, what with polluted air and the lack of adequate outdoor recreational facilities still affecting our inner cities. Nice to know, however, that even in those bleak, Dickensian days there was at least one commentator looking out for the well-being of young ballplayers. In this instance, the youngsters meriting his concern were boys. As we have seen, however, and as will be borne out by further examples below, the majority of references to English baseball in the 1820s identified girls and young women as its primary practitioners.

It was the athletic involvement of British females, or perceived lack thereof, that concerned an Italian resident of London by the name of G. P. Voarino. He claimed to be a professor of gymnastic exercise and to have taught at the Royal Military College with Capt. Peter Heinrich Clias, who was a follower of our old friend, the German educator J. C. F. Gutsmuths. In 1827 Signor Voarino published *A Treatise on Calisthenic Exercises; Arranged for the Private Tuition of Ladies.* Perhaps it was noble intentions that prompted the good signor to take upon himself the instruction of English women in physical exercise. Unfortunately for him, his efforts were not received as noble, at least not by the few London critics who took the time to review his work. "A very objectionable effort of absurdity," wrote a reviewer for the *Times,* apparently not someone prone to mincing his words. He added that Voarino's book might more correctly be called "An Essay on the art of putting young Women into hideous, and not particularly decent, postures."[9] A second reviewer, writing in the prestigious *Literary Gazette and Journal of the Belles Lettres,* took especial umbrage at the Italian author's presumption that British females were somehow deficient in their physical pursuits. His scornful rebuke of Voarino listed some of the numerous games and activities that the nation's women engaged in and chastised the Italian for overlooking them:

Signor Voarino apologises, as a foreigner, for an imperfect acquaintance with our language;—perhaps he was not aware (as few travelers speak of them) that we had diversions . . . as hunt the slipper, which gives dexterity of hand and ham; leap-frog, which strengthens the back . . . ; romps, which quicken all the facilities; tig [tag], a rare game for universal corporeal agility; base-ball, a nonsuch for eyes and arms; ladies' toilet, for vivacity and apprehension; spinning the plate, for neatness and rapidity; grass-hopping, for improving the physical powers; puss in the corner, and snap-tongs, for muscularity and fearlessness:—all these, and hundreds more, not so well known nor so much practised in London, perhaps as in the country, we have had for ages; so that it looks ridiculous to bring out as a grand philosophical discovery, the art of instructing women how to have canes or sticks laid on their backs. We would wager the value of one of our *Literary Gazettes* to its price (a heavy and fearful odds), that Betty the housemaid, uninstructed in Calisthenic exercises, will beat the ablest pupil Signor Voarino can produce, in the twirl of a mop, the lavations of a broom, and all the forces and elasticities of action in the superior as well as inferior extremities. Is it a bet? done![10]

I have not uncovered any data showing how well Voarino's book fared among the English reading public, but I suspect that the *Gazette*'s review did little to enhance its popularity. The British are a proud people, and it is my impression that they are not particularly welcoming to foreigners attempting to instruct them in anything having to do with their sports. My own experience when trying to acquaint individual Britons with the historical reality that baseball originated in their country is that some of them are a little uncomfortable with the idea. They have always viewed the sport as distinctly American and are not overly receptive to having an American inform them that baseball was not only born in England but, unbeknownst to them, a part of their national culture for more than 150 years. I suppose the citizens of most countries would adopt a similar attitude, and Americans certainly have little tolerance for the interference of outsiders in almost anything. In the case of baseball, however, I reckon Britons might be proud to have spawned it, if for no other reason than to give them some currency in the friendly, cross-ocean rivalry. How satisfying, I would think, to puncture the narrative that America's national game was the innovative brainchild of upstart colonials and reframe it instead as a trivial castoff of the mother country.

In defending the physical prowess of English womanhood, the reviewer of Signor Voarino's book saw fit to include baseball among the games well suited for the country's females. Another to share that viewpoint was a physician and school administrator living in the county of Surrey. William Newnham was born in 1790 in the town of Farnham and spent all of his forty-five-year career in practice there, mostly specializing in obstetrics and gynecology.[11] Farnham is in western Surrey, twelve miles in one direction from Guildford where the young diarist William Bray played baseball in 1755, and twelve miles in another direction from Chawton in Hampshire where Jane Austen polished her manuscript of *Northanger Abbey*. This was baseball country, and as a schoolmaster and father of both boys and girls Dr. Newnham would have been familiar with the game. He was also the author of several books on medicine and education, and in 1827 he had one published with the ambitious title *Principles of Physical, Intellectual, Moral and Religious Education*. In the section devoted to physical education, he emphasized to parents the importance of exercise and active play to the health and well-being of their children. He wrote, "The games of cricket, prison bars, foot ball, &c. will be useful as children grow up, and are strong enough to endure such exercise." He then added: "With regard to girls, these amusements may be advantageously supplanted by bass-ball, battledore and shuttlecock, and similar active and playful pursuits."[12]

Although evidence suggests it was not uncommon for boys to play English baseball during the first half of the nineteenth century, contemporary observers tended to associate the game with girls and women. In part, this was based upon the real likelihood that female participation in the pastime during those years exceeded that of males. Coupling this with the fact that English authors who mentioned baseball in their writings prior to 1830 were more likely to be women than men and that the gender of those playing the pastime described in those writings was typically female, it is easy to understand how the presumption that baseball was mainly a game for girls became established. As we shall see in the following chapters, however, the tilt toward female predominance in English baseball, if not the perception of it, began to level out and even reverse itself as the century proceeded.

Indicators of English baseball's presence in the 1820s were relatively bountiful compared with previous decades. Yet these numbers themselves would be dwarfed by hundreds of new references that would document the game's reach and popularity throughout the remainder of the century. Lateral to this, there was a major shift under way in where this new evidence would be found. Up until 1830, what we knew about the game emanated mainly from the pages of English books, journals, magazines, and handwritten documents. Going forward, however, British newspapers would surpass all other media as the principal sources for information about baseball. As the country entered the Victorian era, the once stodgy news industry was undergoing a significant transformation. Newspaper production had long been concentrated along London's Fleet Street and in other major population centers. The contents of those papers almost exclusively reflected the reading interests of the British governing classes, namely, politics, war, religion, commerce, crime, and the social lives of the aristocracy. The papers devoted little space to a range of social and cultural topics that might have been of interest to the broader citizenry. A few regional newspapers had been in operation since the mid-eighteenth century, but those were rarely more than four pages in length and had little room for anything beyond basic national news and advertisements. As the middle of the nineteenth century approached, however, the number of provincial papers increased dramatically, as did the size of each issue.

This expansion was the consequence of several converging factors. One was burgeoning demand, as newly opened National Schools and church-based institutions brought literacy to wider segments of the population. At the same time, publication and distribution of newspapers became less expensive due to improvements in technology, lowered costs for paper and other materials, and the emergence of a modern postal system. Perhaps the biggest single factor in making English newspapers more affordable in the mid-1800s was a sharp reduction in the steep, per-issue stamp tax that had burdened publishers and consumers alike since the seventeenth century. As an example, following the reduction of the tax in 1836 from four pence to one penny, the circulation of English newspapers rose from 39 million in that year to 122 million by 1854.[13] These efficiencies were accompanied by a new focus on subject matter that would appeal to the growing readership, including entire news sections devoted to the affairs of ordinary people living in the villages and towns that dotted England's rural counties. This coverage extended to the most mundane of civic events, including activities of local schoolchildren. And as more of these reports appeared on the pages of newspapers, mentions of English baseball filtered in among them.

10

The Numbers Game

On May 17, 1830, a small display advertisement appeared on the front page of the *Reading Mercury*, a long-established newspaper in the county of Berkshire that had once been operated by John Newbery. The town of Reading, then and now, was a regional economic hub, and its weekly paper served the surrounding rural counties. The ad that day announced an upcoming community event:

> Whitsuntide Amusements.
> at the Seven Stars, Knowl Hill.
> There will be a Cricket Match,
> at the Seven Stars, Knowl Hill, on
> Whit-Tuesday; wickets to be pitched at eleven
> o'clock.—Donkey Racing, Baste Balling for
> Ribbons, and a great variety of other amusements.[1]

What fun! Whitsun is what the Christian festival of Pentecost is called in Britain. It falls on the seventh Sunday following Easter and is considered the first holiday of summer. The week following Whitsun is known as Whitsuntide, a time when local communities tradition-ally hold fairs and public celebrations of various kinds. Residents of the village of Knowl Hill in northeast Berkshire apparently went all out for Whitsuntide in 1830, calling on neighbors far and wide to join them in games and other traditional competitions. Undoubt-edly, the entire community mobilized to stage such an ambitious undertaking. The cynic in me suspects the big party was staged to raise money for local coffers; nor would it have done any harm to the proprietor of the Seven Stars, the most prominent pub in the village. Of most interest to me is the revelation that winners of the "baste balling" match would come away with prizes, revealing that on occasion English practitioners of the game played it for something other than the sheer enjoyment of the experience.

The good citizens of Knowl Hill must have been quite pleased with how their Whitsuntide celebration turned out in 1830 because the following year they decided to stage it again, this time with some particularly colorful additions. Once more, the *Reading Mercury* was their platform of choice for publicizing the event. The new display ad for 1831 reads as follows:

The Knowl-Hill Yearly Recreations
will take place on Whit Tuesday, when the lovers
of sport will find ample amusement. To commence
with a Cricket Match, at 9 o'clock, for ribbons; Base Ball
for ditto; Donkey Racing, Running in Sacks, Gingling,
Dipping for Eels, Climbing for a Hat, Bowling for a Cheese;
a Female Race for a new Gown-piece, and a variety of
other Amusements.[2]

Baseball, yes, but how about all that other cool stuff! I remember as a kid bobbing for apples in a tub of water at birthday parties and not finding the experience especially satisfying. Eels? Um, no thanks. But while the very idea of it might seem a bit gross for our modern sensibilities, dipping for eels was a favorite draw for eighteenth- and nineteenth-century English festival-goers. I'm guessing it was more of a hit for the watching crowd than the actual participants. I've found evidence that eel-dipping was routinely part of local celebrations of major events like the monarch's birthday, and it was among the attractions listed for a grand festival at Cambridge in honor of the coronation of George IV in 1821.[3] "Gingling," by the way, was an alternate spelling of "jingling" and described a contest that seems far more appealing to me than trying to snag a slimy eel. To play it, organizers roped off a large area, perhaps forty yards square, and some number of participants, typically about ten, were blindfolded and placed in the confined area. One additional player who was not blindfolded entered the arena and was given bells that he or she was obliged to ring continuously with both hands while darting around the open space. The challenge was for the blindfolded players to locate and capture the bell-ringer within a designated period that could be as long as an hour or more. The prize went to the one who first managed to grab hold of the ringer, or if none succeeded, to the ringer himself.[4] This game was guaranteed to produce hilarity, although possibly not for those wearing the blindfolds.

Some of the other attractions, such as "bowling for a cheese" and "climbing for a hat," were certain to draw contestants from far and wide, especially those in need of a hat or a round of cheese. As for the "female race for a new gown-piece," this was a widespread English custom that dated at least as far back as the late seventeenth century. Such contests were often referred to as "smock races" and could be seen at fairs, festivals, weddings, cricket matches, and almost any type of celebratory public gathering. Sometimes the races were nothing more than frivolous gambols, but on many occasions they were serious undertakings with prizes worth competing for. Joseph Strutt, in his authoritative 1801 study of English games and pastimes, wrote: "Smock Races are commonly performed by the young country wenches, and so called because the prize is a holland smock, or shift, usually decorated with ribbands."[5] According to one scholarly paper on the subject, women at times faced a quandary over how to clothe themselves for these footraces.[6] If they showed up in the appropriate fashions of the day, they might find that their garments encumbered their performance. Conversely, if they wore garb suitable for athletic activity, they could risk scandalizing their neighbors and being censored for indecency.

The Seven Stars, the pub at the center of Knowl Hill's celebrations, was already more than two hundred years old in 1830 when Whitsuntide revelers played baseball in its shadows. The venerable inn kept serving up pints to thirsty locals until 2012, when declining patronage finally forced its owners to sell. In a sad statement of what passes for progress these days, developers have converted the pub's buildings into several four-bedroom townhouses. The village of Knowl Hill itself remains small and somewhat out of the way, nestled in pretty countryside nine miles northeast of Reading and five miles west of Maidenhead. In my mind, however, its location is central, lying a scant two miles north of the equally small village of Waltham St. Lawrence. That rural outpost, you might recall, is the place where John Newbery was born and raised, he of *A Little Pretty Pocket-book* publishing fame. I've kept tabs on the physical locations of every reference to English baseball that I've discovered thus far. These I've plotted on a map, and their geographic center falls somewhere close to the immediate neighborhood of Knowl Hill and Waltham St. Lawrence. My methods are not entirely scientific, but I like to believe that this peaceful slice of countryside, surrounded on three sides by the meandering River Thames, is where the fledgling game of baseball began.

Knowl Hill was not the only community in its corner of Berkshire to afford citizens the opportunity to make merry. The town of Eton, barely ten miles away and known for its famous school, hosted regular fairs and festivals in a large meadow facing the Thames. These grounds, called the Brocas, offer a stunning view of Windsor Castle across the river and were a regular venue for cricket matches going back to the eighteenth century. Eton still hosts annual fairs on the site, and it remains a popular year-round destination for picnic goers and tourists alike. On a fine day in August 1826, the community hosted a Brocas Festival on the meadow, and according to a newspaper covering the event, "a vast concourse of persons assembled to witness the amusements."[7] This Eton fair served up a smorgasbord of competitive events for attendees. Some were the same as those offered by their upstream neighbors in Knowl Hill, such as cricket, jingling, boys running for a hat, and girls racing for a gown piece. Other contests were equally compelling, such as "boys to eat rolls and treacle" and "a smoking match." For me, of course, the highlight of the day, as described in a bill announcing the festival, was "Girls under 14 years of age to play at Baseball; the Winners to receive 1s. each and a Ribband; the Losers a Ribband each."[8]

The Knowl Hill and Eton celebrations continued for years, but the examples above are the only ones I could find whose advertisements named baseball as one of the amusements. I can't help wishing the *Reading Mercury* or other papers had sent out reporters to cover the events so that we might know the outcomes of the various contests. Who dipped the most eels? Which skillful bowler brought home the cheese? Most important, who won the baseball ribbons? I crave these details. I want to see box scores for those long ago games and scan the latest team standings. Is it not reasonable for us living two hundred years afterward to wonder whether the same team prevailed year after year or to learn how the baseball stars of the day performed? As someone who grew up enthralled by batting averages and on-base percentages, I deeply rue the absence of statistics in English baseball. Yes, I concede that collecting such numbers might prove a bit difficult (i.e., impossible) for a sport never known to have organized teams or leagues, but that is small consolation. I need my numbers. So to cope with the frustration at never knowing who had the best OPS in the Knowl Hill Whitsuntide league, I've had to devise a few English baseball statistics of my own. These may not have quite the cachet of RBI or ERA, but they're the best I can do utilizing the thin selection of data available.

The first of these new stats I've dubbed NFD (newspaper frequency by decade). As described at the end of the previous chapter, newspapers in the mid-nineteenth century began to emerge as the primary sources for references to English baseball. The Knowl Hill ads mentioning baseball in the early 1830s were among the advance guard of this new trend, although they remain the only two known examples from that decade (NFD = 2). The 1840s didn't stack up much better, as my searches turned up only four newspaper mentions of English baseball within those ten years (NFD = 4). But then came the breakout

decades, a stunning eruption not unlike the astonishing and unprec-
edented home run totals Babe Ruth piled up in the 1920s. English
baseball leaped to an impressive NFD of 37 in the 1850s, followed by
61 in the 1860s, 58 in the 1870s, a world record 69 in the 1880s, 67
in the 1890s, 31 in the 1900s, and then fell off abruptly with only 7
more scattered mentions in the 1910s and 1 in the 1920s as the game
faded into oblivion.

Table 1. English baseball newspaper frequency by decade (NFD)

DECADE	NFD
1830s	2
1840s	4
1850s	37
1860s	61
1870s	58
1880s	69
1890s	67
1900s	31
1910s	7

As I slowly unearthed this trove of newspaper articles, I found my
understanding of English baseball's history turning somersaults. The
accumulated evidence taken from them demonstrates that the pastime
enjoyed significant popularity through the full span of the Victorian
era, a remarkable revelation in light of the fact that not so very long
ago I believed the original English game had gone extinct by the year
1860. These newly discovered references also bring with them a wave
of fresh data about English baseball's geographic distribution as well
as the demographics of its players. What they don't do, unfortunately,
is reveal much detail about the nature of the game itself, with most of
the articles doing little more than noting that baseball was among a
group of amusements offered at a company picnic or Sunday school

treat. But while this lack of detail is disappointing, it doesn't deter me from calculating the second of my shiny new English baseball statistics, the all-important EBC (English baseball by county).

To keep track of every reference to English baseball that I locate, I maintain a spreadsheet that lists them all in chronological order, summarizes their content, and cites their sources. As mentioned above, I also note the specific town or village in Britain associated with each entry, as well as the county it falls within. With some entries, this sort of geographic classification is impossible, such as with fictional English works that mention the word *baseball* but give no indication of where the story is based. But since the great majority of references allow me to pinpoint a location, I can use the data to help trace the rise and spread of the game. It also feeds my compulsive statistical cravings by providing numbers for the hard fought, county-by-county EBC competition.

In all, I have identified English baseball references associated with forty British counties as well as London. Distribution of the game among those counties is far from even. For half, including a few as far afield as Wales and Scotland, I've noted only one or two examples over the game's lifespan of more than 150 years (EBC of one or two), a level so statistically insignificant that it is impossible to know whether the game made any sort of impression in those locales. Taken as a whole, however, they suggest that the play of English baseball, at least to a limited degree, fanned out widely across Britain during the course of its history. In the serious contest for EBC leader, however, only a select group of ten counties are in the running, each with an EBC count of ten or higher. The provisional results are these:

Table 2: English baseball by county (EBC)

COUNTY	EBC
Suffolk	55
Buckinghamshire	54
Hampshire	49

Berkshire	29
Sussex (E & W)	28
Norfolk	23
Surrey	21
London	18
Bedfordshire	11
Kent	10

Congratulations, Suffolk, for edging out Buckinghamshire and Hampshire in a very spirited contest! But EBC competition aside, what immediately jumps out about this list is that it comprises the home counties bordering London as well as East Anglia, essentially the southeast quadrant of England. Clearly, this clump of mostly rural counties was the principal terrain of English baseball. You'll notice that there appears to be a soft spot within this grouping. The counties of Hertfordshire, Essex, and Cambridgeshire are absent from the list; indeed, their EBCs amount to only 9, 7, and 5, respectively. One might infer from these numbers that there was less interest in English baseball along London's northeast periphery, forming a gap separating Suffolk and Norfolk from the rest of baseball's heartland. But before one makes such an inference from the EBC data, one must take into account the built-in weakness of my entire statistical system. You see, what I've examined and tabulated are only those references to English baseball that are known to me. And while I can safely say I have studied this subject far greater than anyone else, the pool of information I am drawing upon is only as representative and comprehensive as the available source material from which it itself has been drawn. And there's the rub.

Let me be a bit more specific. Much of my EBC data is drawn from the flood of newspaper reports mentioning English baseball that poured forth in the second half of the nineteenth century. Who's to say that publication of the emerging regional newspapers in which

Fig. 7. The counties with the most references to English baseball. The names Beds and Bucks are shorthand for Bedfordshire and Buckinghamshire.

many of the accounts appeared was evenly distributed among the various English counties? Perhaps Hertfordshire, Essex, and Cambridgeshire sported fewer local newspapers than other counties. Or, for whatever reasons, their papers apportioned less coverage to civic festivals and school outings than did their neighbors' papers. Or that compilers of twenty-first-century digital newspaper databases happened to scan a smaller percentage of their publications. All in all, it is entirely possible the comparatively diminished EBC totals from the three counties are simply the product of a random disparity in source material and not any real difference in the actual level of baseball play.

A similar distortion may well apply to the English baseball NFD statistics listed above. Those numbers appear to suggest that interest in the pastime peaked in the second half of the nineteenth century. A broader measure, one that takes into account every known reference to the game over the course of its history, shows only ten examples of English baseball from the eighteenth century, and twenty-six more from the first half of the nineteenth. These are small totals compared with the more than three hundred examples I've identified in the years following 1850. Yet, notwithstanding the imbalance in raw numbers, it would be fallacious to conclude that English baseball's popularity soared as the century progressed. If anything, I suspect the opposite, that the game ebbed in prominence as the twentieth century approached, if for no other reason than its abrupt disappearance shortly thereafter. I tend to believe that the great increase in English baseball sightings from the 1850s onward is largely due to the parallel increase in the number of local and regional newspapers beginning or expanding publication during those years and not from any actual boost in the game's popularity.

Although it's not something I can prove with quantifiable data, I suspect that English baseball reached its apex somewhere in the early nineteenth century, possibly in the 1820s. This I deduce from an analysis of references to the game from those years, such as Mrs. Marcet's use of the term *baseball* in a science textbook or the literary allusions to the pastime by popular authors such as Jane Austen and Mary Russell Mitford. It has always impressed me that those writers' use of the word *baseball* assumed their readership would readily understand the reference. I contrast that with what I sense to be a decline in familiarity with English baseball as the century progressed, notwithstanding its increased newspaper presence.

The sharpest indicator of this for me is the contemporary reaction of British news reporters to the tours of American professional ballplayers to the UK in 1874 and again in 1889.[9] To those scribes, as evidenced by what they wrote in their papers, baseball was seen as purely an American sport. Almost none seemed cognizant that an English version of a game called baseball was still being played in multiple counties on the immediate outskirts of London and even occasionally in London itself. I suspect that in the days of Jane Austen and Mrs. Marcet, they would not have been so oblivious.

Having now shattered your faith in the reliability of my numbers, I will pirouette and proffer you an exciting new stat that, I believe, carries a marginally higher measure of confidence. Ladies and gentlemen, let me introduce you to the EBGA (English baseball by gender and age). I should acknowledge that after calculating this statistic, I discovered, to my great embarrassment, that it tends to undercut a claim I've been making about English baseball for at least a decade, that girls and women played the game far more than boys and men. Before getting to that, however, let me explain what EBGA entails. In analyzing every known reference to English baseball, I've taken note of the gender and age of the players associated with each. Sometimes boys played the game, sometimes girls. Adults played as well, and I've recorded that information, too. In all, I've broken down these demographics into nine categories and have placed every individual English baseball reference into one or another. The first six are straightforward: boys only, girls only, boys and girls together, men only, women only, men and women together. Then I have a category for "generic children" where the source doesn't indicate the gender of the players, only that they were youngsters. I also have a category for "all" to cover situations where the reference reveals that males and females of all ages were playing the game together, such as at a large public gathering. And, finally, I have a category for "none," which denotes those examples that give no hint as to the makeup of the players or make no mention of players at all.

Here are the results in order of finish:

Table 3: English baseball by gender and age (EBGA)

CATEGORY	EBGA
Generic children	123
All	96
Boys only	39
Men and women	33
Girls only	25
None	25
Men only	20
Boys and girls	18
Women only	7

Further values can be calculated from these numbers, such as a grand total for children regardless of gender (205) and for adults only (60). These results establish that English baseball was practiced far more commonly by youngsters than by grownups. These numbers also suggest that, unlike some sports, English baseball served to satisfy a social need rather than a physical one, often showing up in settings where parties of males and females of all ages were taking their recreation together. This characteristic makes itself evident throughout the game's history, ranging from the coed games played by the Prince of Wales and his family in 1748 and William Bray and his friends in 1755, to an 1899 report of a church group in Princes Risborough, Buckinghamshire, playing baseball at their annual treat. A news account of that event took note: "After an excellent tea, games were freely indulged in, such as base ball, bat and trap, &c., the older folk apparently enjoying the fun quite as much as the youngsters."[10]

I promised you a higher level of confidence with my EBGA numbers, and I believe they're reliable to the degree that they reflect the broad demographics of who played the game of English baseball over the course of its 150-plus years of existence. But what they lack is any insight into whether those demographic proportions stayed consistent across the course of the game's history. This matters to me because it bears upon the embarrassing admission I alluded to above. For many years I asserted that English baseball was primarily a game for girls and young women. This was not something I plucked out of the air but was drawn from my continuing analysis of references to the game as they became known to me. It wasn't until a decade or so ago that I began to notice that English baseball's lifespan extended into the second half of the nineteenth century and even into the beginning of the twentieth. Previously I had believed the pastime had gone extinct by 1860. Back then I was aware of only a relatively small number of references to English baseball, all dating between 1744 and the mid-1800s. I formed my opinions of the game from that limited set of data, including my observation that females were its customary players. The EBGA findings obviously convey a different story, showing that while both genders played the game, male participation was somewhat greater. Trying to make sense of my miscalculation, I went back and tabulated a narrower set of EBGA figures, this time taking into account only those references preceding the year 1830. Here are the new totals, listed in descending order:

Table 4. English baseball pre-1830 by gender and age (EBGA)

CATEGORY	EBGA
Girls only	9
Boys only	4
Generic children	3
Women only	2
None	2
Boys and girls	1
Men and women	1
Men only	1
All	1

Notwithstanding the small sample size, these numbers helped me understand why years ago I was so far off the mark in avowing that girls and women were English baseball's primary participants. They imply that female involvement in the game was relatively greater during the eighteenth and early nineteenth centuries. Yet, even with this explanation, I was troubled by the contrast between the two sets of EBGA numbers. If the earlier data trended toward greater participation by girls and women, it would mean that later references to English baseball would need to be weighted more heavily male to explain how my overall EBGA figures turned out the way they had. As I understand it, English baseball was an informal social game, one played without a bat. It didn't seem logical to me that participation in the pastime would veer in a masculine direction during the latter decades of the nineteenth century. This, after all, was the time when the philosophy of muscular Christianity was taking hold in Britain, when the noble feats of adventurers, soldiers, and athletes were seen as the highest expressions of Victorian manhood. Surely, more than ever, men and boys would have been flooding into the manly sports of football, rugby, and cricket, not upping their stake in a simple picnic game played by girls. How to explain this contradiction?

It got me wondering whether there might be a problem with the reliability of my data. I felt compelled to reexamine every reference to English baseball from the late nineteenth century to make sure I categorized it correctly. This I did, and what I learned was that, indeed, a disproportionate number of newspaper stories and other sources mentioning the game from the 1880s and 1890s identified the participants as men or older boys. I also noticed that many of these male-player reports emanated from two counties in particular, Hampshire and Suffolk. Had I missed something? Had the character of English baseball shifted in some way in the game's waning years that made it more appealing to men and boys? Or were my own appraisals at fault? Had I misidentified references as English baseball when I should have pegged them as instances of British citizens playing American baseball? These were questions I had to answer. But I'm getting ahead of myself here, which is to say you'll have to wait until chapter 21 before I get around to tackling these issues. I began the current chapter with the Knowl Hill Whitsuntide celebrations of 1830 and 1831, and rather than leaping ahead to examine how English baseball in the twilight of its years may have crossed paths with its American namesake, I might better serve you by first sorting out what went on with the pastime in the intervening seven decades.

11

A Class Act

Residents of southern England remained faithful to their homegrown game of baseball throughout the entirety of Queen Victoria's reign, as measured by the numerous times that newspapers, books, and magazines mentioned the pastime on their pages. Strange, then, that almost no one, then and since, seems to have taken much notice. When the royal family sponsored a large public festival to celebrate the birthday of the Duchess of Kent in 1858, dozens of newspapers reported on the festivities. In their coverage, every one of those papers observed that a game called *baseball* was among the amusements offered to celebrants. Over the following decades, many of those same newspapers would report on hundreds of other outdoor events where English baseball was played. I find it astounding then that nary a scribe for any of those papers took note of the fact that the indigenous game of baseball mentioned on their pages bore the same name as the American National Pastime, nor did they question whether the two forms of baseball had any relationship to each other.

But if writers from the national press paid little heed to English baseball, the snub had minimal impact on those playing the game at outdoor gatherings. Older citizens who had practiced the pastime in their youth continued to recall it fondly, sometimes with unusual emotion. One clergyman, writing in an 1833 memoir, wistfully recounted a long ago memory that had come upon him during a recent visit to the Sussex countryside: "The ground over which I now moved was sacred ground,—sacred to friendship,—for there, on former, happier days, I had, either walking or riding, been blessed with the society and conversation of the friends of my heart. . . . My mind turned mechanically to the period when upon the beautiful lawn ... I had viewed, with a moment's pleasurable sensation, my friends bounding over the enameled earth, like the fawns by which they were surrounded, while playing at base-ball."[1]

Some had recollections of the game that were a bit more prosaic. Pritchett Blaine Delabere was one of those. He was a pioneer in the field of veterinary medicine, known as "the father of canine pathology," and is remembered among doggy doctors for, among other things, his "masterly studies of canine distemper and rabies."[2] Dr. Delabere was so successful in his practice that he took an early retirement at age forty-seven. No idler, he whiled away his leisure years with a modest undertaking, that of compiling an encyclopedia of rural sports which, when it finally rolled off the press in 1840, ran to 1,240 pages. He found room on barely six of those pages for ball sports, mostly for overviews of cricket and tennis. Delabere commented that the game of handball was an appropriate activity for both males and females, then added: "There are few of us of either sex but have engaged in *base-ball* since our majority."[3]

The following year, a travel writer offered a more maudlin reminiscence in a magazine feature entitled "Railway Rambles" where he lamented how modernization had despoiled a lovely village in Buckinghamshire: "There *was* a village green some twenty years ago—the prettiest of greens; but now there is a straight road between two hedgerows; and the cheerful spot where the noise of cricket and bassball once gladdened the ear on a summer eve is now silent."[4] Happily, most of those who recalled playing English baseball in their youth expressed rosier memories. A newspaper in the county of Norfolk revealed one example in 1847 while covering the thirty-year reunion of former classmates of the Norwich Free Grammar School. "Here was the true English character exhibited," noted the reporter, "all the frost, and stiffness, and foolery of etiquette gave way before the good old English feeling of boyish reminiscences. Here met again the rival leaders in cricket, camp, hocky, fives, or base ball."[5]

The city of Norwich, in the East Anglian county of Norfolk, would soon be the site of another baseball reminiscence, one documented in the unlikely confines of a court transcript. In the summer of 1851 a hearing was under way in that city to determine whether a recently deceased man by the name of Bailey Bird had been of sound mind in his younger years. At the time of his death, Mr. Bird had been married thirty-three years, and his widow was expecting to receive the comfortable income that Bird had himself inherited from his father. However, challengers to the will claimed Bailey was always feeble-minded and never possessed the mental competency to make legally binding decisions. They maintained his faculties were so compromised that his marriage should be declared invalid. The case must have been a big sensation in Norwich because a local newspaper devoted many columns of precious editorial space to publish a lengthy transcript of the hearing. A procession of witnesses came forth to offer their memories of the late Bailey Bird and whether or not they thought him of diminished capacity. One witness was a merchant named Samuel Beare from Norwich who knew Bailey from childhood. He testified: "He was about 18 years. I used to say, 'well Bailey, how do you?' He would answer or not, as it happened. He was desirous of playing with us as boys, but he was not able; he did not comprehend the game. We used to play base, striking a ball and running to places called homes. Have heard the boys say to him, 'now Bailey, count five.' His answer was, 'don't know.'"[6]

Notwithstanding the evidence of Mr. Beare and others, the judge dismissed the challenge due to the many years that had passed since the wedding and because most of the people who might have been in the best position to know about Bailey's competence at the time were also deceased. But while Mr. Beare's testimony may not have convinced the judge that Bailey was impaired, it satisfied me in other ways. Beare offered only the sparest of detail about the baseball he and his friends had played decades earlier, but it was beyond what I typically find in such fleeting references. He revealed that youngsters in his community referred to bases as "homes," a nice little nugget of information of the type valued by early baseball zealots like me. By informing us that Bailey was eighteen years of age at the time of the long-ago ballgame, Beare also lets us locate English baseball in the county of Norfolk in the first decade of the nineteenth century. I had always supposed the pastime had taken hold in East Anglia by then, but it's nice to have explicit confirmation.

The fact that Bailey Bird, Samuel Beare, and the rest of their childhood circle came from prosperous middle-class backgrounds had little to do with English baseball being one of their favored games. We have seen that the pastime was enjoyed by players representing all ranks of society, from posh, high-born types like Prince Frederick and his sidekick, Lord Middlesex, to the raggedy children described by Mary Russell Mitford in her village stories. Indeed, English baseball appears to have been among the most democratic of ball games. In May 1850, for example, hundreds of laborers affiliated with the London chapter of the Chartist movement joined an excursion to Gravesend in Kent for a "Grand Whitsuntide Chartist Holiday." According to their organizational newspaper: "The spacious grounds of the Bat and Ball Tavern being reached, the company separated—some to visit Windmill-hill and admire Rosherville, whilst others engaged at an exhilarating game of cricket, base ball, and other recreations."[7] The Chartists were a radical political reform movement of the working class whose followers numbered in the tens of thousands across England.

Other reports from that period showed that baseball's popularity worked its way even further down the socioeconomic ladder, engaging some of the most marginalized members of society. An 1854 Berkshire newspaper article describes how local benefactors hosted a summer outing for a group of impoverished schoolchildren and their teachers from the Union Workhouse of Newbury: "They were most hospitably entertained by the respected chairman of the Board of Guardians on the lawn of Shaw House where piles of plum cake and other good things were speedily demolished, after which various sports were introduced, viz., cricket, trap bat, base-ball, kite flying, racing, &c., till night-fall came, when the national anthem being sung, and vociferous cheers given, the juveniles marched off, gratified for that benevolence which had not overlooked the orphan and destitute."[8]

Four years later, baseball appeared again at an event designed to lift the spirits of less fortunate members of the British public. A local landowner in the small Berkshire village of Bray-Wick hosted a "rural fête" on his nearby estate. Those invited included "the children of the Holyport Boys'-school, the Bray-wick Girls' National-school, the children and old people connected with the Cookham Union, as well as the inmates at the asylum at Bray." The Cookham Union was another workhouse for the poor, while the schools mentioned were public or church-funded institutions serving the children of laborers and other impoverished families. A local newspaper covering the event reported that "portions of the assemblage were scattered over various parts of the ground, engaged with games such as base-ball, trap-ball, foot-ball, swings, kiss-in-the-ring, &c., &c."[9]

During the 1850s when staffers at Victorian workhouses were introducing English baseball to the unfortunate children under their care, it was Queen Victoria herself who collaborated in making the game available to thousands of her other subjects. The occasion was the aforementioned seventy-second birthday celebration for the Duchess of Kent, the queen's mother, who was honored in 1858 by a grand festival staged near Windsor Castle under the auspices of the Windsor and Eton Mechanics' Institution and sponsored in part by the royal family. Newspapers reported that the queen "forwarded to the committee £10 10s. towards the expenses." This figure might equate to somewhere between a few hundred and few thousand pounds in today's money, a somewhat paltry sum considering it was her own mum's party. In any case it was a gigantic affair, treated locally as a major holiday. Shopkeepers closed early so that their employees could attend, church bells rang throughout the day, and Her Majesty's bombardier fired royal salutes from Windsor Great Park. Thousands of people showed up for the fun, and the press reported that "amusements principally consisted of cricket, dancing, archery, quoits, football, trap-ball, base ball, swinging, throwing sticks for prizes, &c."[10]

Like her daughter, the Duchess of Kent was named Victoria. She entered the world as a German princess and lived a life marked by oscillating turns of fortune. In 1803, at the age of seventeen, she married her first husband, a forty-year-old German prince who, inconsiderately, died eleven years later, leaving the widowed Victoria with two children. Her prospects brightened two years later when her brother, Leopold, a future king of Belgium, married Charlotte, the Princess of Wales and second in line to the British throne. Sadly, this matrimonial union would be of even shorter duration than Victoria's, as the young English princess died a year later following childbirth. This unfortunate development not only deprived Victoria of a well-positioned family member but it also threw Britain into a succession crisis. Prince George, Charlotte's father and first in line to the throne, was serving as regent for his father, the ailing George III. But with Charlotte's death he no longer had any legitimate living heirs, and neither did his brothers who might follow him in succession.[11]

At this juncture, fortune once again smiled on Victoria with the appearance of another prince charming. This time it was Prince Edward, Duke of Kent, the fifty-year-old fourth son of George III. Edward could count heads, and he realized that if he could produce a legitimate heir, he or she might one day ascend to the throne. Victoria was available, and in 1818 they married. The new Duchess of Kent dutifully gave birth to a daughter in 1819, an event that turned out to be the ultimate resolution of the succession problem. At the time of her birth, however, it was not at all obvious that Alexandrina Victoria would ever become queen. She was fifth in line behind three of her living uncles and her father, and she risked falling even further back in the pecking order if her uncles came up with new heirs of their own. But the biggest jolt for mother Victoria and her infant daughter was yet to come. When Alexandrina Victoria was only a year old, Prince Edward abruptly died. Then, six days later, on the heels of this calamity, came the death of Victoria's father-in-law, the now truly mad and otherwise incapacitated George III. These events elevated George IV to the throne and left mother Victoria a widow with a small child for the second time.[12]

For a royal, she found herself in unusually dire circumstances, having inherited her husband's debts while receiving little financial support from Parliament. She and her daughter were relegated to rundown rooms in Kensington Palace, and the duchess considered returning to Germany where she had family and a palace. But in the end she decided to stick it out in England in the hope that her daughter might one day move up the succession order, a wise decision as it turned out. George IV left no living offspring when he died in 1830. His next youngest brother, the Duke of York (he of "The grand old Duke of York / He had ten thousand men" fame), had passed away in 1827 and also was childless. That left a third brother, the Duke of Clarence, who was crowned King William IV. He, too, would not be long for the world, and when he died in 1837 he left behind eight living children. Unfortunately for them, none were products of his lawful marriage but were born to an actress he had been living with for twenty years. When all the royal dust had cleared, the Duchess of Kent came out golden. Her eighteen-year-old daughter was crowned queen, and the question of succession wouldn't arise again until the twentieth century.

Following teenage Victoria's accession, and once she and her mother smoothed out some frictions in their relationship, the Duchess of Kent slid into the role of revered dowager. Her popularity seemed to advance with her age, and the big birthday bonanza thrown for her in 1858 was emblematic of this. The celebration went off so well that the following year a similar extravaganza was planned for the duchess's seventy-third birthday, also cosponsored by the local mechanics' institution. This time it was held on the Ankerwycke estate in nearby

Wraysbury, immediately across the River Thames from the Runny-mede Water Meadow and in the same vicinity where King John and a collection of barons had signed the Magna Carta more than six centuries earlier. As in the previous year, the 1859 birthday festivities provided a range of amusements for the thousands of attendees. Those included, according to newspaper reports, "dancing, archery, cricket, quoits, trap bat and ball, foot and base ball, swings, boat racing and dinner."[13]

The full name of the outfit that organized the two birthday celebrations for the duchess was the Windsor and Eton Literary, Scientific, and Mechanics' Institution. It was among a new family of educational establishments that emerged in the nineteenth century to arm the British workforce with the technical and engineering skills required by the Industrial Revolution. As with the royal birthday parties, some of these organizations staged annual summer fêtes to promote cordial relations with their neighbors and to serve as fund-raisers. An unusually high number of such gatherings in the mid-nineteenth century included baseball. This tradition appears to have started with the Slough Literary and Mechanics' Institute at their annual rural fête in 1855. Slough is a large town three miles north of Windsor. The *West Middlesex Herald* covered the event and reported that attendees enjoyed "the exciting games of archery, cricket, trap and base ball, rural dancing, &c," adding that these games "presented an interesting picture of old English sports."[14] Subsequent newspaper reports reveal that baseball remained on the Slough fête's list of attractions every year but one between 1855 and 1862.

In 1857 the success of the Slough gatherings caught the eye of a member of the neighboring Windsor and Eton Mechanics' Institution, who wrote a letter to his local paper questioning why their organization couldn't stage a fund-raising fête similar to the one held by their close neighbor to the north. The correspondent noted that "there need be no lack of amusements. For music we have at least equal facilities with neighbouring places. Dancing, . . . recitations, songs, even a speech or two (if not *dry*), trap and base ball, and dozens of ways of passing a pleasant afternoon will suggest themselves to every one."[15] Thus the Windsor and Eton annual fête made its successful debut that year with baseball as one of its attractions. Then, the following year, its organizers realized they could extend the event's appeal to a wider audience by linking it with celebration of the Duchess of Kent's birthday, all the while continuing their commitment to baseball.

English baseball's presence at summer events hosted by mechanics' institutes spread beyond the Slough and Windsor operations. Newspaper evidence shows that similar organizations in the nearby towns of West Wycombe and Maidenhead featured the game in their respective annual fêtes in 1865.[16] Also joining the bandwagon was the Mechanics' Institution based in the town of Basingstoke in Hampshire. For three consecutive years, beginning in 1857, planners of that group's annual "rural fête" chose to include baseball among their list of offered amusements.[17] In 1859, organizers staged the Basingstoke fête in a local park. Evidently the writer for the *Hampshire Chronicle* who covered the event was so moved by what he/she witnessed that nothing less than the following rapturous (and nearly unending) sentence could capture his or her enthusiasm:

> During the afternoon various amusements were introduced, consisting of cricket, archery, bowls, lawn billiards, foot-ball, quoits, base-ball, and other innocent recreations, which were carried out with right good humour and unflagging spirit by old and young, who all appeared determined to devote the few hours provided for them to real enjoyment, free from the cares and toils of every-day life, and a most gratifying spectacle it was to see so many hundred happy faces and merry hearts, of both sexes and all ages, thus brought together to participate in the cheering and exhilarating pleasures which such social meetings, when properly conducted, are sure to afford, and which never could be experienced in greater variety or purity than on this occasion.[18]

Clearly, baseball remained ingrained in the rural social life of mid-nineteenth-century England or at least within that grouping of southern counties where the game had established its deepest roots. This pattern would continue for the remainder of the century. Far from being confined to newspaper reports of picnics and festivals, evidence of English baseball in this period seeped into all manner of written media, including the pages of fiction. And, knowing my fetish on the subject, you might not be surprised to learn that this road again intersects with the mystique of Jane Austen.

12

Literary Allusions

Jane Austen's contribution to our knowledge of English baseball did not end with her mention of the game in *Northanger Abbey* nor even with her death if you credit the power of genetics. When, following a long battle with a debilitating illness, Jane finally succumbed in July 1817, the event brought deep sorrow to members of her close-knit family, not the least to her brother Francis.[1] With less than two years of age separating them, Jane and Francis had formed an enduring bond as children that extended into adulthood. When Frank and his wife, Mary, welcomed a newborn daughter into their household a year following his sister's death, they paid homage to Jane's memory by christening the girl Catherine Anne. Those are the names of the heroines of *Northanger Abbey* and *Persuasion*, respectively, the two novels published posthumously in December 1817.

Frank died many years later at the age of eighty-nine, having outlived all seven of his Austen siblings. He was the only one among them whose celebrity approached that of Jane's, albeit in a very different sphere. His accomplishments were nautical, first as a successful Royal Navy captain during the Napoleonic Wars and then gradually rising through the ranks in a long career that saw him appointed Admiral of the Fleet.[2] All this activity kept him away from home much of the time, and when his wife died shortly after giving birth for the eleventh time in 1823, the care and raising of his ten surviving children fell to fellow family members. Cassandra, Frank's only surviving sister, was among the most forthcoming of these. She never had offspring of her own but built a warm attachment to her many nieces and nephews. Cassandra Austen made a point of familiarizing her young charges with the works of their late aunt, reading to them from Jane's novels as well as from her shorter works. Catherine Anne Austen grew up proud to be wearing the names of two of Jane's heroines. She became especially attached to the stories Cassandra read to her, and as she approached adulthood she made the decision to follow in the literary footsteps of her accomplished aunt.[3]

First, though, as with most women of the era, she needed to provide for her own security by finding a husband. John Hubback was a young lawyer and friend to several of her brothers. Catherine married him after a lengthy courtship, settled in London, and began having babies. John showed great promise in his profession, and everything looked bright for the young couple. But then in 1848, John suffered a mental breakdown. He never responded to treatment and lived out his life in various asylums and institutions. Catherine was left with three young sons in her care. Fortunately, she and the children were welcomed into her father's large household, and as a senior admiral he had the monetary resources to support them and pay for the boys' schooling.[4]

It was during this period that Catherine began to write. She retained a vivid memory of an unfinished manuscript of Jane's that her Aunt Cassandra had read to her often while she was growing up. As her first project, Catherine took it upon herself to complete the novel, a somewhat presumptuous undertaking for such an untrained and inexperienced author. She no longer had the manuscript in her possession, as ownership of it had passed to an older cousin, but she was able to recall most of it with uncanny accuracy, almost line by line.[5] She finished the work in 1850 and saw it published under the title *The Younger Sister*. The novel was about the Watson family, whose adventures followed the same themes and whose lives unfolded within the same sort of social and cultural milieu that would be familiar to readers of Jane Austen. As for readers of mine, who may be wondering where I am headed with all of this, please take note of the following bit of prose from *The Younger Sister*, an otherwise forgettable sentence but for the inclusion of a certain word: "Emma, drawing little

Charles towards her, began a confidential conversation with him on the subject of his garden and companions at school, and the comparative merits of base-ball and cricket."[6]

Like her Aunt Jane before her, Catherine Anne Hubback took the unusual step of working a reference to English baseball into her novel. I say unusual because, to my knowledge, it was only the fifth time this had been done. Remarkably, and perhaps not coincidentally, three of the five novelists were women members of the extended Austen-Leigh family, the third being Cassandra Cooke (*Battleridge*, 1799), who was the first cousin of Jane and Frank's mother (hence Catherine Anne's first cousin, twice removed). Another unusual aspect of *The Younger Sister*, one that would not remain unique for very long, is that Catherine endeavored to attract readers to the book by informing them of her connection to Jane. This she did under the guise of a dedication: "To the memory of her aunt, the late Jane Austen," she wrote, adding, "This work is affectionately inscribed by the authoress who, though too young to have known her personally, was from childhood taught to esteem her virtues, and admire her talents."[7]

I don't think I'm being overly cynical about Catherine Anne's intentions, as this was not the only time she would demonstrate a willingness to exploit her aunt's reputation. Twenty years following the novel's publication, and after moving to Oakland, California, to take up residence near two of her adult sons, she began writing short stories for submission to *Overland Monthly*. When the magazine published the first of these, she wrote to her third son, John, who was still in England. "I mean in the future to have my name printed Mrs. C. Austen Hubback and make believe the A. stands for that. I never have written it *at length*—so nobody knows, and Austen is a good *nom de plume*."[8] Despite feeling comfortable brandishing the Austen name, she apparently never acknowledged in print that *The Younger Sister* was based on a partial manuscript from the hand of her famous relative.

By invoking her aunt's name in the novel's dedication, and by adopting her later pen name, Catherine had seized upon a good idea. One modern commentator has credited her for producing "the first published Austen fan fiction" and labeled her "the founding mother of a genre whose exemplars now fill groaning shelves in bookstores everywhere."[9] Even in her own time she was not alone among her cousins in hoping to get some benefit from Jane's works and prestige. James Edward Austen-Leigh wrote a biography of his famous aunt with the cooperation of various siblings and cousins that was first published in 1870. A second edition followed soon afterward, in which he featured, as an added bonus, several of Jane's previously unpublished works, including the novella *Lady Susan* and the manuscript fragment that his cousin Catherine had shaped into *The Younger Sister* years earlier. Now the fragment had a name, "The Watsons." Subsequent to that printing, another Austen descendant divided the original manuscript into two parts, one of which passed out of the hands of the family and eventually wound up in the collection of the Morgan Library in New York. The second, larger section of "The Watsons" would appear in print several more times over the next 140 years, including an edition published in 1928 with an introduction by Edith Brown, who was Catherine Hubback's granddaughter. Apparently Edith was unaware that her grandmother had adapted the manuscript into *The Younger Sister*. The portion of "The Watsons" still held by Austen descendants eventually turned up at a Sotheby's auction in 1978 and then again in 1988. In 2011 Sotheby's auctioned it for yet a third time, and this time the document was snatched up by Oxford's Bodleian Library for the bargain price of £1 million.

If Catherine intended to exploit Jane Austen's reputation by dedicating *The Younger Sister* to her aunt, the familial connection escaped the notice of the reviewers. They did, however, greet the work positively for the most part. One writer, from the *New Monthly Review and Humorist,* offered that "*The Younger Sister,* a novel by Mrs. Hubback, is characterised by more straightforward common sense, and less of the maudlin sentiment and mere fanciful sketches of character which inundate the pages of too many ladies' novels."[10] I suspect that the literary qualities this reviewer observed in the completed novel were inherited from Jane Austen's manuscript, which formed the basis of the work's first five chapters. Catherine Hubback's further contributions to *The Younger Sister* were less impressive, which perhaps explains why the novel achieved limited success in its time and has been almost completely forgotten today.

One question about *The Younger Sister* that tickled my interest years ago when I first learned of its baseball reference was whether Catherine Hubback found the term in Jane's manuscript and carried its use forward into the completed novel, or whether Catherine, on her own, chose to mention the game. A digital search of texts of "The Watsons" then available failed to detect the presence of baseball (in any of its spellings), but I wasn't certain those texts represented the entirety of Jane's document. More recently, with both the Morgan Library and Bodleian Library fragments fully available, I searched them and once again found no mention of baseball, suggesting that it was Catherine Hubback who wrote the game into her book. Evidently, baseball remained as familiar a part of the world that she grew up in as it was during her Aunt Jane's own upbringing some forty years earlier.

The Younger Sister was but one of a varied collection of fictional works published in the second half of the nineteenth century whose authors chose to mention English baseball. None of these works would be remembered as a literary treasure. The majority, perhaps half a dozen in number, are novels and short stories targeting a juvenile readership, and in one of them the author's baseball reference is particularly odd. It surfaced in a short story entitled "Along Fleet Street" that appeared in the April 1871 issue of a children's magazine, *Merry & Wise*. The piece, written by someone identified only as "Old Merry," includes the following sentence: "Arthur wanted to know where the old Fleet Prison used to stand, and if it was the veritable place where Mr. Pickwick went to, and if it wasn't where he met Mr. Jingle, and whether people did not play racquet and base-ball there, and pay for their own lodgings, etc."[11]

Finding this, and not having read *The Pickwick Papers* since my school days, I was truly puzzled. I had no recollection of Dickens mentioning baseball. Had he done so in such a widely read work, it would surely be known to me and to other baseball historians. It might well have attained the iconic status of Jane Austen's use of the term in *Northanger Abbey*. Even so, when coming across the baseball reference in the short story, I was instantly motivated to check out its author's suggestion. What in Dickens's novel could have driven "Old Merry" to imply that baseball was played in Fleet Street prison? Consulting an early London edition of *The Posthumous Papers of the Pickwick Club,* I came across what appeared to be the relevant passage: a description of a grim and filthy open area within the prison that served as an impromptu "racket ground." Dickens wrote: "Lolling from the windows which commanded a view of this promenade were a number of persons; some in noisy conversation with their acquaintance below; others playing at ball with some adventurous throwers outside; and others looking on at the racket-players, or watching the boys as they cried the game."[12]

Dickens's reference to "playing at ball" is a bit vague. Was he implying baseball? Old Merry seems to have deciphered it that way. By parsing Dickens's words, one might infer that the "playing at ball" action was taking place separately from the rackets game. But even if this was his intention, there is nothing to confirm his "playing at ball" was a euphemism for baseball. In the end, I chalked up Old Merry's interpretation as another of the fanciful phantom baseball sightings that seem to crop up occasionally in Victorian writings.

That said, Old Merry was not the only nineteenth-century fiction writer, nor the most prominent, to allude to the presence of baseball in a prison setting. So did the prolific Scottish novelist Henrietta Keddie, who often employed the nom de plume Sarah Tytler. (I can't resist mentioning that Ms. Keddie took a holiday from fiction in 1880 to pen a biography of Jane Austen, notably the first of these not written by a family member.) In her novel *Lady Jean's Vagaries,* published anonymously in 1894, Ms. Keddie unfolded a plot set in the days of the French Revolution. At one point in the story, she described her eponymous well-born heroine venturing to a dank prison in the Southwark district of London to visit her debtor husband: "She knew every grimly solid piece of furniture in the receiving room; which was at least spacious enough for the various incongruous groups that were wont to be congregated there; she could have made her progress unguided, as she went—the tall, nodding feathers in her beaver hat adding to her height, her train drawn through her pocket-hole—smilingly picking her way in her high heeled shoes past the base-ball court and the skittle ground, acknowledging the humble salutations made to her with the unwearying affability of one born to state and condescension."[13] This is fiction, of course, but as we shall see in chapter 20, the presence of baseball in a debtors prison was not such a far-fetched notion.

Other nineteenth-century English literary connections to baseball come with their own touch of quirkiness. In 1891 a biographer of the English poet Robert Browning made a surprising claim about the poet's father, also named Robert Browning. She wrote: "Mr. Browning enjoyed splendid physical health. His early love of reading had not precluded a wholesome enjoyment of physical sports; and he was, as a boy, the fastest runner and best base-ball player in his school."[14] The biographer was Alexandra Leighton Orr, a close friend of the Brownings. Her source for much of the background on the lives of family members was Sarianna Browning, the poet's sister, someone who might be considered a reliable authority on the details of her father's childhood. The senior Robert Browning passed his schoolboy years in Camberwell, a district of south London that was then a rural village. This was during the 1790s, a time when playing baseball would not have been an unusual recreational option for English students of either gender. Still, claims from one hundred years in the past, no matter how plausible, much be treated with skepticism. From such a far remove there is really no way of knowing whether Robert Senior was truly the baseball phenom of his era or whether Sarianna Browning or Alexandra Orr contrived the claim to embellish his memory.

Another curious case involves Maria Louise Ramé, a popular nineteenth-century English author who wrote under the pen name Ouida. Her best-known work is the 1867 novel *Under Two Flags*, which was turned into a Broadway play in 1901. It was also the basis of four films, including one in 1936 that starred Ronald Colman, Claudette Colbert, Victor McLaglen, and Rosalind Russell. As its crowning honor, *Under Two Flags* was released as a Classics Illustrated comic book (#86) in 1951. Ouida spent her childhood near Bury St. Edmonds in Suffolk, apparently not the most stimulating environment for an aspiring author, or so she implied years later when describing her hometown under a thinly disguised fictional name: "That neat, clean, quiet, antiquated town, that always puts me in mind of an old maid dressed for a party; that slowest and dreariest of boroughs, where the streets are as full of grass as an acre of pasture-land, and the inhabitants are driven to ringing their own doorbells lest they rust from disuse."[15]

Notwithstanding her later disapproval of the place, she seems to have enjoyed some happy moments there. Writing in her diary with breathless enthusiasm at the age of thirteen, she described an 1852 summer outing to Ickworth Park: "We lighted the fire and then spread the cloth on the grass [and] we had glorious fun for the little spiders got into the tea and all manner of disasters happened—some cows then frightened Grandma and Arnie by coming near us but we frightened them in return with the Cornet and they all took to their heels, after that we had a game of Bass Ball then Rick got on the donkey and I made it gallop and finally we all returned home."[16]

Ickworth Park was an appropriate setting for young Ouida's baseball experience. It surrounds Ickworth House, the hereditary estate of the Hervey family. On those premises, in an earlier manor house, resided Mary Lepel, Lady Hervey, who in 1748 penned the famous letter describing the Prince of Wales and family playing baseball. Ouida's participation in the game as a child fits right in with what we know about Bury St. Edmonds and, indeed, all of Suffolk, which is that it was rock solid baseball country. In fact, Suffolk can boast more historic references to English baseball—more than fifty—than any other county.

English baseball also found its way into odd bits of English verse during the nineteenth century, sometimes for reasons that seem curious to this poetically untrained reader or just outright inexplicable. One such example is a poem entitled "Polling" that appeared in an 1880 issue of the British humor magazine *Fun*. Actually, it is more a song than a poem and a satirical song to boot. Here are its first verse and chorus:

> A season it was once of good fun and fashion,
> And folly, no doubt, but the follies still live;
> Lawn tennis alone was a prevalent passion—
> With cotillions, maybe, or *Sara la Juive*.[17]
> It served for the mothers' and modistes' consoling,
> Distending the bills and disposing of belles;
> And now they have given it all up to polling,
> To bill-sticking, bouncing, and yawnings and yells.
>   *Chorus of Mayfair Maids and Matrons.*
>   Polling, polling,
>   Keep the base ball rolling,
> Never mind your sisters, nor your cousins, nor your aunts,
>   So you "stump" for,
>   "Split" or "plump" for
> Candidates that mock you with their miserable vaunts.[18]

The anonymous writer's use of the term *baseball* here is puzzling; it seems almost gratuitous, as if he or she were reaching for any handy word to fill in the line. The song makes reference to other sports as well—lawn tennis, cricket, and polo are all named in various verses—but, unlike with baseball, there appears to be recognizable purpose behind the placement of those games among the lyrics. It is obvious that "Polling" is both an homage to, and parody of, Gilbert and Sullivan's popular musicals. The line in the song mentioning "sisters," "cousins," and "aunts" mimics a well-known lyric from the operetta HMS *Pinafore*, which had completed its initial run of 571 performances only two months prior to the publication of "Polling." The magazine *Fun,* in which the poem appeared, was a rival to the better-known *Punch*, the former directed more toward a lower-middle-class audience rather than *Punch*'s posher readership.

As I write this, the American 2016 election has just come to its unthinkable end. The ugliness and insanity of the campaign season and its repugnant results are fresh in mind and will be, I suspect, for a long time to come. "Polling" finds humor in a far different type of electoral scene, one from late nineteenth-century Britain that I assume was more genteel. The writer presumed to voice the point of view of the well-bred ladies of Mayfair, who are aghast at the behavior of their menfolk during the campaign. They fret at the men's willingness to cast aside all matters of true importance, such as balls and cotillions, in the thrall of almighty politics. Had they foreseen how immeasurably more malevolent and dangerous the stakes of elections would present to countries in the future, and indeed to the entire world, they might not have protested so much.

English baseball made another poetic appearance, this time in 1892 and with yet another connection to the royal family. On January 14, Prince Albert Victor, the Duke of Clarence, died suddenly in the midst of an influenza pandemic. He was the eldest son of Albert, Prince of Wales, and grandson of Queen Victoria, and as such he was second in line to the British throne. His death came only a week after his twenty-eighth birthday and barely a month after becoming engaged to Mary of Teck, a German princess and, like the Duke, a great-grandchild of George III. The luckless Duke had the further misfortune of being the subject of merciless rumors both before his death and afterward. But despite these, the nation mourned his passing. One unnamed, sorrowful citizen channeled his grief by writing and publishing a poetic eulogy in a British newspaper. This is an excerpt:

The Death of the Duke
  January 14th, 1892

The Duke is dead!' So ran the cheerless
Tidings round the whole domain—entering
Hall and cot, and laying its heavy
Burden upon us all. Rude boys—alas!
Accustomed to street cries—yet mindless
Of the due import of what they told to-day—
Tossed the sad intelligence from each to
Each—as though they played at base-ball
Mid sunshine. 'Twas otherwise with men.[19]

The poem went on to describe how word of the Duke's death shocked and saddened the men of Britain, and as best as I can tell, the poet seemed to be contrasting the strongly felt impact of the death upon the older and wiser citizens of the country to that of the boys in the street who tossed the news back and forth among themselves with no more care than if it were a "base-ball." His decision to use baseball for his analogy, rather than cricket or football, is a curious one, given the other two sports enjoyed much greater popularity in Britain. Then again, maybe he was suggesting that throwing a baseball back and forth was a more casual form of play, one that made his metaphoric point more precisely than tossing around a cricket ball or football.

As to those rumors, some journalists had attempted to link the duke to the Cleveland Street scandal having to do with a gay men's brothel in London, and rumors of his alleged homosexuality persisted long after his death. These accusations were probably unfounded, as no evidence ever surfaced showing he visited the brothel or was gay. His fiancée, Princess Mary, seemed unconcerned by the insinuations and, according to contemporary newspaper accounts, was devoted to him and took his death very hard. Not so hard that she didn't recover from her mourning quickly, it would seem, because barely a year later she became engaged to the duke's younger brother, Bertie, who later in life would be crowned George V, with Mary becoming his queen. Other rumors besieged the Duke in his short lifetime, branding him as lazy, feeble, or completely idiotic. But the worst rumor surfaced seventy years after his death when several authors stirred speculation that Albert Victor was Jack the Ripper, the infamous serial killer of the 1880s. Even though indisputable evidence proved it was impossible for him to have been the killer—he was five hundred miles away in Scotland when several of the crimes occurred—the rumor persisted in film and fiction and did nothing to improve his already battered reputation.

One final instance of baseball's presence in nineteenth-century English poetry is one from 1898 that fits in just under the wire. It is a long, maudlin verse, unsigned, that expresses the feelings of a working man who returns to his boyhood village of Redgrave, in Suffolk, after an absence of sixty-four years. He anguishes over all the changes: the familiar sights are gone, the houses are decaying, industrialization has taken a heavy toll, and the laboring classes and the poor are worse off than ever. Here is his opening stanza:

Doggerel Lines by the Son of a Labourer

Now 64 years from my own native home,
Had a wish to visit once more
The haunts of my childhood, I longed to roam
Recalling the days of yore;
I know all the places, and names can tell
Where we played at the close of each day,

Baseball, prison bars, and cricket as well,
Quite green in my mind now I'm grey.[20]

Sixty-four years prior to 1898 would place this working man's
baseball-playing days in the early 1830s, a realistic claim since baseball was listed in Edward Moor's 1823 glossary *Suffolk Words and
Phrases* as one of the games played regularly in the county. Indeed,
Suffolk had long been one of the hotbeds of English baseball. But as
the nineteenth century progressed, some Suffolk citizens began to fear
that opportunities for their children to play baseball and other games
were facing an existential threat. Defenders of the games took to the
columns of newspapers to complain that authorities were limiting
access to playgrounds. In 1884 a writer for the *Ipswich Journal* protested the inadequacy of the few recreational areas in one neighborhood. "All the old places in that district are being gradually enclosed,"
he complained, "so that in future young Ipswichians will have to take
to the streets."[21] He lamented some of the former venues no longer
available for play: "As for the Racecourse, that best of all playgrounds,
who does not remember the summer evenings when cricket, baseball, 'hunt-the-hare,' and football . . . were favourite games on both
sides of the course, and where literally hundreds of children of both
sexes were engaged in joyous play unmolested?"

Nine years later, another columnist for the same paper took issue
with Ipswich town employees fencing off the Old Recreation Ground,
a popular field on the banks of the river Orwell, and posting "No
Trespassing" signs:

> For several years past the youngsters have here, unchecked by
> frown of officious caretaker in brass buttons, indulged in the
> hearty enjoyment of their games of cricket, football, base-ball,
> and many other healthful pastimes which are the delight of
> every true juvenile Briton. Here were no trees to damage, no
> grass on which they might not tread, no flowers to pluck, no
> seats to damage, and consequently they were left entirely alone,

unable to do any kind of mischief, as there was nothing they could possibly harm. No wonder, then, that when the schools were closed this patch of ground became a perfect elysium to the liberated youngsters.[22]

Perhaps the old laborer, who through his poetry expressed dismay over the loss of former childhood haunts, would have enjoyed some small measure of comfort had he known that some of his fellow Suffolkites were rallying to the cause.

13

Glorified Rounders of Antiquity

In 1874 two American baseball clubs decided to show off the great National Pastime to their former colonial rulers in Britain. At the initiative of prominent player and manager Harry Wright, who was himself English born, players representing two premier professional teams, the Boston Red Stockings and the Philadelphia Athletics, boarded a ship bound for England. They were on their way to play a series of exhibition matches organized in conjunction with several English cricket clubs. It was the expectation of the tour's American sponsors that when Britons witnessed the exciting game of baseball firsthand they would hasten to begin playing it themselves. The planners also banked on earning a tidy profit from the undertaking. They struck out on both counts. Attendance at most of the matches fell well below projections. Moreover, many of the writers reviewing the American game for British publications found artful ways to belittle it. It would take the passage of another fifteen years and a second international tour showcasing the pastime before American-style baseball established any type of foothold in Britain.

Not all British commentary about American baseball in 1874 was negative. Some observers praised the speed of the game and the agility and skills of fielders.[1] Others found favor in the relative brevity of baseball matches when compared with cricket's marathons.[2] Still, it should come as no surprise that almost every British reviewer took pains to emphasize the superiority of cricket. What was more layered, however—and what most interests me—were the comparisons various writers made between American baseball and rounders. By 1874 rounders was well established in Britain as an activity for boys and men, although it was still a relatively young pastime. My research suggests it separated from its parent game, English baseball, in the late eighteenth century and acquired the label "rounders" in the 1820s after subsisting for several decades under the simple name "bat and ball." By the time of the American tour of 1874, most Englishmen were intimately familiar with rounders. Having played it as youths, they would have had no reason to think it hadn't been around for centuries. So when American baseball showed up on their doorstep, and when news writers noticed its similarity to rounders, they quite naturally commented on that likeness, albeit not always favorably.

Several columnists gave grudging credit to American baseball for being more "scientific" than rounders.[3] One from the *London Daily News* framed it as "the old game of rounders considerably elaborated."[4] Others were reluctant to go even that far. "It is now generally agreed that base-ball is rounders under another name—with certain complications," conceded a writer for the *Western Daily Mercury* of Plymouth.[5] Many papers were simply content to repeat the common catchphrase that baseball was "glorified rounders," or in the words of a columnist from the *Southern Reporter* of Selkirk, Scotland, "Base ball is only 'rounders' after all—'rounders gone mad' or 'rounders glorified'—and the American form of it is no improvement, notwithstanding its parade of science, on our own boys' game."[6] The *Graphic*, an illustrated newspaper published in London, took it a notch further:

> Base-Ball. We have now seen enough of this game on the London cricket grounds to enable us to form a definite opinion of its merits, and we must say that that opinion is not a favourable one. The game cannot be compared with our own cricket, being only a refinement on the "rounders" of our schoolboy days. There is not much scope for real science in base-ball, and hence it will never be as popular among us or draw such crowds of spectators to witness it as cricket. In fact it is a game better suited for boys than men.[7]

But what was missing from all this, and what these newspaper commentators failed to point out, was that English citizens themselves had long been practicing a form of baseball. I find it astonishing that the newspaper writers who so willingly critiqued the display of America's National Pastime in Britain in 1874 were, by all appearances, completely oblivious to the fact that England's own brand of baseball prospered at that very moment in the southern counties surrounding London. They clearly dropped the ball in not including this homegrown baseball among the list of domestic games meriting comparison to the one the Americans were showing off. Thankfully, not all members of the British public who consumed these newspapers were equally obtuse. Several of them wrote to their local papers to protest the omission of England's indigenous form of baseball from articles discussing the American version.

One such letter appeared in the *Times* of London under the heading "Base-Ball." The paper identified the correspondent simply as "Grandmother." She wrote: "Sir,—Some American athletes are trying to introduce to us their game of base-ball, as if it were a novelty; whereas the fact is that it is an ancient English game, long ago discarded in favour of cricket. In a letter of the celebrated Mary Lepel, Lady Hervey, written in 1748, the family of Frederick, Prince of Wales, are described as 'diverting themselves with base-ball, a play all who are or have been schoolboys are well acquainted with.'"[8]

Grandmother displayed unusual acumen in recalling Lady Hervey's reference to baseball, but stumbled in failing to note that the original eighteenth-century pastime was still being played. On the same day her letter appeared, however, another citizen writing to a competing London newspaper, the *Daily News*, avoided repeating Grandmother's error by correctly observing that some English residents were still practicing a domestic form of baseball. Unfortunately, in doing so, the correspondent, J. C. Read, introduced a few questionable claims of his own. He wrote:

Sir,–The notoriety recently acquired by our Transatlantic cousins in connection with the above game . . . [has] led to the belief on the part of many . . . that the game owes its origin to America. . . . It may inform some and remind others that base ball is thoroughly English, and during the sixteenth century occupied a foremost place in the list of our national sports. It is alluded to by Shakespeare and other writers as an old rustic game, and was an indispensable accompaniment to the amusements provided for the festive May-day gatherings on village greens during the reign of the Merrie Monarch and . . . his successors. . . . However, the game of base ball gradually lost its patrons, and is now known to a comparative few. The knowledge of the game . . . lingers chiefly in our most remote rural districts, including some villages in the county of Suffolk, where, more than thirty years since, it was a common game between the lads and lasses. . . . I have no desire to depreciate the ability and skill of the Americans in playing this game, being only anxious to remove the prevailing impression that it is an importation from another country.[9]

While giving credit to Mr. Read for recognizing that villagers in Suffolk were still playing English baseball, we must also marvel at his colorful imagination. To my knowledge, there is not the slightest evidence to support a claim that baseball was practiced as early as the sixteenth century in England nor anywhere else for that matter. Mr. Read evidently fell victim to the same confusion between baseball and the game of prisoner's base that has tripped up many others before and since. His remark about Shakespeare's reputed allusion to baseball is what gives him away. The Bard's mention of a game called "base" in the play *Cymbeline* was almost certainly a reference to prisoner's base, as were all similar uses of the term dating from that earlier era.

Mr. Read would not be the last to allege exceptionally early beginnings for English baseball. In a speech entitled "Old English Sports and Customs" given in 1883, an alderman from the Yorkshire town of Hull claimed that "base ball . . . used to be played in the streets of London in the seventeenth century."[10] Three years later, a writer for the *Cornishman*, a Penzance newspaper, seemed to agree, maintaining that the game was high on the list of raucous Whitsuntide amusements encouraged during the reign of King James I. Of those he wrote: "Outdoor amusements naturally predominated, and we read of gay picnic parties and rude musical gatherings, and games of every kind of sport were freely indulged, one of the most popular being base-ball."[11] Less flamboyantly, a journalist writing a column for a London newspaper in 1873 was content simply to name "baste ball" as one of "ye ancient sports of Albion," without identifying which "anciente" era he had in mind.[12]

Then there was the school headmaster in Kent who creatively managed to work a reference to baseball into an 1892 lecture about the English Reformation. The Rev. George J. Blore brought up the topic of the "boy king," Edward VI, who ruled Britain as a child for six years in the mid-sixteenth century. Alluding to the king's immaturity, Blore stated that "he recorded his experiences in a curiously methodical journal, where he entered with equally matter of fact brevity great matters of State, and the games of baseball got up for his amusement."[13] This mind-boggling assertion is, of course, fanciful and is rooted in the same venerable fallacy that afflicted J. C. Read. Edward, the young and highly intelligent son of Henry VIII, did, indeed, keep a detailed journal during his short life (he died from what was probably pneumonia at the age of fifteen). The journal notations that Reverend Blore interpreted as being about baseball were entered by Edward on two successive days in the year 1550. The first, on March 31, reads, "A chaleng made by me that I, with 16 of my chaumbre, shuld runne at base, shote, and rune at ring with any 17 of my servauntes, gentlemen in the court." The outcome of the challenge was revealed the next day, April 1: "The first day of the chaleng at base, or running, the King wane."[14] Quite clearly, these entries make reference to the running game of prisoner's base, not baseball. The Reverend joined an expanding list of those getting the two games confused.

Even though Reverend Blore backdated the imagined beginnings of English baseball to the sixteenth century, his was not, by a long shot, the oldest reference to the game. The author of an 1888 book registered an earlier one in his work entitled *The Illustrated History of England from the Earliest Times to 1887*. Writing about the sports and pastimes of the fourteenth century, the author, Henry William Dulcken, asserted: "The present games of schoolboys and children had also their prototypes in those days. Thus the game of hoodman-blind is the medieval form of blindman's buff, baseball and stool-ball, etc. are perpetuated in hockey, trap-ball and similar games."[15] How Mr. Dulcken knew that baseball was played in the age of Robin Hood he does not say.

But the prize for backdating English baseball to its earliest point in history must surely go to an 1891 history of the medieval town of Burford in western Oxfordshire. Its author, W. J. Monk, included the following sentences while discussing ancient hunting rights in the town: "From time immemorial the townsmen had possessed the privilege of hunting in Wychwood Forest on Whit Sunday. The custom, no doubt, originated in the early days of the Church, and when the Sabbath was not so rigorously kept as it is now. So long as Mass was attended in the morning, every one was free, as on other days, to indulge in base ball, football, or any other game."[16]

So let me see if I get this. Mr. Monk looks through his time machine's magic periscope and observes that "in the early days of the Church," not only was everyone a Sabbath-breaker, but they were also free to play baseball on Sunday afternoons, just like on all the other days. His designated time period is somewhat vague, but since Christianity arrived in Britain in the first or second centuries CE, I suppose we can place the "early days" somewhere within the following few centuries, perhaps during the Dark Ages. That opens up the possibility that Arthur, Guinevere, and all that lot might have played baseball. Interesting thought.

In contrast to these rather imaginative accounts, an 1873 book describing an ancient town in Berkshire named Wallingford offers a more solidly grounded historical depiction of baseball.[17] The work is entitled *Rambles in the Neighbourhood of Wallingford* and was written by William Allnatt. He recalled spending his childhood in the town a half-century earlier: "Games . . . were annually held here on Mayday, and many a comely and buxom girl have I witnessed on such occasions vigorously throwing the bass-ball to a fellow maiden near her, and all were full of frolic. This latter game I have discovered is nearly, if not completely, gone out of fashion now about here which is to be deplored, as I am one who would willingly see a revival of such like harmless sports."[18] One wonders whether in Wallingford it was only the comely and buxom girls who played baseball, as Mr. Allnatt suggested, or perhaps it was only the young ladies with those attributes who attracted his gaze. Regardless, we are grateful to him for bearing firsthand witness to baseball's early presence in that rural Thames valley community and for his obvious appreciation of the game.

In the wake of the American baseball tour of 1874, while J. C. Read and Grandmother were protesting that the supposedly newfangled Yankee pastime of baseball had actually been meandering around England for centuries, it fell to a humor publication to put the whole matter into perspective. Shortly after the Americans departed for home, *Punch* magazine printed a letter written, ostensibly, by a resident of the county of Suffolk. It appeared under the heading "Baseball in the Vernacular":

Worlton, Nr. Ipsidge, Suffolk
August, 1874

Dear oad Poonch,
What fules you Lundoners be! You're allus ridy to swaller any thing a furrenner hoads afore yar jaw. The newest thing I see in the peapers is that the hool country be a gooin to luze thar wits about the game o' base ball.

I'm nigh furty year oad, and I ha' plaed base ball, man and boy, for more un thirty-five year, as any o' yar folks there could hev sen if tha'd ha come to our village—or fur the matter o' that, to furty other villages hereabouts—any evenin' a summer time. I'll try and tell yow the wai we plae base ball.

We make the base at the oad Church wall, and chuze sides, then we toss for In or Out; them ut git out stop outside the base-bounds, and hev to field, same as in cricket, and them ut get in stop in and take ball. Then the pitcher puts his men in the field where he chuzes, and then delivers the ball to fust man in base. If he doant hit it wi his stick or his hand, and the ketcher behind him ketch it, he is out, and a dead man for t' innings, but if he hit, he must run like t' oad un to fust bounds, which in our place is t' corner o' public-house wall (the Feathers), and if the next man hit the ball, the fust man runs nation hard to 'tother end o' public-house wall, and second man runs to where he left, and so on, to as many bounds but one, as there are men to the innard side. If the field men ketch the ball, the fellar ut struck it is out, same as in cricket.

Blarm me if I doant think them there Yankees hev ben down here and larnt the game, jest to gull yow Cockneys wi', or else some Suffolk emmergrunts ha' goon and larnt them Merricans the game, and they're a lettin' yow hev it second-hand. Carnt you get 'em to come and plae agin our village?—I think thar'd git thar match.

Yours to command,
Saml. Plant
Cow-parstur' farm
Worlton, near Ipsidge, Suffolk

P.S.—We eent got much munney, but we'll plae em for harf a gallon, all round, o' Cobbald's best Brighteye, jest to let 'em know we doant want folks to come thousans o' miles to larn us what our granfarthers larnt our farthers, and thae we.

How is it none o' yar young fellars who come to Fillixter a summer times doant tell the folks about base ball?

Bust and blarm my skin if I eent riled to see such a fuss made about nought.[19]

This letter confronts me with a dilemma. As a satirical piece published in a humor magazine, I should, by definition, disqualify it as a legitimate historical source. Yet within its lines there are details that reveal its author possessed unusual insights into the state of English baseball at the time it was written. Nowadays I would ponder the propriety, if not the sanity, of anyone citing *Mad Magazine* or the *Onion* to support a scholarly thesis. Yet such a course of action, though I tremble to admit it, is what I am about to take with *Punch*.

In all likelihood, the mock letter's writer was a staff member based in the publication's London headquarters. The practice of printing a piece written in such an exaggerated, homespun Suffolk dialect was not new for *Punch* in 1874. A database search shows the magazine had used the technique multiple times in years past when poking fun at a topic related to the county. Other publications occasionally employed the folksy dialect for humorous effect as well, including several newspapers based in Suffolk itself. The staffer who wrote the baseball letter for *Punch* displayed a familiarity with Suffolk culture that went beyond his or her ability to spoof its dialect. This is implied not only by the accuracy of the piece's parody but also through its plausible depiction of baseball's stature in the county. The writer clearly was aware that Suffolk residents had been playing a simpler, more rustic version of the pastime for many years before the 1874 arrival of the American players. He or she also appeared well acquainted with the fundamentals of Suffolk baseball and the ways it differed from the American-style version, such as that it could be played without a bat or that all players on a side had to be put out before a change of innings, as in cricket.

All told, it must have been a great disappointment for the organizers of the 1874 American baseball tour to Britain that their undertaking did not win the hearts and minds or the pocketbooks of the British public. The only suggestion that any Brits were impressed enough by what they witnessed to actually begin playing the American-style pastime was the appearance a couple of years later of several baseball clubs in and around the city of Leicester in the English Midlands.[20] But apparently those clubs did not survive more than a year or two, and in any case, there is no hard evidence their creation was a direct outgrowth of the 1874 tour. For British journalists who covered the visiting Yankee ball players, the consensus about the shiny new bat and ball game being showcased was that it was a reworking of something they had seen before, namely, their "old friend" rounders. For a smaller group of British citizens who took the time to write letters to newspaper editors, the American pastime was also nothing to get excited about, because, as they rightly observed, a version of baseball had long been practiced in England. In their own ways, both factions hit the ball right on its sweet spot: American baseball was not original. It derived from an earlier presence in England. Several months after the Americans departed for home, a writer for the *Daily News* of London published a column that discussed how certain terms that are assumed to be Americanisms were either derived from other languages or were imported English provincialisms. In the course of the piece, he summed up the British attitude toward the sport they had seen displayed on the recent tour: "These terms flourish on American soil, till their use is taken for a sign of American nationality, just as the old English game of base-ball met us this summer with a new face as a native Transatlantic institution."[21]

14

Summertime Treat

On September 30, 1843, a brief article in the *Berkshire Chronicle* informed readers that a parish church in the town of Reading had hosted a summer treat for boys and girls attending its summer school. According to the paper, "The children, above 200 in number, assembled in a meadow adjoining the Forbury [a public park], where they amused themselves with cricket, base ball, and other recreations during the afternoon, and were afterwards assembled at the school room in the churchyard and were regaled with buns and tea."[1] The content conveyed by this sweet little notice, in itself, was nothing remarkable. English children playing baseball at school outings in southern England was a common sight in the nineteenth century. Yet prior to the 1840s, newspapers had ignored these gatherings, thus lending special significance to this otherwise innocuous report. It marked a milestone. Never before had a British newspaper described a school event where children played baseball. Many dozens of similar reports would follow.

English newspaper coverage of schoolchildren's recreational activities during the nineteenth century varied widely from paper to paper and region to region. Big city dailies ignored these functions almost entirely. Even if a major paper such as the *Times* of London had deemed school picnics worthy of coverage, which it never would have, it could not possibly have spared a fraction of the space needed to document the activities of thousands of educational institutions in its metropolitan area. Readers of provincial and local newspapers, by comparison, were more apt to expect and receive this sort of reporting. The *Bucks Herald* of Aylesbury in Buckinghamshire was one such publication. It began operation in 1832 under its original, tongue-stretching name of the *Bucks Herald, Farmers' Journal and Advertisers' Chronicle for Bucks, Beds, Herts, Berks, Oxon, and Northamptonshire.* It is still in operation today. The *Herald* was one of the first English papers to offer broad coverage of day-to-day social events within its reporting area, a territory that was initially quite as expansive as its name suggests.

The *Herald* published its first story mentioning English baseball in 1845, and by the end of the century it had covered almost twenty other gatherings where children or adults had played the game, ten of those being school outings. On August 18, 1860, for example, the *Bucks Herald* covered the annual festival of parochial schools in Chesham, Buckinghamshire, noting that "the meadows were well filled with the townspeople and others from the surrounding neighbourhood, and the usual games such as cricket, football, bassball, and bat-trap, were entered into with great zest and continued till the close of day."[2] Only a week later, the paper reported on the "annual feast" of the Church Sunday School of Stoke Mandeville, another town in Bucks. The writer for the *Herald* peppered his article with the kind of neighborly chit-chat that would be valued by his audience: "After partaking of beef and plum pudding, the children adjourned to a meadow kindly lent them by Mr. Gurney, and were soon scattered in every part—some playing cricket, foot-ball, and base-ball; whilst others were racing for handkerchiefs, kindly given by Mrs. Edwards."[3]

Like in Buckinghamshire, English baseball also became a frequent presence at school-related functions in the county of Hampshire, with more than a dozen events garnering newspaper coverage. The *Reading Mercury* reported one such occasion in August 1850, when several hundred schoolchildren gathered in the town of Andover to celebrate the birthday of the local vicar's daughter. According to the paper, "After tea, the boys amused themselves by playing at cricket and other games, and the girls by playing at base ball, &c."[4]

Over the years, newspapers seemed to pay greater attention to particular towns when it came to reporting on school events involving baseball. Perhaps this was due to school authorities in those communities doing a better job of notifying editors of upcoming activities, or perhaps it was just a matter of baseball enjoying greater popularity in those locales. One of these towns was Princes Risborough, a small Bucks community nestled at the foot of the Chiltern Hills. On September 13, 1879, the *Bucks Herald* took note of the annual treat held for ninety students attending the town's British School, reporting that "among the sports were cricket, base ball, races, and scrambles, the latter for a good stock of sweets and biscuits."[5] Ten years later, on August 3, 1889, a *Herald* article described another summertime treat for children in Princes Risborough. This time several schools and churches joined forces to hold a single event for their combined flock. The *Herald*'s report mentioned that "after tea, cricket, base ball, rounders, races, jumping, scrambles, &c., were held, affording considerable amusement, not only to the children but to the large number of neighbouring residents and parents of the scholars who were now present."[6] For this treat, the organizers gave youngsters the option of playing either English baseball or rounders. This choice was not typically offered because of the similarities between the two games. Yet it is situations like these, where newspaper coverage identified English baseball and rounders being played side by side, that bolster my theory that the two were separate and distinct pastimes.

Before the end of the century, the *Herald* would cover two additional school treats in Princes Risborough where English baseball was one of the offered amusements. Clearly, the game had been a popular option for picnic planners in that Bucks community. Still, they had a long way to go to match their counterparts in Framlingham, a market town in Suffolk, where English baseball seems to have been something of an obsession. Framlingham is a small place—only a bit more than three thousand residents today—yet newspaper accounts document at least twenty-two instances during the Victorian years where schoolchildren in the community played baseball at summer gatherings. That number almost certainly represents a tiny fraction of the actual times that Framlingham youngsters played the game, as the great majority of picnics, treats, and other outings held there—or anywhere else—would have passed without any press attention at all. One of the earliest of the Framlingham baseball events reported in print was a combined annual treat held in September 1866 for students of the local Wesleyan Sabbath School and the Band of Hope. The *Framlingham Weekly News* covered the gathering and reported that the children "marched in procession through the principal streets of the town, flags and banners flying, to the Castle yard, where the afternoon was passed in various games such as swinging, cricket, baste-ball, kissing in the ring, racing, jumping &c. At five they were all regaled with buttered rolls, plum cake and tea."[7] Spelling baseball as "baste ball" was not an uncommon practice in England, although it seems to have gained more favor in Framlingham than anywhere else. In fact, newspapers chose to use that spelling in nineteen of the twenty-two articles mentioning English baseball's presence at school events in the town between 1865 and 1902. This oddity cannot be dismissed as the particular whim of an individual writer, editor, or newspaper because several publications did the reporting.

Decade after decade, county after county, local papers in southern England continued to identify baseball among the amusements enjoyed by schoolchildren at summer gatherings. Altogether I've found close to 200 articles documenting this phenomenon between 1843 and 1910. Most of them describe events in counties like Buckinghamshire and Suffolk where the practice of English baseball was commonplace. But I've also identified occasional reports from other locales where the game may not have been as deeply rooted. One of them is an article published in the August 26, 1878, issue of the *Bristol Mercury and Daily Post*. It describes an annual treat for children attending parish schools in the town of Clevedon in Somerset, a location well to the west of "traditional" English baseball territory: "On arriving at the Vicarage several games were indulged in. About 500 sat down to a substantial tea. A large tent was erected for the visitors. The children entered with spirit into the games, consisting of swings, cricket, football, baseball, running, jumping, &c., until evening, when they were marched to the front of the Vicarage-house to receive a bun each from Mrs. Marson."[8] Equally far afield from English baseball's typical turf was an example reported in Hull, a city in southern Yorkshire. A brief article in the *Hull Packet* dated July 7, 1882, describes an anniversary celebration of the Wesleyan Sunday School based in the nearby village of Winteringham in Lincolnshire, and notes that "football, cricket, base-ball, and other sports of various kinds were kept up to a late hour."[9]

As the nineteenth century rolled toward the twentieth, reports of English baseball activity among schoolchildren in far-flung British communities seemed to pop up with ever greater frequency. A second Lincolnshire example surfaced in the *Grantham Journal* issue of July 18, 1891. In its coverage of the annual outdoor "feast" for students attending the National Sunday School in the village of Waltham, Lincolnshire, the newspaper described how following a "well-provided tea . . . groups were formed for various games, and cricket, jumping, base-ball, &c., were freely indulged in."[10] Four years later, the same newspaper reported on an annual treat for students attending the Board School of Cropwell Bishop, a village in neighboring Nottinghamshire. The paper described how the party of students traveled to the grounds of a local stately home that had been lent to them for the occasion, where "the young people quickly commenced their various games of cricket, skipping, base-ball, &c."[11]

Planting its flag even further north, English baseball in 1889 made an appearance at a summer outing in County Durham.[12] The *Northern Echo*, a newspaper based in the large market town of Darlington, reported in its August 30 issue that the Rockhope School, located in the rural village of the same name, had recently held its annual treat: "On Friday," wrote a reporter, "the annual gathering of Vicar, wardens, teachers, scholars, parents, and the young men of the village took place in the Vicarage field, where a substantial tea was enjoyed.

The customary games of cricket, base-ball, wrestling, races of all sorts, long ropes, and the high jump were indulged in."[13]

It may only be coincidental, but earlier that same year, Albert Spalding and his world-touring troupe of professional American baseball players arrived in Great Britain and played a series of exhibition matches, among them ones in the northern English cities of Liverpool and Manchester. A reasonable question arising from this is whether the incidents of schoolchildren playing baseball in neighboring English counties that I've described above were influenced by, if not inspired by, the method of play demonstrated by the touring Americans. That is, were the youngsters playing something more akin to American baseball than the traditional English version? While I cannot dismiss this possibility, I consider it highly remote. There is no conclusive evidence that the display of American baseball in large English cities had any measurable impact on the neighboring citizenry and certainly not the immediate cultural jolt it would have taken to excite children in scattered rural communities to embrace the American game. Besides, in the article about the Rockhope School, the writer named baseball among a list of "customary games" played in the village. No clear-eyed observer of nineteenth-century rural England would ever attach this descriptor to the American version of the pastime.

County Durham may be far to the north in England, but Northumberland is even farther. On March 31, 1894, the *Morpeth Herald* of that county covered the annual outdoor gathering of students and teachers connected to the North Seaton Wesleyan Sunday School, and, yes, baseball was played there. According to the paper, "They met at the school, where the children were presented by their teachers with two oranges each, after which they marched to the above field, where the fun started. The smaller scholars ran races for nuts and sweets, given by their teachers, and the girls contested by skipping for their share. Some amused themselves with the football, and some with the game of baseball, also some with kissing-ring."[14] With that, having now ascended to the northern border of the country, is it reasonable to ask whether we've reached an endpoint? Does Northumberland mark the farthest extent of English baseball? The answers to these questions are ultimately semantical. We must decide whether use of the label "English baseball" is only appropriate for describing the game as played within the borders of England. Since I'm the one who coined the term in the first place, I grant myself the right to make such a determination. But before I do, we must consider the following.

On September 11, 1879, the *Southern Reporter*, a newspaper published in the town of Selkirk in the Borders region of southern Scotland, carried news of a Saturday picnic for students of the Free Church Sunday School in the nearby town of Innerleithen. "The weather being exceptionally fine, there was a large turn-out of children, teachers, and friends. Football, cricket, base ball, races, leaping, swings, skipping, and a number of other games were gone into with great spirit."[15] Eleven years later, the *Aberdeen Weekly Journal* reported on another picnic, this one for youngsters attending the Established Church Sabbath School in the village of Old Deer located some thirty miles to the north of Aberdeen. The article notes that "a very pleasant afternoon was spent in running, jumping, base ball, and other games, for which prizes were liberally given."[16] Finally, on September 25, 1894, the *Inverness Courier* reported that the Free Sabbath Schools of the small Highland village of Rogart, located some fifty miles north of Inverness, treated its students to an end-of-summer outing. According to the paper, "After tea, all set off to the glebe [parish land], where a most pleasant afternoon was spent in skipping, playing base-ball, running exercises, and other games."[17]

So Scottish baseball? Probably not, at least not as a separate game. Barring evidence to the contrary, there's no reason to think a game called baseball that schoolchildren played at picnics in nineteenth-century Scotland was materially different from the identically named pastime that youngsters enjoyed south of the border. That said, there might be a reason to question this assumption in regard to the final Scottish example above, the school treat in Rogart. As mentioned, the Highland village lies approximately fifty miles from Inverness, but only forty miles from the smaller community of Dingwall. It is not widely known that Dingwall was the spot where the first documented game of American-style baseball was played in Great Britain. An American historian, Bruce Allardice, made this discovery in 2013, and a British baseball researcher, Joe Gray, filled in the details. What they found was that in May 1870 a group of men in Dingwall organized a club to play the American game. They were influenced by an Inverness-born man named Andrew K. Brotchie who had emigrated to Massachusetts as a child and then returned to the Highlands as an adult, carrying with him a love of America's National Pastime. On July 9, 1870, the *Inverness Advertiser* reported that two teams made up of Dingwall club members faced each other in a match in which a total of ninety runs were scored.[18]

This discovery set me wondering whether the doings in Dingwall might have impacted how baseball was played in the surrounding neighborhood, including the village of Rogart. After all, the home terrain for the original English game lay six hundred miles to the south. Still, everything else about the Rogart treat and the other two Scottish examples smacks of English baseball. There is no mention in their respective newspaper reports of terms associated with American baseball, such as club, bat, diamond, umpire, nine, etc., nor do they give the game the novelty treatment that would befit a recent import from afar. Instead, they list baseball no differently than any of the other conventional childhood pastimes, such as cricket, jumping, running, and swings. This is precisely how newspapers reported English baseball's presence at dozens of comparable school events throughout England. It is easy to conclude from this that the Rogart game and the other Scottish examples, other than the Dingwall exception, are nothing more dramatic than instances of the original English baseball having drifted far from its roots.

Notwithstanding these occasional reports of children playing English baseball at school picnics in England's northern regions and in Scotland, the great majority of such sightings continued to emanate from the southeast. That's where the game started and where it retained its greatest popularity. However, a factor that might shift this calculus, at least to a small degree, is that in parts of England and Scotland, baseball wasn't always necessarily called baseball. Students of the game's history in North America will recognize this phenomenon, will know that in parts of the young United States early versions of baseball acquired the names "town ball" and "round ball." As we shall see in chapter 17, Britain, too, had its own unique collection of alternate labels.

15

People's Pastime

If I've left you with the impression that English baseball in the second half of the nineteenth century had become the sole property of youngsters indulging themselves at school outings, then I've misled, you badly. Quite the opposite is true. Indeed, it's hard to imagine any activity appealing to a broader demographic spectrum than did English baseball during that era. Evidence shows that it was played, altogether or separately, by men, women, boys, and girls, by the wealthiest of the queen's subjects and by the poorest, by church groups and mutual aid organizations, by choirs and harmonic societies, by temperance groups, fraternal organizations, and political parties, by art, literature, and lecture societies, by industrial workers, sales clerks, fishermen, carpenters, bakers, and brewers, by cycling and athletic clubs, by journalists and police officers, and by members of the military. Yet despite this widespread appeal, or maybe because of it, English baseball was taken for granted. The game was such a familiar sight at summer picnics during the Victorian years that nobody gave it much thought. Perhaps this is why chroniclers of the era ignored it almost completely; it was such an unremarkable and ordinary presence that it never occurred to them to leave behind descriptions of it or commentaries about its place in society.

Even though journalists and historians in the nineteenth century largely disregarded English baseball as a topic worthy of attention, casual references to the pastime pepper the published record. The same sort of community newspaper coverage that revealed the extent of baseball play among children also disclosed the breadth of the game's popularity among adults. I have already described how newspapers documented baseball's presence at the Whitsuntide celebrations in the village of Knowl Hill in the early 1830s, as well as the numerous times that mechanics' institutions incorporated the game into their popular fêtes during the 1850s and 1860s. These were beginning signs of a widespread presence of English baseball in public life. The year 1857 alone offers a variety of examples. On April 18 the *Sussex Agricultural Express* described a gathering of those it called "teetotallers." The event was held near the village of Washington in West Sussex, and "nearly 200 met and enjoyed a dance on the green sward; others amused themselves at cricket and base ball."[1] Three months later, the *Luton Times and Advertiser* in Bedfordshire described an outing sponsored by the local Harmonic Society: "About one hundred of the members and their friends in holiday trim engaged in various *pic-nic* recreations. Quoits and cricket in one part of the field, and base ball, thread-the-needle and the like in another."[2] Then, on August 29, the *Bucks Herald* covered an afternoon outing of more than one hundred citizens and tradesmen from the town of Chesham: "Cricketing commenced at about one o'clock, and from that time to the close of the day continued with little intermission. There were also several games, such as bat-and-trap, and bass ball, which occupied the attention of the majority of the ladies during the afternoon."[3]

On May 4, 1858, the *Kentish Gazette* of Canterbury announced a "grand picnic party" to be held for members of the New Brompton and Gillingham Reading and Lecture Room Society. The article disclosed that the event would unfold on the grounds of an inn in the nearby town of Sittingbourne, adding that "cricket, baste ball, a concert, and dancing on the green, with other sports of a rustic character will form part of the day's amusements."[4] Then, in 1859, a newspaper in the county of Norfolk reported on "one of those friendly and much to be admired re-unions between employer and the employed." The owners of a textile factory in Norwich, "Messr. Clabburn, Sons, and Crisp," staged an "annual treat for those immediately in their employ and their jacquard weavers." The event was held in the small village of Whitlingham, and according to the newspaper, "The sports began in good earnest with rowing and running matches, jumping, quoits, base, trap and ball, and other out-door amusements, which in conjunction with fresh air and the delightful scenery of the neighbourhood, fully prepared them to do ample justice to a most splendid dinner."[5] And yes, I am aware that some of you may protest that the word *base* is not followed by *ball*. I've discovered, however, that English newspaper writers in the second half of the nineteenth century occasionally employed the solitary term *base* as shorthand for the more typical *base-ball*. In earlier centuries, use of the term *base* would be assumed in most instances to be a reference to the venerable tag-like, ball-less game of prisoner's base. But by the Victorian era, the once-popular prisoner's base had fallen out of favor in most parts of Britain.

The temperance movement was a significant social force in nineteenth-century England, but lest anyone think those involved in the cause were killjoys, a study of their outdoor parties would allay the concern. One such gathering was a Whit Monday gala staged in 1862 by a Temperance Society chapter in the Suffolk city of Ipswich. A reporter covering the event for a local newspaper revealed the spectrum of fun and games provided for attendees: "The Rifle Band, under the direction of Mr. Gunning, was in attendance, and to their music not a few 'led the merry dance,' whilst foot-ball, base-ball, cricket, swinging, see-saws, Aunt Sally, and, of course, kissing in the ring—(this being a great occasion for such mutual interchanges)— were going on in different parts."[6] English newspapers from the 1850s to the end of the century documented many more events sponsored by organizations dedicated to combatting the evils of liquor, with more than a dozen identifying baseball among the offered amusements. One gathering in 1885 treated attendees to a robust selection of entertainments. It was labeled a grand "United Temperance Picnic" and was staged in a local regional park by a coalition of temperance and Band of Hope societies in the Aylesbury Vale district of Buckinghamshire. In describing the event, the local paper reported that "after the refreshments, the company dispersed about the Park.

There was no restriction. Some proceeded to the lakes, and with a rod and line baited for fish, others, and these were in several teams, pitched wickets and enjoyed a game at cricket, others played quoits, bass-ball, and other sports, indeed it may be imagined with the large company the amusements were of endless variety."[7]

The operators of English industrial plants in the nineteenth century were known on occasion to organize sizable summer picnics for their employees and their families, similar to what I described with the Norwich textile factory. I don't doubt that some of the production workers would have gladly foregone those outings in exchange for wage increases and better working conditions, but in lieu of such choices they thronged to the picnics to take advantage of rare opportunities to relax in the countryside with their colleagues and families. A significant industrial business that regularly staged events for its workers was the Orwell Works, a manufacturer of agricultural machinery in Suffolk and employer of thousands. The firm's annual fête, or "gipsy party," was a big production, and baseball was often among its attractions. An article in the *Suffolk Chronicle* described the entertainments available at the Orwell gathering in 1862:

> The usual preparation had been made for the amusement of young folks. Round-a-bouts had been improvised out of the works of horse thrashing machines and stout beams; swings were suspended from some of the stoutest trees; and cricket, base-ball and other games were freely indulged in; and that game of games in which both sexes can take part, and which, be it said, seemed to be highly relished—kissing in the ring; whilst for those who felt inclined to "trip the light fantastic toe," ground had been staked off and roped off, so that the merry dance could go on without interruption.[8]

The same newspaper noted that the Orwell Works party in 1864 again included "various games, such as cricket, baste ball, and the much patronised one of kissing in the ring."[9]

Owners of certain English commercial and retail establishments in the nineteenth century also made efforts to build goodwill with their employees by hosting annual outdoor parties. The proprietor of Hannington's Department Store in the seaside resort of Brighton in Sussex was one such enlightened entrepreneur. In 1866 he staged an all-day picnic for his workers in the nearby village of Hurstpierpoint. The *Brighton Gazette* dispatched a reporter to the scene, and here's what he encountered: "Arrived on the ground it was found that a large tent had been erected, casks of beer were visible, as were bottles of ginger beer, by the gross, and various other comestibles, evidently intended for the day's consumption. The 'weed' was freely indulged in, and all parties prepared themselves for the amusements of the day. Some betook themselves to a game at quoits, others to trap and base ball, others fond of 'the gentle art' betook themselves to ponds and lakes in the vicinity and proved themselves apt disciples of Isaak Walton."[10]

Hannington's was a major commercial enterprise with more than two hundred employees, and it was long nicknamed "the Harrod's of Brighton." It closed in 2001 after two hundred years of operation. In the event any of you reading this are admiring the liberal attitude of Hannington's in providing "weed" for the enjoyment of its employees, please note that in those days the term was almost certainly an allusion to cigars or other forms of tobacco.

Other sectors of southern England's working population benefited from organized summer outings as well, with baseball often among the attractions. In 1864 it was some Brighton fishermen and boatmen who ventured off for their annual excursion to the countryside. Joined by family and friends and by fellow seafarers from the nearby town of Worthing, the party proceeded to a park in the Sussex community of East Grinstead. According to an article in the *Brighton Gazette,* "Baseball, cricket, bowls, and a variety of other games were carried on with much vigour, while the elder portion smoked their pipes and were highly amused with the various sports."[11] A year earlier it had been the turn of carpenters working for the South Eastern Railway Company, whose employer treated them to an annual holiday picnic in the Surrey village of Shalford, just south of Guildford. The *West Surrey Times* covered the event and reported that "the party, numbering about ninety, arrived at the railway station at eleven o'clock, and immediately proceeded to the common, where cricket, trapbat, base-ball, quoits, Aunt Sally—the old lady's first appearance at Shalford, need we add she was warmly received—and other games were carried on with immense vivacity, till dinner was announced."[12]

Industrialization transformed British society in the nineteenth century, and the expanding working class formed new types of organizations to meet their needs. Among these were mutual aid groups, also known as friendly societies, which arose to provide working people with what we now call a social safety net, a responsibility that had not yet been assumed by government. These operated by having members who were healthy and holding down jobs make small regular payments to the society, and then when individuals or families suffered injury, illness, or death, they were provided modest financial relief. Many of these groups adopted organizational characteristics similar to fraternal societies and periodically hosted parties and celebrations for their members and their families. Not surprisingly, games of English baseball could be spotted at these gatherings. One particularly colorful example was an anniversary party held in 1866 for families and friends of the Providence Lodge of the Loyal Order of Ancient Shepherds of Soham, a small town in eastern Cambridgeshire. The *Bury Free Press* reported that "the members, accompanied by the Soham band, adjourned to the orchard, and were then joined by their wives, children and friends to the number of about two thousand. Rural sports were commenced in great variety and carried on with much spirit, including pony, mule, and donkey races, jumping in sacks, foot races, hurdle races, aunt sally, &c., concluding with a wheelbarrow race in the river, for all of which good prizes were given. Mr. Wilkerson burnt a variety of coloured fires. Kiss-in-the-ring, bass-ball, and other games were introduced, and the Soham band frequently played some good music."[13]

Other friendly societies and fraternal organizations in the nineteenth century hosted gatherings offering English baseball, among them the Royal Order of Foresters, the Good Templars, and the Odd Fellows. So did some mutual improvement societies, another type of group unique to the times. These differed from the mutual aid and fraternal groups in that their objectives were educational and political rather than humanitarian and philanthropic. They were structured democratically, and their mission was to provide basic schooling for otherwise uneducated workers, often with more highly schooled workers serving as teachers. They also were deeply rooted in the radical labor movements of the times, with the Owenists and Chartists among the political forces backing the societies. But the zeal and seriousness of their undertakings did not preclude them from throwing a good party from time to time, and on these occasions they were apt to incorporate baseball. On August 13, 1870, the *Ipswich Journal* described the annual fête of the Mutual Improvement Society of Framlingham: "From the lawn in front of the house is a beautiful slope, studded with trees, and well adapted for fêtes and pic-nics, and when enlivened with flags, marquees, and nearly a thousand persons engaged in various sports, of croquet, quoits, baseball, cricket, football, and youngsters swinging under the shady branches of the trees, formed a beautiful picture of English enjoyment on a gala day."[14]

But it didn't require fancy fêtes and highly organized summer outings for adults to enjoy English baseball, as the game could appear at almost any type of modest gathering. For example, when members of the Liverpool Association of Science and Art convened for their first meeting of the summer in 1885, they decided that rather than stay indoors, they would avail themselves of the nice weather and adjourn to the countryside. Members residing in Liverpool took a ferry cross the Mersey [really] where they gathered with the rest of the group in Birkenhead, and then the party proceeded by wagonette to the picturesque town of Heswell.[15] A notice in the *Liverpool Mercury* revealed, "After returning from a ramble along the Dee side a very substantial repast was provided. An adjournment to the lawn followed, where several games of old English sport rapidly and cheerily succeeded each other, the ladies proving the victors in the game of baseball."[16] I don't know whether women regularly bested men while playing the pastime in those days, or whether the male members of the Liverpool Association of Science and Art were particularly inept, but this example reveals that at least some females in England still retained the prowess at the game their foremothers had demonstrated in the earlier years of the century. It is also noteworthy that even as far afield as Liverpool and at this relatively late date, baseball was still being recognized as an "old English sport."

In 1888 another mixed party of adults played baseball under unusual circumstances. Members of the Southsea Rowing Club of Portsmouth decided to invite patients from a local asylum to join them for a day's outing to the nearby village of Portchester. Under the headline "A Picnic for Lunatics," the *Hampshire Telegraph and Sussex Chronicle* acknowledged that the gesture, which they praised as a "generous act," was "entirely a new departure from the ordinary run of 'treats.'" The paper described the unfolding events: "Once there, wickets were soon pitched for cricket on the green under the shadow of the ancient Castle, and the contest 'Southsea Rowing Club v. Lunatic Patients' was commenced amid a good deal of interest. The Club representatives, however, had the best of the game," the final score being Club 107, Patients 29. The *Chronicle* reported that the whole party then sat down to a nice tea, followed by speeches from local luminaries. One alderman, Mr. Cudlipp, rose to say that he believed another alderman, Sir W. D. King, "was never more at home than when he was among those who were in the asylum." It's not clear from the context whether he was joking. According to the paper, "The party had then another stroll around the green, and while many of the ladies and gentlemen resumed the game of base-ball, the patients were greatly amused with shying at cocoa nuts."[17]

In 1889 the Spalding tour of professional baseball players from the United States landed in Great Britain and demonstrated the American game in a series of exhibition matches played in a number of cities across the island as well as in Ireland. From that point onward, the complexion of baseball in England became a bit more complex. Schoolchildren and some adults continued to practice the original game of English baseball in rural regions of several southern counties. Concurrently, an effort was under way to implant the American version of the sport, especially in the Midlands. The overlapping of these two forms of the pastime in the 1890s, along with the sudden appearance of yet another variety of baseball, provided a challenge for me in trying to complete my story of the original domestic game. In chapter 21 you'll see how it all unfolded.

16

Rules Don't Apply

Now that I've given you a taste (or, perhaps, engorged you with a seven-course meal) of how English citizens from all walks of life enjoyed playing baseball in the eighteenth and nineteenth centuries, you may be thinking to yourselves: "Fine, but isn't it about time he gave us a description of the game itself?" This is a fair question, and I admit that up until now I've been dodging it. It's not as easy a task as it might seem. You see, for all the hundreds of times that books and newspapers mentioned the game during its 150-plus years of existence, few offer any hint as to how it was played. Without a stockpile of descriptive data to draw upon, I've had to cobble together a picture of the pastime from the limited resources available, a meager trove containing one significant document and a handful of clues extracted from a variety of others.

You may recall that I thought I had this problem solved in 2001. It was my first big discovery, a 1796 book written in German by J. C. F. Gutsmuths that included seven pages of rules for a pastime called *das englische Base-ball*. The author described a bat and ball game that was roughly recognizable as baseball, and I had no reason to doubt the faithfulness of his account. This, indeed, was how English baseball was played, I wrote confidently in my 2005 book, adding that the game's familiar features, as described by Gutsmuths, proved that the hitherto little-known eighteenth-century game was the immediate forerunner of American baseball. But with the passage of time, I reluctantly came to recognize that the specifics of baseball described by Gutsmuths differed in some respects from the impression of English baseball I was forming from other sources. Indeed, the German author's portrayal seemed more akin to what would later be known as rounders.

Still, I find it amazing he was describing something called baseball in the eighteenth century, and his account remains a valuable asset for those studying the game's origins.

Unfortunately, by not fully trusting Gutsmuths's contribution, I'd left myself with only one substantial source. It is an obscure children's book, first published in 1875, that bears the charming but exhausting title *Jolly Games for Happy Homes: To Amuse Our Girls and Our Boys; the Dear Little Babies and Grown-up Ladies.* In my own little lonely world of researching English baseball, this book is a biggie. When writing my first book, I celebrated *Jolly Games* and the significance of its baseball description. In those days, however, I thought that English baseball had gone extinct by the time *Jolly Games* was published, which led me to characterize its baseball content as a "time capsule" of how the English had practiced the pastime in the eighteenth century.[1] Now that I know that English baseball was still very much alive in 1875, I can appreciate that *Jolly Games'* descriptions were intended as an active guide for instructing children in how to play the game and not the vestige of bygone days that I once believed.

The one really odd thing is that *Jolly Games* contains not one description of the game but two. The first appears on page 110 among a group of "Indoor and Outdoor Games for Girls and Boys." Inexplicably, a separate and somewhat different description shows up on page 247 in a section labeled "Forfeit Games, etc." There is no logical explanation for why the author, or the editors, chose to include two distinct sketches of the pastime, and one can only conclude it was the result of careless editing. As you will see, the two appear to be the work of separate authors whose respective approaches to describing baseball vary somewhat in writing style and treatment of detail. Here is the first one:

BASE BALL

This is a healthful exercise and a never-tiring game. Say it is played in a garden or a field. Two leaders are chosen, who stand at a distance apart, and walk towards each other, placing foot against foot as they step, the heel of one foot touching the toe of that before, and perfectly straight. As they thus advance together and space decreases, of course ultimately one is unable to get room to plant her foot. She is consequently out. The party is divided equally between the two leaders.

The one who is "out" throws the ball, which the one who is in receives "in" her hand as if it were a bat, bats it away and starts for the first base, or station. The garden or field has previously been divided into bases or stations, duly marked at convenient distances.

The business of the followers of the leader who is "out" is to act as scouts, to catch up the ball thrown—after which they can all start if they like—and hit the runner with it as she passes from base to base. If she is so hit she is "out," and must remain dormant till there is a change in the ministry of the game. Her business is to make good her passage from base to base without being hit, and for this purpose to keep an eye on the enemy and the flying ball. If she is hit on reaching or whilst stationary at a base, it counts for nothing. Each member of a party runs in turn. When all members of a party are out, the game recommences, passing into the hands of the other party, and so on.[2]

And the second:

BASE-BALL

In the West of England this is a favourite and healthy out-door amusement for girls in a large garden or play-ground, with a soft ball. The bases, or stations, must be arranged according to the locality, and must be fixed, either by a distinct object for a boundary determined on, or by a mark purposely placed.

The subjoined diagram shows the ground which we will suppose to consist of four bases, *a,* the starting-point, *b, c,* and *d.* The

c

d   b

e

a

players are divided into two equal parties, who determine by drawing lots, or any other method chosen, which shall be "in." The bowler and leader of the party "out" stands at *e*, and tosses the ball to the leader of the party "in," who stands at *a*, and who receives the ball on the flat of the palm of her hand, as with a bat. If she misses three times, or if the ball when struck falls behind *a*, or be caught by any of the party who are "out," and who all stand about the field except one, who stands behind *a*, she is out, and another takes her place. If none of these events take place, on striking the ball, she runs toward *b*, or, if she can, to *c*, *d*, or even to *a* again. If, however, the bowler or any of the "out" players who may happen to have the ball, strike her with it in her progress from *a* to *b*, *b* to *c*, *c* to *d*, or *d* to *a*, she is out. Supposing she can only get to *b*, one of her partners receives and strikes at the ball in turn. While the ball is passing from the bowler to *a*, if it be missed, or after it is struck, the first player gets to the next further goal, if possible, without being struck. If she can only get to *c* or *d*, the second runs to *b* only, or to *c*, as the case may be, when a third player begins. As they get home, that is, to *a*, they strike at the ball in rotation, until they all get "out"; then, of course, the "out" players take their places, and go "in."[3]

Other than on minor matters such as how to choose which side is "in," or by the fact that the second description gets a little more specific, the two are in notable agreement. Together they outline an image of English baseball that is consistent with my own impressions of the game formed during the years I've been studying it. They also confirm what many writers from the early 1800s onward had observed about English baseball, that it was an activity well tailored for girls. And, not least, the descriptions offer significant support to the notion that players struck the ball with their bare hands rather than with a bat.

Based upon these *Jolly Games* accounts and other input, here is my best stab at describing the game: English baseball was played with a very soft ball and—in most situations—no bat. Bases were located and placed (with no standard arrangement), and sides were chosen. One side, the "ins," had the opportunity of batting first. The opposing side, the "outs," provided a bowler and positioned the rest of its players around the field. The bowler served the ball to strikers of the "ins" side whose job was to swat it with the palm of the hand and advance safely to one or more bases. The mission of the "outs" was to make the "ins" fail at this by getting them out. (The dual use of the term "out" is a little confusing, but anyone familiar with baseball can discern the difference.) Members of the "outs" could put out a batting opponent by catching a struck ball on the fly or, failing this, by retrieving the ball and successfully catching a runner from the "ins" between bases and then hitting her with the ball. Members of the "ins" would also cause themselves to be out if they missed striking the ball after three attempts, or if their struck ball fell behind them. Batters from the "ins" took turns in succession, attempting to strike the ball and proceed from base to base until all were out. At that point the sides exchanged places and the pattern repeated.

Obviously, this summary omits the game's finer details and neglects to spell out certain critical elements such as how scores were tallied and winners determined. I have long assumed that something like "runs scored" was the likely measure of success in English baseball, but whether a run was counted for each station advanced, as in cricket, or only for reaching the home base, as in American baseball, I've never determined. The *Jolly Games* descriptions overlook these basic points, as do all other references to English baseball I have examined over the years.

Those readers who have studied the early history of games in the baseball family might spot something familiar about the second description in *Jolly Games*. Its format and some of its wording appear to be lifted directly from a description of the game rounders that appeared in an early nineteenth-century children's book, *The Boy's Own Book*, which was published in London in 1828 and was the first work written in the English language to describe any baseball-like activity.[4] Whoever contributed the second description of English baseball in *Jolly Games* cloned text from *The Boy's Own Book* as a starting point and then removed references to the use of a bat and made other minor modifications. But in carrying out this act of repurposing, the perpetrator appears to have been somewhat lackadaisical in her cutting and pasting. She failed to excise the introductory words "in the West of England" from the earlier rounders description. As any well-informed follower of English baseball in 1875 would have known, the pastime's center of popularity was not in the west; indeed, it lay far to the east in the counties surrounding London.

Another unusual note about *Jolly Games* is that, despite its obscurity, its descriptions of baseball came to the attention of a nineteenth-century American professional baseball player, John Montgomery Ward, who cited them in his own 1888 book. Ward was straining to justify his argument that baseball was indigenous to North America. He sought to wave away the inconvenient base-ball references in Lady Hervey's letter of 1748 and Jane Austen's novel *Northanger Abbey* by shamelessly and nonsensically asserting that they couldn't possibly be related to the vigorous American game because they involved the participation of girls. He then tried to explain away the similarities between American baseball and the baseball in *Jolly Games* by claiming the latter was "a modern English conception" of the American game.[5]

The title page of *Jolly Games for Happy Homes* identifies Georgiana C. Clark as its author, although, as the book's two distinct descriptions of baseball imply, she seems to have relied on contributions from other writers. I couldn't find any background data about Ms.

Clark that might provide insight into why she chose to include the otherwise overlooked game of English baseball in her book. *Jolly Games* was not her only published work, as she also produced the memorable classic *Serviettes: Dinner Napkins and How to Fold Them.* She followed this groundbreaking book with other notable titles, among them *Wool and Paper Flowers, and How to Make Them* and, of course, *Gifts, Knick-Knacks, and Pretty Trifles, for Fancy Fairs and Homes of Taste.*

Even with their limitations, the *Jolly Games* descriptions should be recognizable to anyone familiar with rounders or American baseball, especially the earlier forms played prior to the establishment of organized ball clubs in the mid-nineteenth century. One salient feature of English baseball that distinguished it was that it was commonly played without a bat. Years ago, I did not fully appreciate this distinction. I knew that practitioners of English baseball sometimes dispensed with the bat, but I assumed its use was optional. In this I was influenced by the presence of a short, one-handed bat in Gutsmuths's account of *das englische Base-ball*, not recognizing at the time that English baseball and rounders were separate entities and that the German author was describing a game that I have come to believe was more closely related to rounders.

The more I studied English baseball, the more convinced I became that the *Jolly Games* descriptions captured the essence of the game. Still, I knew I wouldn't be satisfied unless I found corroborating evidence. I especially felt a need to locate additional sources confirming my controversial contention that, in most situations, strikers in English baseball swatted the ball with their bare hands rather than a bat. I was motivated, in part, by a fellow researcher of early baseball who doubted my theory and challenged me to prove it. To bolster my case, I examined more than 350 references to English baseball I had come across in the fifteen years I'd been studying it. Most of them revealed nothing either way, with only two offering any suggestion that players might have employed a bat. One was Gutmuths's *englische Base-ball*, a source that I had come to suspect was an outlier. The second was the 1874 letter from *Punch* magazine that spoofed England's reaction to the visiting American ballplayers. Amid the writer's goofy use of exaggerated dialect to explain how baseball was played in Suffolk, he slipped in the observation that when a ball is delivered, a batter's job is to "hit it wi his stick or his hand."[6] By suggesting that using a bat was an optional choice, the letter's author introduced an element that differed from other references in my files, including the *Jolly Games* descriptions. I have been reluctant to trust the *Punch* letter as reliable evidence because of its satirical makeup, yet the author's seeming familiarity with baseball in Suffolk meant that I couldn't ignore it.

On the other side of the equation, my survey of English baseball references turned up two new examples that attested the pastime was played without a bat. One dates from the time of the first tour of American baseball players to Britain in 1874, the same event that triggered the mock letter in *Punch*. Writing in a Yorkshire newspaper, a contributor challenged the notion that the game being showcased by the visitors was a novelty. In making the protest, the writer worked in some valuable details about the original English game:

> Base-ball, which the American's claim to be their national sport, is known to every inhabitant of the North Riding of Yorkshire and to most of the North of England as a game in which both sexes enjoyed on the old holidays—Easter Monday, Shrove Tuesday, and others. Some of the rules are slightly altered, the most important is the striker; the originals strike the ball with the hands, the Americans with a mallet. As regards the Bases which give the American name to the game the Yorkshire people call them the holds, signifying the stop[p]ing places, what the American's call their bowler, was called by us the potcher, who stood nearer to the striker than the American's do, doing the American's wicket keeper part also. The Yorkshire party was

all out with the first person, the American's with the third. All the other rules are the same.[7]

I was baffled and bemused by the columnist's allegation that "every inhabitant" of Yorkshire was familiar with English baseball. My research has uncovered only five scattered references to the game in the entirety of that county, the largest in the UK, which leads me to question the writer's claim of ubiquity. I suspect that in his community the label *baseball* may have been used interchangeably with the more common name *pize-ball*, a sibling game popular in northern England. A tipoff was his comment that in Yorkshire a "party was all out with the first person." This was a characteristic of pize-ball and differed from the method specified in the *Jolly Games* descriptions where a side remained in until all its players had been put out.

Still, for the most part, the Yorkshire correspondent's description of baseball/pize-ball seemed on the mark, including his emphasis that the striker hit the ball by hand. In this he gave welcome backing to my hypothesis and also supported the observation of another English journalist, who was focused on a different sport altogether, tennis. In the midst of recounting tennis's history in an 1883 newspaper column, he stated: "The game is known in France as 'paume' (being formerly played, like base-ball, with the palm of the hand instead of a racquet)."[8] In comparing *paume* to baseball, the writer obviously assumed his audience would know that English baseball was played without a bat or racket.

For years I believed that the visual evidence of English baseball, such as it is, also buttressed my case. But as I was nearing completion of this book, I spotted a small object in one of my images that might possibly be a bat (oh no!). My initial reaction was one of concern: would this discovery undermine my long-held notion that English baseball was usually played without the implement? I soon calmed down and counseled myself that, before leaping to any radical reassessment, I first needed to verify that what I was seeing was really a bat. If it was, I had to consider the implications of its presence within the larger context of everything else I had learned about the game over the previous decade.

This illustration of English baseball was important to my story because, to say the least, I didn't have many of them from which to choose. In all the years I've been researching the pastime, I've found only two images of it. One accompanied the earliest known reference to baseball, John Newbery's *A Little Pretty Pocket-book* from 1744. That engraving shows three boys playing the game, one of them holding a ball. No bat is evident. More than a century would pass before the second illustration appeared. This one flowed from the brush of William Henry Knight, a well-known artist from the town of Newbury in Berkshire who specialized in painting scenes of children at play. In June 1854 the *Art-Journal,* a London magazine, published brief reviews of works on display at the 86th Exhibition of the Royal Academy, one being: "No. 265. 'A Game at Baste Ball,' W. H. Knight." The reviewer stated, "As this seems to be a game of activity as well as address, the point of the picture is action. In execution it is worked up to an enamel surface, and it is rich in colour."[9] The artist's local newspaper, the *Reading Mercury,* praised the painting the following year, hailing it as "first rate evidence" of Mr. Knight's "genius and rapidly rising talent."[10] Perhaps the most vivid commentary on *A Game at Baste Ball* comes from a piece about the artist from an 1863 issue of the *Art-Journal.* Describing the painting as "a small picture with figures full of action," the author then added: "The excitement of the contest is capitally sustained by the combatants, who are drawn with vigour and truth of action not to be surpassed."[11] Unfortunately, while dishing out their compliments, none of these reviewers provided any details about what the subjects in the painting were actually doing.

Auction records show that the picture, variously called *Boys at Bass Ball* and *A Game of Base-ball,* exchanged owners several times in the ensuing years, most recently at a Sotheby's auction in 1981 where it sold for £4,500.[12] I tried and failed to track down the work's pres-

Fig. 8. *A Game at Baste Ball*, an 1854 painting by W. H. Knight (shown in color on cover). Is the girl with the baby also holding a bat?

ent whereabouts, even after gaining the help of experts at the British Library's art department and the Victoria and Albert Museum. I assume it sits in someone's private collection. For years, the only glimpse I had of the painting was a poor quality copy downloaded from the Internet. It pictures several boys playing a game in a country lane, but many of its details were hard to make out.

Then, in early 2018, I located a commercial art library in the UK that was offering a high-resolution digital photo of the painting.[13] I leaped to purchase it, and when it arrived I immediately opened the file. It was dazzling, with bright colors and sharp detail. But as my eyes scanned the image, I gulped, because that's when I noticed that one of the children in the scene held something in her hand that might be a bat. The painting depicts what is, presumably, a game of English baseball, but the pictured action does not readily make clear how the roles of the individual players mesh with each other. The child holding the bat-like object is a girl. Since she is also clutching a small baby in one of her arms it is unlikely she was participating in the game herself. Yet she appears ready to hand over what looks like a rolling pin, minus one of its handles, to a boy standing next to her who is rolling up his sleeves as if preparing to enter the game. Before viewing the high-resolution version, I thought the object in her hand was a toy for the baby. But if it actually is a bat, as I now suspect, it is a very small, stubby one, perhaps the smallest that I've ever seen in any ball game this side of ping-pong.

The painting shows six boys playing in an unpaved lane bordered by two thatched-roof cottages. Several other children stand watching off to the side including the girl with the bat. Three of the boys are in the background: one falling on the ground while reaching for a ball, one standing behind him and apparently preparing to pounce on the ball if the first one missed it, and the third running away from the other two in the direction of three other boys in the foreground. Of these latter three, one is kneeling on the ground near what might be a base, a second is standing next to him and rolling up his sleeves as if getting ready for some action, and the third is running toward them and the base on the same course as the running boy in the background, who is well behind him. The layout of the bases and the extent of the playing field are not readily apparent.

In addition to this painting and Newbery's engraving, there is one other piece of visual evidence that provides an impression of how the game might have appeared to an onlooker. The reason I don't deem it a "baseball image" is because, technically, it isn't. It is an illustration labeled *La Balle empoisonnée*, or poisoned ball, that is taken from a French book of games published around 1815.[14] Compared with the Newbery engraving and the Knight painting, it offers, in my view, a much clearer sense of how English baseball was played. It pictures a group of boys arranged on a playing field, with three bases designated by piles of clothing and hats. A striker is shown standing in the foreground at a fourth base, and with upraised palm awaits the

Fig. 9. *La Balle empoisonnée* (poisoned ball), as pictured in the French children's book *Les Jeux des jeunes garçon*, ca. 1815. This game closely resembled English baseball.

arrival of a ball that has just left the throwing hand of another boy positioned a short distance away. Two more boys stand between bases in the field, seemingly ready to respond if the ball comes their way. A French text describing *La Balle empoisonnée* accompanies the image. I included a translation of this description in *Baseball before We Knew It*, and even a cursory reading shows it to be similar to the accounts of English baseball from *Jolly Games*. It is obvious that the two were kindred pastimes.

Over the years I had become deeply attached to my conclusion that English baseball was a game played principally without a bat. But when that high-resolution copy of *A Game at Baste Ball* hit my inbox and revealed what appears to be a bat, my confidence wavered. True, the painting was only one piece of evidence, yet it is one I had relied upon to support my theory and now it seemed to do just the opposite. After allowing myself a brief moment of self-pity, I cleared my head and set about trying to understand the implications of this discovery while weighing it in the context of other things I knew about the game. One of those was that I always assumed English baseball, like any folk game lacking standardized rules and practiced in dozens of far-flung towns and villages, might well acquire local idiosyncrasies. Quite possibly, the act of introducing a bat into the game in some communities was one such variation, one that Knight captured in his painting. Still, while acknowledging that the bat shown by Knight— along with the supporting evidence of Gutsmuths's *englische Baseball* and the *Punch* letter—tends to undercut my notion that English baseball was played almost exclusively without a bat, I am not quite ready to abandon my hypothesis altogether. The weight of evidence I've collected still persuades me that in most situations the ball was struck by hand. I concede, however (and it's never easy to accept even the tiniest diminution of one's pet theory), that use of a bat may not have been the very rare phenomenon I once thought it to be.

While we can assume that the precise method of playing varied from community to community, at least to a small degree, the lack of detailed evidence about English baseball makes these differences difficult to track. One exception to this comes unexpectedly from a region of Great Britain where the pastime was hardly played at all, the western counties of England and the country of Wales. According to suggestions found in several newspaper reports, the game's few practitioners in that geographic area appear to have played it against a wall. One clue comes from an 1882 Somerset newspaper article otherwise devoted to eulogizing a recently deceased vicar from the Dorset town of Gillingham. The article praised the vicar for putting an end to desecrations of the Sabbath permitted by his predecessor, adding: "Frequently, old people tell us on Sunday afternoons men would come down from other places and play baseball with men of this parish against the church tower. Happily, such scenes as that have passed away."[15] Three years later, the *South Wales Daily News* of Cardiff reported on a field excursion by members of the Cambrian

Archaeological Association to a site in Monmouth in Wales. According to the article, upon visiting St. Thomas Church, the vicar pointed out a hagioscope at the side of the chancel arch "and mentioned that some years since the street front of the building, now showing a beautifully restored late Norman doorway, consisted of a blank wall, which served as the goal for players of base ball."[16] In 1886, a newspaper from the city of Exeter in Devon provided one final confirmation of this feature. The paper was in the midst of reprinting a glossary of the local dialect in serialized form under the title "Provincial Words and Expressions Current in Devonshire." The definition given for the word *base-ball* was "A game at ball, usually played against the wall of a building."[17] Other than agreeing with each other about the wall, none of these three references offer any clue as to how this English (or Welsh) "wall baseball" might have been played (although, undoubtedly, some of you Americans reading these words may have practiced equivalents of it in your childhoods, as did I). The fact that these references all originated in western locales may just be a coincidence, yet they represent the majority of the very limited number of English baseball sightings from that corner of the island. None of the hundreds of other references to the game from other parts of Great Britain mention a wall being involved in its play.

The simplicity of English baseball meant that, in most cases, it could be played with just a ball, unlike cricket with its minimum need for bats and wickets. This may account, in part, for why baseball was a popular choice for spontaneous play in many situations. The ball itself had to have been fairly soft so that players being hit by it wouldn't be bruised, and thus much softer than the "softball" used in the modern sport of that name. I always assumed the balls would have been strictly of the homemade variety, constructed from a soft cover of cloth or leather and stuffed with rags. I was quite surprised, therefore, when I came across an advertisement in an 1866 issue of a newspaper from the town of Luton in Bedfordshire. The ad was for a tradesman by the name of John Spratley who was the manufacturer and purveyor of wooden implements for various purposes, including bats, wickets, and mallets for cricket, croquet, and trap-ball. At the bottom of his display advertisement, after listing his prices, the seller added: "All Kinds of Cricket Balls supplied. Also Trap, Tennis, Base and Foot Balls."[18]

My immediate thought upon seeing this was that these baseballs must be for the American version of the game. Yet this seemed improbable given there's not a speck of evidence that residents of Britain played American-style baseball anywhere in the country prior to 1870. The only other explanation was that English baseball must have attained sufficient popularity by the mid-1860s to persuade at least one entrepreneur that producing balls for its play was a good commercial investment. It's unknown how Mr. Spratley fared from selling baseballs, although we can probably take a clue from the fact that no other manufacturers immediately jumped to follow his example. Over time, however, I discovered that other English outfitters had begun selling American baseball equipment in the mid-1870s, and this prompted me to reconsider that earlier 1866 advertisement. Ultimately, it led me down a new path of inquiry that caused me to rethink another one of my basic assumptions about the history of baseball in England.

17

The Old Ba' Game

Ever hear of Beezie? How about Pie-ball or Soulum? These are not the names of the guys down at the pool hall. Nor are they the horses who ran out of the money in the ninth race at Pimlico. Give up? As it happens, each of them is the name of a British game played with a ball. And if some rambler in the nineteenth century happened to come across a group of youngsters playing any one of them, he might think he had stumbled upon something that looked like baseball.

Before it rose to the stature of America's National Pastime, early baseball in North America was a patchwork of locally based proto-games. These differed in makeup from community to community and region to region, united only by the shared characteristics of pitching, batting, fielding, and baserunning. The names of these pastimes varied as well, with some towns choosing *town ball* or *round ball*, while others settled on the more familiar *baseball*. In Britain, a similar assortment of labels was affixed to regional versions of the original game of baseball, albeit ones that were far more plentiful and colorful than those in the former colonies.

We have already seen how the spellings and formulations of *baseball* itself were constantly in flux. *Baseball* as a single word dates at least as far back as 1768 in England, when it appeared in *A General Dictionary of the English Language*. The hyphenated *base-ball* goes back to *A Little Pretty Pocket-book* in 1744. *Bass-ball* made its first appearance in the 1749 newspaper report of the Prince of Wales playing the game with Lord Middlesex. We can cut the *bass-ball* spellers some slack given that the homonyms *base* and *bass* continue to vex young orthographers today. *Baste-ball* also dates to the eighteenth century, first showing up in a 1788 essay adulating the characters in Homer's *Odyssey*. All of these arrangements and spellings were evident throughout the game's early history in North America as well, although in the case of American writers, their preference until the end of the nineteenth century was to represent it as two words, *base ball*.

Readers of *Baseball before We Knew It* may remember that I paid special attention to an obscure pastime called tut-ball. I cited evidence of that game's antiquity and illustrated its apparent similarities to English baseball, speculating that it might be the missing link in baseball's evolutionary lineage. Now, even after spending another fifteen years studying this topic, I still have tut-ball at the top of my list of baseball's possible progenitors. But while tut-ball may have given rise to baseball, I've concluded that by the nineteenth century, whatever differences that might once have distinguished the two no longer existed. Moreover, I now recognize that a statement I made about tut-ball in my earlier book was incorrect. The game did not go extinct by the late nineteenth century. Just as I misjudged the longevity of English baseball, so too my allegation of tut-ball's death was greatly exaggerated.

When authors of dictionaries and glossaries produced thumbnail definitions of tut-ball, they rarely got it straight. Some claimed it was similar to stool-ball and some to other ancient games, but most compared it to rounders. (They often defined tut as a small chunk of brick or sod used as a base.) Fortunately, a small number of publications during the nineteenth and early twentieth centuries produced more detailed descriptions of tut-ball, and these make clear that it was not the same game as rounders. They document that tut-ball was played without a bat, as was common with English baseball. One such account appeared in an 1874 issue of the *Manchester Guardian* in a piece timed to coincide with the arrival of touring American ballplayers. After comparing the American game to rounders, the author cited a local game played in the West Riding of Yorkshire that he believed related to rounders but with notable differences. He referred to it as "touch ball," a common alternate spelling for tut-ball. "It is called in the West Riding 'touch-ball.' The children in those districts play it without a bat or club; they strike the ball with the open hand, and have posts or stones at the corner of the playground, which correspond to the 'bases' of the American game. If the ball was caught before it reached the ground, or the fielders could hit the striker with it before he reached the touch, he was out."[1]

Local newspapers and dialect societies in the English Midlands continued to offer up various takes on tut-ball. In one 1924 example, a writer for a Staffordshire paper referred to the game in the past tense, but made a point of distinguishing it from rounders:

"Tutball" was a similar game in which the bat was dispensed with, and the open hand used to smite the ball—once highly popular with the poorer children of the Black Country whose means precluded the possibility of providing other apparatus than a penny ball. The sport was played as follows: A number of players having been selected in much the same fashion as has already been described [in rounders], stones or bricks were placed at intervals in a ring, which in most places were called tuts, from which the game was called "Tutball." Here, however, the players instead of throwing the ball into the air with the left hand and striking it with the bat as it descended, placed one of their number in front of the striker to bowl the ball for striking, and when the ball was struck the striker ran round to the various tuts or stations as in the game of rounders.[2]

This and other tut-ball descriptions closely resemble the ones of English baseball that appeared in *Jolly Games for Happy Homes*. And, in most ways, tut-ball lived an existence parallel to that of English baseball, with two dozen newspaper references spanning nearly a century attesting to its play at school treats, factory picnics, and other like gatherings. The game also appears in fictional works, including a 1902 novel by Arnold Bennett, *Anna of the Five Towns*, which is set in the Staffordshire pottery district. Bennett observed that tut-ball was "a quaint game which owes its surprising longevity to the fact that it is equally proper for both sexes."[3]

Tut-ball was a localized game with virtually every reference to it deriving from the central English counties of Staffordshire, Derbyshire, and Yorkshire. The city of Sheffield in Yorkshire appears to have been the pastime's epicenter. Curiously, only a short distance away in the same county, youngsters were playing a game with a different name that in other respects seemed remarkably similar.

One phrase kept popping up in the course of my tut-ball research, that the game "was called pize-ball in the neighbourhood of Leeds."[4] The word *pize-ball* was not unfamiliar to me, having crossed my radar often over the years. I chose to omit mention of it in my first book because, lacking evidence of its existence prior to the nineteenth century, I couldn't put it forward as one of baseball's predecessors. Now with a different objective in front of me, I have approached pize-ball with renewed interest. A broad examination of nineteenth- and early twentieth-century newspapers and other sources reveals that pize-ball was every bit as popular as tut-ball. My findings confirmed that the comparisons between the two I encountered in my tut-ball research were right on the mark: by all appearances, the games were identical.

Multiple descriptions of pize-ball published in the nineteenth century bear this out. One representative example appeared in an 1888 work, *A Glossary of Words Used in the Neighbourhood of Sheffield*, by Sidney Oldall Addy:

> Pize-ball: a game at ball. Sides are picked, as for example, six on one side and six on the other, and three or four marks or "tuts" are fixed in a field. Six go out to field, as in cricket, and one of these throws the ball to one of those who remain "at home," and the one "at home" strikes or pizes it with his hand. After pizing it he runs to one of the "tuts," but if before he can get to the "tut" he is struck with the ball by one of those in the field, he is said to be burnt, or out. In that case the other side go out to field.[5]

Curiously, it seems that pize-ball achieved its greatest popularity in the Yorkshire city of Leeds, located barely thirty miles north of tut-ball's principal stronghold, the city of Sheffield. The large town of Barnsley, situated between the two cities, appears to have been the demarcation line, with newspaper reports showing residents of that community using the names interchangeably. From Barnsley, pize-ball's domain stretched northward to Northumberland. And just as tut-ball had its "touch-ball" and English baseball had its "baste-ball," so did pize-ball have its variants. In fact, the formal name *pize-ball*, as it was spelled in regional glossaries, was largely ignored by newspaper writers. In Leeds, the spellings of choice were *pise-ball* and *pies-ball*.[6] Further north, especially in and around the city of Newcastle-on-Tyne, the *s* was dropped and writers referred to the game simply as "pie-ball."[7] There is little doubt from their contexts that all of these variations applied to the same game.

The people of Leeds seem to have harbored fond feelings for their regional pastime. Signs of it still being played lingered into the mid-twentieth century, and local columnists mentioned it with nostalgic longing. Alan S. C. Ross, a Leeds-based linguistics scholar, became so enamored of pize-ball that he made it the focus of an academic paper published in the *Proceedings of the Leeds Philosophical and Literary Society*. Entitled simply "Pize-Ball," his 1968 paper detailed historical references to the game paired with elaborate descriptions of ways in which it was played. These were based in large part on responses he received from advertisements he ran in Yorkshire newspapers soliciting information about the pastime. Not surprisingly, given his linguistics background, he also delved into the etymology of the word *pize*. While first stating that "*pize* is a word entirely without etymology," by which he presumably meant within the English language, he then devoted several pages to discussing its possible derivation from an obsolete Dutch word, *pisen*, which he maintained was a game of some type. In the end he came to a remarkable conclusion: "The thesis of the present article is that the Yorkshire word *pize* and the game of Pize-ball is a borrowing of MDutch [middle Dutch] *pisen*, a ball game about which we know nothing but about whose central nature we may assume to have been somewhat the same as that of Pize-ball. I think that this thesis may now be considered established."[8] Hmm. Not so fast, buster. His claim that pisen was a ballgame was a total leap based on nothing other than it was something Dutch people in the fifteenth century placed bets on. For all we know it could have been a card game. His fixation on pize-ball in Leeds, and his multi-page diversion into the catacombs of medieval Dutch, consumed so much of his article that he barely gave any thought to exploring the virtually identical pastime of tut-ball in neighboring Sheffield, nor even hint at both games' similarities to English baseball. Then again, perhaps I'm being too hard on Mr. Ross. Editors of the current version of the *Oxford English Dictionary* seem to hold a better opinion of him, as he was the only source cited for their own hesitant etymology of *pize-ball*: "Origin uncertain," they wrote; "perhaps cognate with or borrowed from Middle Dutch *pisen* to play the game of 'pisen,' of unknown origin." OED or not, I'm still not persuaded. In the Yorkshire dialect, the word *pize* had other uses as well, such as in mild oaths like "a pize on you!" or "what the pize!" I suspect its true origins lie somewhere in the cultural history of that county rather than as a Dutch stowaway from across the North Sea.

Neither Hadrian's Wall nor the Scottish border hampered the northward propagation of games resembling tut-ball and pize-ball. As we have seen, schoolchildren in Scotland from the Borders area up to the Highlands occasionally played the original English baseball. However, in certain regions a mishmash of homegrown variations were more the norm. The historical record of these pastimes is often confused, with sources contradicting each other in describing them, making the task of detecting their precise nature a bit of a challenge. Many of their names are derivatives of the term *bases*. For example, the 1818 *Dictionary of the Scottish Language* defined the word *ba'-baises* as "the name of a particular game at ball." Not a particularly helpful description, needless to say, but revealing in that the word *ba'* (or *baw*) in Scottish English equates to "ball." That transforms "ba'-baises" into "ball-bases," which is essentially baseball backward.

A serialized short story for young readers published in 1878 by an Aberdeen newspaper teased us about this pastime. In this instance, the game's spelling was *bazies*:

> On the present occasion a band of boys happened to be play-ing at the "Bazies" (Bases), a game of ball, which to most of our readers we need not describe. William contemplated this active and exciting game with speechless delight, and besought Miss Robinson to allow him to ask permission to join it. Miss Robinson with some reluctance consented. Most willingly and respectfully the young "Lord Bredoyne" was admitted to the play, and a "man" to match him introduced into the opposite side. As William was ignorant of the game, every boy eagerly instructed him in the details, and he picked up his lessons with an intuitive rapidity. As the play proceeded, his interest in it increased, and he ran, struck the ball, caught it, aimed it at an opponent, and went through all the parts of the game with such an ardour of soul, that he felt himself borne along on wings in a transport of wild delight. William had never before felt the springs of his nature let loose in such streams of rapture.[9]

Frankly, I've never before felt the springs of my nature let loose in such streams of annoyance. What about us, Mr. Author? What about those of your readers for whom you *do* need to describe the game? Well, at least he gave us clues to some of its characteristics—running, striking, catching, etc.—and from these we can infer that bazies may well be similar to the other pastimes in the English baseball family. The author's phrase "struck the ball" is just vague enough to leave us guessing whether it was struck by bat or by hand. There's no ambi-guity in his portrait of the boy, William, however, as we learn that it only takes one good ball game to propel him into an ecstatic state.

Nearly seven decades later, in 1946, a writer for the same Aberdeen newspaper mentioned the game in a column evoking memories of nineteenth-century country life, this time referring to it as "ball and baisies."[10] And as recently as 1967, a newspaper in the northern town of Buckie revealed yet another formulation for what was likely the same pastime. In an interview with a local old-timer about his childhood, the paper quoted him recalling: "We played fitba, an' tackie, an' the quines [girls] an' wifies played bessie ba'."[11] Nothing else is known of bessie ba', but by my reckoning its name equates to "bases ball."

The city of Perth in central Scotland had its own variation called "ball paces" as described in an 1836 cultural study, *Traditions of Perth*. The work's author wrote that "ball-paces was formerly much played; but is now almost extinct." He depicted the game as a hybrid of baseball and the old British pastime of trap-ball. Runners were positioned at three bases, and a batter standing by a fourth used a simple lever on the ground to elevate a ball into the air and strike it. Opposing team members would then try to catch it or chase it down, while players on the base paths sought to advance as far as possible before the ball could be returned to the home base.[12] Unlike the other games mentioned above, this one used a bat. A 1901 work on games and amusements in the western Scottish region of Argyleshire described a somewhat similar pastime. It, too, used a bat and was more like rounders than the previous example in that a bowler served the ball to the batter. The author wrote that the game was known in Gaelic as *Iomairt air 'an Stainchair* and was identical to the pastime known as "bases" in Aberdeen. He also declared it "the game from which has developed the national American game of Base-ball."[13] He would not be the first or the last to raise such a claim.

Another localized Scottish ball game was dubbed with the unfortunate name "dully," according to the author of an 1881 English book on games and sports. He compared dully to both rounders and baseball and claimed the name was coined by "Edinburgh street boys."[14] A second reference to the game appeared in an 1886 Glasgow newspaper story describing a summer sojourn to Loch Lomond by members of a large Bible class, where "the old regretful, oblivious games of 'dully' and 'rounders' were revived by both sexes."[15] The writer, in this instance, obviously regarded the two games as separate. Then, in 1891, a whimsical article with the not-to-be-taken-seriously headline "Pastimes for Elderly Ladies" appeared in several newspapers. Its author—in an attempt at humor that would not stand the test of time—breezed through a long list of games and sports accompanied by droll commentary regarding each one's suitability for older women. He then dropped the following tidbit: "There used to be a capital game in old Edinburgh known as Dully, which in minor respects resembled Rounders, but was a far superior pastime. One of its special charms was chipping another player while he was yet on the skip. If you were playing with a new 'twopenny dumps' and succeeded in nailing your friend, or rather your companion, at the foot of his spine, or what is recognized by schoolboys as such, your feeling of mirth was perfectly unalloyed."[16]

I've struggled to decipher this passage, and your own interpretation is likely as good or better than mine. Ordinarily I would assume that the phrase "on the skip" referred to a dumpster, but that doesn't make sense in this context. If pressed, I would hazard that "chipping another player while he was yet on the skip" equates to striking an opponent with a ball or other object while he was between bases. A "new twopenny dumps" may refer to a blank metal coin the size of a tuppence that boys of the era used in various games. It certainly would sting if one struck you in the backside, and I suspect that the writer's choice of the term *unalloyed* was an intentional pun. Dully, it would seem from these references, was something other than rounders, but hardly dull.

And then there is "beezie," a true enigma. It is mentioned in books and newspapers with greater frequency than all of the other Scottish games combined, and yet none of the sources describe how it was played. It is absent from all of the dictionaries, glossaries, and guides to traditional Scottish folklore that served as sources for other games. I'm quite certain that *beezie* derived from *bases* as did *bazies* and the others, but what little else I know about it comes from bits and pieces of information I've scavenged from various written works that mention it. Because virtually all of these references emanate from the city of Dundee and its surroundings in eastern Scotland, it is reasonable to conclude that beezie was particular to that region. My earliest findings of it date from the late nineteenth century, with some sources indicating that Dundonians were still playing beezie in the mid-twentieth century, a later time frame than most of its fellows.

So how was it played? There seems to be no consensus. Several sources equated it with rounders, while at least one indicated that it was separate and distinct from rounders.[17] An April 29, 1939, article in the *Dundee Evening Telegraph* quoted a local prosecutor as saying that "the game of 'kick ball' as far as he could see was merely the old game of 'beezie.'"[18] Yet that same paper six weeks later, in its June 9 issue, referred to "the old hand-ball game known in this quarter as 'beezie.'" None of the nearly twenty references to the game I've located indicate the presence of a bat. We do know that all segments of the population played it. The *Dundee Courier* reported that on Easter Sunday in 1939, "old and young flung themselves with amazing abandon into the time-honoured game of 'beezie.'"[19] One character in a novel published in 1921 with the title *Carroty Broon* observed, "At times boys and girls played together. Beezie was a popular mixed game."[20] And in 1908, a writer for a paper in Arbroath, about thirty miles up the coast from Dundee, reported on what he called an "old folks outing." He wrote that "games that did not make too great a demand on their energy—such as 'beezie' and 'jolly miller'–were set in operation and engaged in by such of the company as were so disposed."[21] Elsewhere one source called it a "violent exercise," another described its players as "ladies," and still another tabbed it "a manly sport."[22] Everybody in the area loved it, or so implied a writer for the *Dundee Evening Telegraph* in his coverage of weekend festivities at the seaside town of Monifieth in July 1930, where he reported that "football, cricket, and the more popular 'beezie' form part of the day's enjoyment."[23] It is frustrating to me that we don't have enough detail about beezie to know whether it falls in the tut-ball/pize-ball category or the rounders family. My instincts lead me to suspect the former, but unless some previously unknown description of the game comes to light, we may never know for sure.

As we bid Scotland a fond farewell, we'll pause again briefly in the far north of England to consider a mysterious game called soulum. I spotted it within the writings of an English antiquarian named George Tate who described some boys playing it in his 1866 multi-volume history of the Northumberland town of Alnwick:

> Soulum, a peculiar game, played [in the public marketplace of Alnwick] by boys or lads, not by girls. . . . [It] was played by two parties one out and the other in, and with bat and ball as in cricket; but there were no wickets, and only three bays. The object of the party in was to run as often as possible to the three bays, after the ball had been successfully struck, and of the party out to hit the runner with the ball, or to throw it to the first bay before the runner reached it. I have not learnt that the name Soulum is in use in any other part of the kingdom; nor can I say whence it has been derived.[24]

Nor have I found any other reference to it, but I suspect its name derives from the old Norman game of la soule.[25] In any case, from Tate's description and by its use of a bat we can place soulum squarely in the rounders family. In my first book I described two other obscure English games—feeder and squares—that, like soulum, appeared to be related to rounders. I also took note of a couple of French games in this category, but rather than repeating them here, I would rather take us in a different international direction—across the Irish Sea.

On March 25, 1889, the visiting American baseball players staged the penultimate exhibition game of the Spalding world tour in the city of Belfast. The match received extensive coverage the next day in Irish newspapers, including a long report in the Dublin-based *Freeman's Journal and Daily Commercial Advertiser*. Near the bottom of a gloriously overwritten article, in which the author equated Spalding's conquest of the world to that of Alexander the Great, he got around to describing how the American pastime was played: "Of the game itself it is only necessary to say for the benefit of the uninitiated that it much resembles our old Irish game of rounders or towns, the towns being represented by what are called bases, four in number, at corners of a diamond, and represented by small, square, semi-stuffed sacks."[26] While reading this, I was reminded that present-day devotees of Ireland's sporting history celebrate their domestic version of rounders as a hallmark of their national culture. When the Gaelic Athletic Association came into being in 1884, it named Irish rounders as one of its foundational sports, along with Gaelic football, hurling, and Gaelic handball. But the name *towns* was new to me, and seeing it equated to rounders prodded me to do some digging. Frankly, I didn't find much. Nor could I uncover any record of Irish rounders itself prior to 1884. A fellow baseball historian, Howard Burman, also set out to investigate Irish rounders and met with the same disappointing outcome. The reason, he mused in an article posted to the Protoball.org website, may have been because Irish newspapers in the nineteenth century were controlled by the English, "who were wont not to comment on things Irish."[27]

Irish rounders is still played today and more closely resembles American baseball than does the present game of English rounders. Burman consulted with officials of the Gaelic Athletic Association who insisted that not only have the Irish played rounders for hundreds of years, but that it was the ancestor of American baseball. Really? My wife and I visited Ireland for three weeks in 2017 and were charmed by its natural beauty, its people, and its music. We also learned that the Irish culture is replete with many colorful legends. It may be that the ancient pedigree of Irish rounders is one of these, as it is not borne out by any evidence known to me. It is far more plausible that the game sprung from the migration of baseball or rounders across the Irish Sea from Britain sometime in the eighteenth or nineteenth centuries. I should speedily add, however, that my supposition too is devoid of supporting evidence. As for the game of towns, the only thing I could dig up that possibly sheds any light on its backstory is a brief entry in an 1880 glossary of dialect words from the counties of Antrim and Down in the north of Ireland. It describes a game called town-stinker: "Played with a ball. The 'town' is marked by a circle on the ground and two parties of boys take possession of it alternately, according to their success in striking the ball in certain directions."[28] This isn't much, and the only reason we might consider this stinker game to be part of the baseball-rounders family is because of the ensuing reference to towns that appeared in the aforementioned *Freeman's Journal* article eight years later.

Overall, the historical record of games in the baseball family in Ireland is far skimpier than in either England or Scotland. Even so, among the few existing references are several oddities. An 1863 article in the *Cork Examiner* describing conditions for boys in a local reformatory noted, "At play-hour they were pretty much the same as other boys; engaged in the mysteries of long-ball, foot-ball, and the other games in which youngsters delight."[29] Long-ball is a bat and ball game related to baseball's origins. Varieties of it circulated around northern Europe for centuries, including in Norway and Denmark, but there is no previous evidence of the Irish playing it. Why it popped up in this one Cork example is anyone's guess, although we can look to ancient history for one speculative explanation. In the tenth century, a party of seagoing Vikings departed their homeland in what is now Denmark and Norway to settle the area around Cork, and it is just possible that the 1863 sighting of long-ball might be a vestige of that visit.

Another unexpected Irish find was the one-word headline "Baseball" that showed up on the pages of the *Freeman's Journal* one day in

September 1881. It announced the formation of the Leinster Baseball and Hurley Club.[30] Little information was provided, but articles over the next several months in the *Dublin Daily Express* informed readers that the group was active and playing regular interclub matches.[31] The reports neglected to specify what type of baseball the Leinster club members were practicing, although I strongly suspect it was the American version based on the fact that these were adults and that there is no record in Ireland of homegrown games akin to English baseball. Newspaper coverage of the club ended in December 1881 with no indication of whether it formally disbanded or just dissipated. Still, that it existed at all was startling. Unbeknownst to them, these Leinster baseball and hurley guys joined the rarest of fraternities, one that included an isolated club founded in the Scottish Highlands in 1870 and two others formed in the English city of Leicester later that decade. They are the only known groupings of local players mustering themselves into formal clubs to practice American-style baseball anywhere in Britain or Ireland prior to 1889. Moreover, they set a benchmark for the earliest documented baseball activity of any kind in Ireland.

Unless, that is, we trust the words of a YMCA official from the Irish city of Waterford. In March 1888, a year prior to the Spalding tour's arrival in the country, the chairman of the local Y addressed an annual reunion of organization members. As reported in the *Waterford Standard*, the speaker, Reverend R. H. Christie, emphasized the importance of providing opportunities for athletic sports to deter youths from "being allured into places where no Christian young man ought to be seen."[32] He added, "We must remember that we are a *Young Men's* Association, and while our forefathers were satisfied with a game of bass-ball, we must suit ourselves to the times by establishing those innocent amusements and keeping them in our own hands which are in many of our homes, such as tennis-court, gymnasium, etc."[33]

This is a head scratcher. Disregarding the confusing latter part of that sentence, I have no idea what he meant by their forefathers' connection to baseball. He seems to be implying that by 1888 Irish people had been practicing baseball for generations. Of course, Irish immigrants were then playing the game in the United States, but the clergyman seems to be referring to baseball activity from a more distant time. That would be big news if it were true, although it is hard to believe that such historic game playing could pass without leaving any footprints. After some digging and some critical help from fellow baseball researcher Bruce Allardice, I learned that Reverend Christie traveled to Australia as a young man to serve as a missionary. He returned to Ireland in 1886 to accept the first of several clerical postings. It's quite possible his familiarity with "bass-ball" derived from his experiences in Australia, where the game had been played competitively since the 1850s. In preparing his oration for the YMCA audience in 1888, it may not have occurred to him that baseball would be unfamiliar to many of his Irish listeners. That is pure speculation, of course, but this is all I can offer for this particular baseball mystery. Fortunately, there are plenty of other mysteries to keep us occupied, and one that I found especially entertaining takes us back across the Irish Sea to England.

18

Strange Diversions

In June 2013 I once again found myself sitting at a computer terminal in the British Library keying in one of my never-ending searches. As results from my query appeared on the screen, one of them directed me to an 1887 newspaper article from the Sussex town of Hastings on England's southeastern coast. Hastings, of course, is the name forever linked to the pivotal battle of 1066 when William the Conqueror and his army of Norman invaders overwhelmed the Anglo-Saxon defenders. It was also the setting for the British television series *Foyle's War*, beloved by many, including me. But, as you might imagine, the reason the story caught my attention had nothing to do with these things but with English baseball. The article described a large public festival held in Hastings where organizers had arranged a selection of games for the benefit of children, baseball among them.

This festival did not actually take place in 1887. In fact, it had happened thirty-one years earlier, and for some unspecified reason, perhaps to fill space, the paper's editors decided that 1887 was a fine time to reprint an old story about it. The event, it turns out, had been one of many gatherings held throughout the country in 1856 to celebrate the successful conclusion of the Crimean War. After digesting this, I thought, fine, now I have an English baseball reference dating decades earlier than it first appeared. But, as is my habit, I decided to check out the original report from 1856 to make certain it truly mentioned baseball, as had its 1887 reprint. Right off, I encountered a small obstacle. The 1887 reprint appeared in the *Hastings and St. Leonards Observer*, but the original article was from a different paper, the *Hastings and St. Leonards News*. This latter publication, I discovered, had not yet been scanned and digitized and, therefore, could not be retrieved from a database. Fortunately, because I was already in England, and because the British Library's newspaper annex had not yet moved from Colindale in London to Boston Spa in Yorkshire as it would later that year, I was able to plan a visit to the branch without great inconvenience. The newspaper issue I was seeking resided in the library's microfilm collection.

Once I scrolled up the original 1856 story on the screen of my film reader, I spotted something unexpected in its pertinent sentence: "There were scrambling for nuts, marbles, &c., and racing amongst the girls as well as boys for toys, footballs were bounding all over the hill, blindman's buff engaged one circle, and drop-handkerchief excited some interest in others, while ball-bias and other games engaged the attention of the rest."[1]

You will notice that instead of baseball, the report mentioned something called "ball-bias." I compared this sentence with its counterpart in the reprinted version and found they were identical except that the compound word *ball-bias* from the original 1856 article had been replaced by the compound *base-ball* in 1887. My initial assumption was that the writer, or editor, of the 1856 article was confused about the word *base-ball* or had misspelled it, and years later in 1887, while preparing the piece for reprint, another editor reached the same conclusion and corrected it. Feeling comfortable with that being the likely explanation, my attention turned to other matters, and it wasn't until some weeks later that a mental itch nudged my thoughts back to this apparent case of misspelling. Something felt wrong about it; not only was *bias* a strange way to scramble the word *base*, but the two terms were reversed in order. Out of curiosity I began conducting searches of books and newspapers for *ball-bias* and was startled by my results.

Not a misspelling! There actually was a game called ball-bias. What's more, it seems to have been a member of the baseball-rounders family. Yet I had never heard of it, nor to my knowledge had it crossed the radar of other baseball researchers or social historians. My searches turned up fifteen references to it, not an inconsiderable number for a heretofore unknown game. The earliest of these came from an obscure 1844 novel about the adventures of a teenaged Jewish girl. The book, *Rebecca Nathan; or, A Daughter of Israel,* included the following sentence: "Emilie . . . anxiously looked in all directions for Edward, whom she at length espied at a short distance before them, superintending a game of ball-bias."[2] This obviously tells us nothing about ball-bias, nor, to my frustration, do most of the other sources that mention the game.

Chronologically, the last of them was a short piece in the July 26, 1889, issue of the *Kent and Sussex Courier* that describes a summer treat held for younger members of the Band of Hope from the town of Wadhurst in East Sussex. The paper reported that "the boys' races were exceedingly well contested, and the three-legged races, sack races, and obstacle races caused a great deal of merriment. The visitors and elder children appeared to enjoy themselves immensely with French tag, ball-bias, the jolly miller, and other games, while many swings and see-saws were in constant requisition." The format of this reference, itemizing ball-bias as one of several amusements offered at an outdoor event for schoolchildren, is replicated in most of the other mentions of the game produced by my search. Coincidence or not, this mirrors how English baseball often appeared on similar lists. This shared trait, however, is hardly enough to claim that the games themselves were related.

My searches showed that most uses of the term *ball-bias* emanated from a relatively narrow geographic area. Some reports mentioning the game placed it in the vicinity of Hastings. Others located it in the county of Kent. When plotted on a map, these markers of ball-bias's territory sketch a rough triangle formed by the towns of Hastings, Maidstone, and Sevenoaks, the latter two in Kent.

The Kent connection prompted me to conduct some further searches, and through them I discovered yet another pastime unique to that county, stroke-bias. This turned out to be an ancient game, and several published sources, including one dating back to the year

1700, described stroke-bias as having considerable resemblance to prisoner's base, which leads me to suspect that the term *bias* in the context of these Kentish games equates to the word *base*.[3] Intrigued by all of this ball-bias and stroke-bias business, I contacted authorities with knowledge of the social and sporting histories of Kent and Sussex and was disappointed to learn that none of them had ever heard of either of these "bias" games.

Eventually, my research turned up a couple of clues that led me to make a tentative identification of ball-bias. One came in an 1875 essay that appeared in a London magazine called *Belgravia*. The essay was entitled "Upon Sticks," and the topic expounded upon by its anonymous author was how his countrymen love their sticks. "The Englishman has always been fond of something in his fist in the way of a stick," he wrote, as he delved into the various staffs used for walking and sporting purposes. "The cricket-bat is simply the 'crooked stick'; it is merely a development of that game of ball, other forms of which exist in ball-bias, base-ball, rounders, hockey, *cum multis aliis*."[4] While letting us know, unambiguously, that ball-bias was played with some type of a bat, the author's mention of the game fell short of helping me categorize the pastime any further. True, he mentioned it in the same phrase as the safe-haven ball games of baseball, cricket, and rounders, but diluted this hint by mixing in the unrelated sport of hockey. Still, the wording of his sentence helped me infer that ball-bias was a separate game from either rounders or baseball (and I assumed he was probably referring to American baseball, since it uses a stick or bat). I came across a second and somewhat more helpful clue in *The English Dialect Dictionary*, which reprinted a brief definition for ball-bias that originally appeared in a nineteenth-century glossary of terms of the Kentish dialect. It simply stated that ball-bias was "a running game, much like 'rounders,' played with a ball."[5] Combined with the "stick" information from above, I feel comfortable classifying this previously unknown game as a member of the extended baseball family, although evidently it was closer to rounders than to English baseball. Moreover, it did not escape me

that the word *ball-bias* was not very different from the names of some
of the Scottish games, such as ba'-baises, even though their respective
territories were far apart. Ultimately, it is nearly impossible to follow
the wanderings of folk games like these that are seldom documented
in print and whose roots may be hundreds of years in the past.

Even more puzzling than ball-bias is another curiously named pastime, brace-ball. I first spotted this oddity in a June 1865 newspaper
squib announcing that members of the Brighton Sacred Harmonic
Society would be holding their annual picnic in the countryside.
Then and now, the Sussex city of Brighton was a popular seaside
destination. For residents of the town celebrating their own summer
holidays, however, it was probably a good place to escape from, and
in this case the choir members chose the inland town of Henfield
for their outing. The event's announcement mentioned that "a match
of cricket is to be played between the married and single gentlemen.
Trap, brace ball, and singing will form some of the amusements of
the day."[6] Surely this *brace ball* must be a misspelling, I thought. But
as with ball-bias, I felt obliged to exercise due diligence and check
whether this term could be found elsewhere.

My searches turned up two further mentions of brace-ball almost
immediately, and both came from the pages of the *Leicester Chronicle,*
a newspaper in the English Midlands. Curiously, they appeared only
a week apart in 1882, and both related to events that took place in the
deliciously named Leicestershire market town of Ashby-de-la-Zouch.
The first of these appeared on August 12 in a sentence describing how
townspeople there celebrated a recent bank holiday: "Games of various kinds were provided, such as cricket, quoits, brace ball, swings,
&c."[7] One week later, a second similar story described a Church of
England Sunday School festival in the same town, where "games of
various kinds were provided for the youngsters, such as cricket, football, swings, Punch and Judy, round-about horses, brace ball, &c."[8]

Reading these, I felt certain that they must have been misspellings
as well. Someone from that small town probably submitted articles

about two local events to the regional newspaper in Leicester twenty miles away, and that person likely misspelled *baseball* both times. There really was no other likely explanation, unless you suppose that an otherwise unknown game named brace-ball could have been so elusive that it only surfaced on three occasions, once at a picnic in rural Sussex and twice more at public gatherings in a small town 170 miles to the north. Since this defies belief, I concluded that the brace-ball references in Ashby-de-la-Zouch were meant to be baseball. This then raised the question of which version of the pastime the townspeople there were playing. Ordinarily I would assume that mentions of baseball in an 1882 English newspaper, without clues to persuade me otherwise, would indicate English baseball rather than the American game. But in this case there was a possible mitigating circumstance. Only a few years before the Ashby-de-la-Zouch references, American-style baseball had a brief dalliance in Leicestershire. This occurred during the years 1876 and 1877 when a couple of baseball clubs formed in and around the city of Leicester, one of the rare documented manifestations of the American game in Britain prior to the 1889 Spalding tour.[9] I had to weigh the possibility that residents of that county continued to practice the American-style game informally after those clubs disappeared, especially considering that the original English baseball never had much of a presence in that part of the country.

Aside from that small ambiguity, and feeling that I had the whole brace-ball matter sewed up, I moved on to other topics, only returning to hunt anew for brace-ball references at random moments. On one such occasion, I was surprised and a bit thrown off when an unexpected wrinkle appeared. A search directed me to an article in an archaeological journal, written in 1883 by Frederick Ernest Sawyer, Esq. What I found upended my previous assumptions about brace-ball. The vehicle for Sawyer's mischief was a piece entitled "Sussex Folk-Lore and Customs Connected with the Seasons," in which he described how residents of that county observed the various holidays.

For Easter Monday, he wrote: "Mr. Rolf tells me that skipping takes place on this day as on Good Friday, and this is the second 'Long-Line Day,' for the women, whilst the fishermen indulge in 'brace-ball' (base-ball)" [parentheses his].[10] Could this be the undoing of my assumption that *brace-ball* was a misspelling? By putting it in quotes, Mr. Sawyer indicated that his spelling of the game's name was deliberate. Moreover, by following *brace-ball* with the word *base-ball* in parentheses, he let us know that, in his view, the game practiced by Sussex fishermen equated to baseball. With this new twist I now had to reconsider whether the use of the term *brace-ball* in the earlier 1865 Sussex article about the Brighton harmonic society's picnic was really a misspelling after all. Unfortunately, my supply of brace-ball examples was now exhausted, and the sample size was too small for me to draw any firm conclusions about the word.[11] Regardless, I'm still inclined to believe that the two 1882 sightings in Ashby-de-la-Zouch, which is nowhere near Sussex, are the result of some well-intended and possibly hard-of-hearing local newspaper correspondent who may have heard the word *baseball* spoken aloud, but to whose ears it sounded like *brace-ball*.

These were hardly the only quirky diversions I encountered on the road to researching English baseball. For example, the *Illustrated Sporting and Dramatic News* of London ran an unusual story in its issue of July 13, 1878: "The members of the Ranelagh Club on Tuesday last enjoyed some outdoor sports, consisting of tilting at the ring on polo ponies, base ball on horseback, and military pastimes. . . . The base ball was a most interesting feature, especially as the generality of the competitors were renowned horsemen."[12] The Ranelagh Club was newly formed that year as a split-off from another organization and would soon become the largest polo club in the world. How its members managed to play baseball on horseback is not quite clear, notwithstanding a confusing hint offered up by another newspaper the following year. A writer for the *Weston-super-Mare Gazette* (how do the English come up with such wonderful names for their towns?)

reported in 1879 that "Polo has had its innings, its sensations, and, I regret to add, a heavy score of victims. A new sort of joust or tournament *à cheval* is, I hear, about to be started soon. It will not be unlike the old schoolboy game of baseball, but a hurdle or two will be introduced into the *enceinte*."[13] Maybe it's a lack of imagination on my part, but I was already having trouble envisioning how baseball on horseback might work before being further bewildered by this hurdle-jumping element. My compliments if it makes any sense to you.

In a similar vein, the *Morning Post*, another London newspaper, carried a front page advertisement in 1874 announcing "A Great Swimming Fete and Competition" to be held August 24 at the famed Crystal Palace. The list of promised attractions included swimming races of various distances as well as novelty performances such as "Exhibitions of Ornamental Swimming by Professor Beckwith."[14] But what jumped out at me was one item on the program identified simply as "Water Base Ball." No further elaboration was given, but evidently it was an idea whose time had come because only a month later a newspaper in far off Yorkshire announced that "a game of base ball" had been played as part of a swimming *fête* held at a bathing venue in the town of Dewsbury. Additional references to baseball aquatics would appear in English newspapers over the next several years, including one from the town of Kettering in Northamptonshire in 1883 where two clubs faced off at a swimming meet. "The entertainment concluded with a base-ball competition from which much amusement was derived," the *Northampton Mercury* reported, adding, "But as the sides were not clearly distinguishable, it was hard to tell which of the two gained the advantage."[15] For a time I was a bit mystified about what this water baseball might be and how it was played, but all became clear once I extended my searches for "water baseball" into the twentieth century. A 1908 newspaper article revealed that when the game—later to be known as water polo—"was first introduced into this country about 1870, [it was] under the title 'water baseball.'"[16] Aha! One mystery solved, but that led immediately to another. Why on earth was it affixed with the name baseball? Water polo is a game with goals, where one side defends its own goal while trying to breach its opponent's. So, too, are traditional polo, football, hockey, and any number of other pastimes. But not baseball, which, along with cricket and rounders, belongs to an entirely different family of activities classified as safe-haven games. I could find no evidence to explain why or how the English came to tag water polo with the misnomer "water baseball," but as we know, not everything in life is guided by logic.

In general, the original English baseball was a harmless pastime, but sometimes those who played it paid insufficient heed to how their behavior impacted others, drawing not only the disapproval of fellow citizens but also, on occasion, the law. Under the headline "Ball Throwing Nuisance," one particularly aggrieved resident of the Landport district in the city of Portsmouth wrote to his local paper in 1879 to complain:

> Sir,—By the medium of your paper, I should like to ask how much longer the inhabitants of Landport are to be subject to the above nuisance which in some places has become unbearable? Take Central-street or Church-path for instance. Every evening for the past two months or more, from about half past six, a party of youths from sixteen to twenty years of age, make it a practice to indulge in a game of baseball until it is too dark for them to see. If you escape being knocked down by them or struck by the ball you cannot close your ears to the disgusting and obscene language which they make use of at the same time, and until the police make their appearance. Unless the ringleaders are made an example of we cannot hope that it will be much better. Hoping it will not be very long before something is done. I remain yours truly, A Resident."[17]

Similar letters appeared from time to time, and the police took notice. Newspaper accounts reveal more than ten instances between

1869 and 1905 where English youngsters playing baseball unlawfully in the streets, or otherwise causing havoc while engaged in the game, were taken to court and penalized.

The pastime could also pose dangers to the players themselves. In 1888 a Kent newspaper reported that some visitors to Canterbury were playing baseball in the Dane John Gardens when one of them broke an ankle. But that person was more fortunate than a young Yorkshire woman, as reported by the *Hull Daily Mail* in 1902: "The tragic death of Edith Eliza Fennellow (21), 9, John-street, Hull, at the Cliff, Humber-side, Hessle, on Saturday, formed the subject of an inquiry. . . . She had gone for a stroll, and was playing baseball when she fell and expired. Dr. S. H. Johnson testified that death was due to syncope [fainting], and a verdict of 'Natural causes' was returned."[18]

On the brighter side, English baseball made its way into the diary of a young man writing about a romantic dalliance with his future wife. The diarist, an eighteen-year-old medical student named John Henry Salter from the town of Arundel in Sussex, inscribed the following entry for August 2, 1859: "*Aug. 2.* A boating party with myself as Captain. After dinner, archery, and cricket, then separation and a stroll. Laura and I found a beautiful sequest[er]ed spot, and never did time pass more quickly and delightfully. She vowed she loved me—God knows I do her. She gave me a ring to wear for her sake when absent, and I will wear it too so long as I have a finger. After tea base-ball and bat-and-trap. After a bit the damp came on and it was time to pack up and be off."[19]

Now that we've seen English baseball's association with love and death, how about beauty? Or weakness? Perhaps vitality? Frankly, I've been having a little trouble deciphering the meaning of a certain paragraph dropped into a Norwich newspaper column in 1858. The paragraph was anonymous, untitled, and unconnected to the stories above and below it. I'm leaning toward one possible explanation, but I present it here in its entirely so that you can form your own opinion of what the author was trying to convey:

A little go of sports had been got up by the little boys of the present day, in a meadow near the Ferry, which, as far as they went, showed a certain amount of agility and strength. Such play has been honoured by the fine name of 'æsthenic,' but is as far from the athletic sports of olden time as base, cricket, bandy, and camp, and the jumping, where broken shins, and sometimes broken heads and arms were got, and where determined energy of character, and vigorous activity of muscle, were brought into play unfettered, as the amusements of an age of hardihood can differ from an age of words. "Æsthenics" were not then invented, but nature found the strength and the power, and boyhood the energy and the spirit, which has continued to maintain the glory of England in India, and in the Crimea, and on the broad blue ocean, under a less sounding title than æsthenic.[20]

First of all, there's no such word as *æsthenic*. I searched high and low for it, and as far as I can tell, it was the author's invention. He obviously had some particular word in mind, but whatever it was, he got it wrong. Then the question is: what word was he seeking? In my mind, the leading choices are *æsthetic, asthenic,* or *sthenic.*

If the word he was trying to dredge up began with the grapheme *æ,* then the logical answer would be *æsthetic.* But does that fit with the paragraph? *Æsthetic* can mean "art for arts sake" or perhaps "designed to give pleasure through beauty." That doesn't seem anything close to what he was trying to convey. A more likely premise is that whatever term he had in mind would have been extracted from the Greek word *sthenos,* which means "strength." The word *asthenic* sounds about the same as *æsthenic* and is derived from *sthenos,* but its leading syllable of *a* marks it as an antonym of *sthenos,* giving *asthenic* a meaning of "weak or debilitated." By my interpretation of the paragraph, this seems the exact opposite of the point the writer was trying to make, although, we should acknowledge, the writer was eminently ineffective at getting his point across. That leaves the word *sthenic,* which

I've just learned, thanks to a dictionary, means "tending to produce vital or nervous energy." This seems closer to my best guess of what the writer was trying to impart through his paragraph.

So this is what I think he was trying to say: While the games boys play in the present time have some vitality and energy to them, they were nothing like in days of yore when rugged sports like cricket, base, et al., or other violent activities, were the norm, where young players could get serious injuries, but where they could nevertheless engage in this type of muscular play without limitation. These experiences built the character and energy of the participants so that they were then prepared to conquer the world for the British Empire.

If I've got it right, the author's message is akin to the old adage that "the Battle of Waterloo was won on the playing fields of Eton," a quote falsely attributed to the Duke of Wellington but which seems to have come into use around the same time as the puzzling *æsthenic* paragraph above. In any case, even if the author had the adjective *sthenic* in mind, there was no such thing as *sthenics*. As far as his use of the term *base*, the author could have been harkening back to the game of prisoner's base, especially since he was discussing pastimes from the "olden time." My intuition, however, tells me it is at least as likely he had baseball in mind. For one thing, I noticed he reduced the word *camp-ball* to the simpler *camp*, and I suspect he took the same shortcut with baseball. For another, he wrote his little opinion piece for a newspaper audience in East Anglia where English baseball had been a familiar presence for decades.

Having led you through some of the metaphorical sidetracks I encountered in my English baseball adventure, I'll now share an experience that began with me being stranded, literally, on a sidetrack.

19

The Third Baseball

This is a story of strangers on a train. It begins in November 2004 when I was returning to San Francisco from Los Angeles aboard Amtrak's Coast Starlight. As those who have made that particular journey will attest, it's a lovely and comfortable ride, but not the best option for passengers who value timeliness. The Union Pacific company owns the tracks traveled in California by the Amtrak route, and whenever the Coast Starlight converges with a freight train along its journey it is required to give way and wait on a siding until the freight train passes. In the years when I used to travel that route with regularity it was common for the scheduled eleven-hour trip to stretch to sixteen hours or more. Such was the case on that particular November day in 2004 when the Coast Starlight's customary tardiness was distended beyond its normal bounds, the unfortunate consequence of colliding with a fruit truck stalled on a grade crossing somewhere north of Santa Barbara. Happily, no one was injured, but it took several hours to clear the tracks before we were able to proceed.

When the dinner hour arrived I was seated at a table in the dining car with two young women from the United Kingdom who were on holiday in California. With all the time in the world on our hands, we introduced ourselves and settled in for a leisurely conversation as one does in those situations. In due course, I mentioned I had written a book and that it was about to be released. They, naturally, asked what it was about, and when I replied, "The origins of baseball," they looked at each other with knowing smiles and then laughed with approval. Seeing the bewildered look on my face, one of them, who lived in Wales, blurted out that she, in fact, was a baseball player. She had participated in the game for years as a member of various pub teams in the city of Cardiff. The kicker in all this was that she and her fellow baseball players did not practice the American game but something quite different, an alternate form of baseball that had quietly carved its own history stretching back more than a century.

This was the unheralded third form of baseball I mentioned in the introduction to this book. Back in November 2004, I was vaguely aware of a pastime known as "Welsh baseball," but had never spent any time familiarizing myself with it. Since then I've learned far more about it and determined that a more suitable name for it is "British baseball." That label captures the realities that the sport is played in both Wales and in England and is different from either the original English game or American baseball. Its history is intertwined with that of rounders, and just as the origin story of American baseball had to be rescued from the mythic tale of Abner Doubleday, so did British baseball's enduring creation legends need to be stripped away to arrive at its true beginnings.

But as I was conversing with my dinner companions, I knew nothing of that background. I eagerly ingested what they were telling me about this flavor of baseball that was unfamiliar to me and hungered for more. When we parted, they left me with their contact information and invited me to get in touch if I wanted to pursue the subject further. The next day I reported to my wife about my educational dinner and mentioned it had got me thinking about visiting Wales to learn more about its esoteric variety of baseball. I should acknowledge that in those closing months of 2004 I was experiencing twinges of anxiety in anticipation of the upcoming release of my first book. Never having been published before, I had little idea how it would be received. I was especially worried about possible pushback from baseball historians given that some of my findings overturned long-held assumptions about baseball's origins. It might be a slight exaggeration to describe me as bouncing off the ceiling, but that's how it may have seemed to my loving and patient wife, Barbara, whom, I realize in hindsight, I was driving a little crazy. Now, many years later, I can no longer remember if it was she or I who first suggested that I take the Wales trip immediately, but it was the perfect solution. It would give me something to do to distract me, and she'd get this nutcase out of the house.

So within a couple of weeks I departed for the United Kingdom, the first in what was to be a series of eight research trips I would take there over the next dozen years. I contacted the two young women from the train and made plans to meet them. The English one worked for the BBC, and in London she gave me the name of a colleague who worked as a sports producer for BBC Wales. I met the Welsh baseball player along with some of her teammates at a pub in Cardiff. Being that it was December, witnessing them playing a live game was impossible, but she introduced me to officials of the Welsh Baseball Union as well as to the sport's longtime historian. On that visit I also met with the BBC sports producer in Cardiff who was an avid follower of the local form of baseball as well as a big fan of the Kansas City Royals. That gentleman, Lawrence Hourahane, was a fount of information about British baseball, and we have stayed in touch over the years to my great benefit.

Regarding the game itself, I won't weigh you down with its full rule book here, but at first glance one might think it resembles a hybrid of American baseball and cricket. Each team has eleven players, a game lasts two innings, all players need to be retired before a side is out, and a run is counted for each base advanced. These are all cricket-like characteristics. Its American baseball traits include a diamond-shaped infield and four bases. A bowler stands in the center of the diamond and serves fast, underhanded pitches to an awaiting striker. The bat is flat on the hitting side, but with a narrower face than the one used in cricket. The ball resembles an American baseball though slightly lighter, and the bases are marked by poles in the ground, as in rounders. Struck balls can be aimed fairly in all directions, even behind the batsman, as is the practice in cricket. Other than the catcher (or backstop), none of the fielders wear gloves.

Yet despite its superficial resemblances to cricket and America's National Pastime, British baseball's immediate ancestor was the game of rounders. You may remember that back in chapter 6 I laid out my theory of how and when rounders got its beginnings. I theorized that the sport was a spinoff of the original game of English baseball, emerging sometime in the late eighteenth century when English youth began applying the use of a bat to a formerly bat-less pastime. The name *rounders* itself didn't appear in print until 1828 when the writer of a guidebook on games, *The Boy's Own Book*, first used the term while providing a description of it. Baseball historians have known about this 1828 reference to rounders since 1939 when the pioneer baseball researcher Robert W. Henderson cited it in his landmark essay "Baseball and Rounders." It is somewhat astonishing to me that despite the passage of so many decades since Henderson's revelation, and notwithstanding the vast reservoir of full-text, searchable databases of historic books and newspapers that have become available in recent years, no earlier reference to rounders has surfaced. I doubt that anyone has been as obsessive as I was in trying to find one, but the best I can show for my efforts is one example that comes close.

I found it in a magazine piece written by a young Englishman in 1829 who was recalling his student years at Cambridge University between 1819 and 1821. He described the cultural adjustments he experienced leaving public school for college, among them exchanging "ring-taw and rounders for hunting and tandem-driving."[1] More references to rounders appeared sporadically in books and newspapers in the years following these two earliest examples, but it wasn't until the 1840s that mentions of the game in print became commonplace. It was also during that decade that British publishers sought to replicate the success of *The Boy's Own Book* by releasing a swarm of new titles devoted to games and sports for boys. Invariably, these included descriptions of how to play rounders, a game that was rapidly becoming a pastime of choice for the country's youth.

Men began playing rounders as well. One early sign of this came in a letter written by Charles Dickens to his future biographer John Forster in the summer of 1849. "I . . . have had great games of rounders every afternoon," he assured his friend while enjoying a holiday on the Isle of Wight.[2] The *Glasgow Herald* of June 1, 1855, printed a letter from a British soldier on deployment in the Crimea who described playing rounders with his comrades near the port city of Sebastopol.[3] The *Bells Life and Sporting Chronicle* issue of May 9, 1858, reported that eleven men representing the Garrick's Head pub in Cheltenham were accepting the challenge of a neighboring pub, the Five Awls, to a rounders match for a stake of not less than £20.[4] By the 1860s it was evident that the pastime was becoming a significant recreational choice for men. A brief notice in the *Western Daily Press* of Bristol in August 1864 announced that "a few young men" of the city had come together to create the City of Bristol Rounder Club.[5] This was the first of many clubs that men in seaports up and down the west coast of Great Britain would form over the next three decades.

Historians of British baseball have overlooked the pioneering role of Bristol men in organizing the first rounders clubs, their efforts predating by several years similar undertakings in south Wales and Liverpool. Initially the City of Bristol players had no other rounders clubs to compete against and had to satisfy themselves with intra-club matches or contests against makeshift teams of cricket players. Evidently the cricketers had no difficulty picking up the game because the *Western Daily Press* reported on May 24, 1865, that players from several clubs in nearby Bedminster faced up against an equal number of City of Bristol members, and in a three-hour match they lost to the more experienced rounders men by the narrow margin of one run.[6]

Another report the following year documented an event where forty to fifty members of the City of Bristol club gathered for a field day. Besides playing an intraclub match, they also hosted a sort of rounders mini-Olympics for themselves, friends, and families. In addition to the games themselves, they staged races at different distances, as well as competitions in various rounders skills. These included "throwing the rounder ball," where the winner threw it eighty yards; "striking the rounder ball," winner eighty-six yards; and a "race around the rounder wickets" (distance eighty-four yards), winner thirteen seconds.[7] Craving outside competition, the rounders men sent out new challenges to neighboring cricket clubs, and the nearby Horfield club accepted. The outcome of the first match versus this new opponent is unknown, but in August 1867 the *Western Daily Press* published the results of a return engagement between the two. The paper's report included a box score that showed the City of Bristol rounders men drubbing the Horfield players by a margin of seventy-seven runs.[8] In 1870, after functioning for six years in a semivacuum, the pioneering City club finally acquired some regular competition when two other rounders clubs formed in the Bristol area.[9]

No records seem to have survived of what specific rules and field dimensions governed the matches played by the Bristol clubs. Most published descriptions of rounders from that era depict a pentagon-shaped infield with a home base, or batting crease, where the striker stood, and four other bases evenly spaced about twenty yards distant from each other. The eighty-four-yard "race around the rounder wickets" reported above suggests a seventeen-yard separation between bases, assuming the Bristol players utilized the traditional five-base arrangement. It is possible, however, they had already made the switch to a four-base diamond format akin to American baseball that would later become a standard for British rounders clubs, in which case their bases would have been twenty-one yards apart. A July 7, 1869, article in the *Western Mail* of Cardiff reported that bases for a rounders match between two teams of men in the Welsh town of Pembroke Dock were set twenty-five yards apart. The article also boasted that "some thousands of persons of all classes [were] present, all of whom seemed to take much interest in the game."[10] The same paper reported a "large assembly" at another match on April 18 of the following year.[11] Articles appearing that spring of 1870 in both the *Cardiff Times* and

Western Mail revealed that men in south Wales had joined their counterparts across the Bristol Channel in organizing formal clubs to play rounders, reporting on at least four contests between the Tubal Cain Club and the Hearts of Oak Club.[12]

The rapid expansion of rounders in the nineteenth century did not always proceed without upsetting the social equilibrium. As early as 1836 boys in Devonshire were arrested and fined for playing the pastime while trespassing on private land.[13] Then, in 1861, one aggrieved citizen wrote to a London newspaper to vent a lengthy but entertaining complaint about the game:

TO THE EDITOR OF THE *MARYLEBONE MERCURY*

Sir,—I do not know whether you are an admirer of the manly game of "Rounders," as it is termed, I believe, but I should like you to hear my case, if you will kindly give it publicity.

Paddington-green is a well-known spot, and although its glories have faded in one sense, they flourish vigorously in another, for it is here that the game of "Rounders" is seen to the greatest perfection. "Tip-cat," also, is pursued with the liveliest zeal, and the ingenious sport of "Three Hole" has its numerous votaries too, which, with the pursuit of "Cross Touch," "Hare and Hounds," "Shuttlecock," "Marbles," and "Cricket," help to vary the monotony, and fill up the leisure hours of our working population.

Now, I have no objection to the game of "Rounders" as a theory, which, indeed, traces from the earliest antiquity, and is a healthy and invigorating pastime, but I have a most decided objection to the practice of it when it is played on the middle of a *cross path* crowded with passers-by, who have as much right to be there as the players themselves, and who, as the tip-cats fly about, and the balls shoot over their heads, are in momentary fear of having a black eye or swelled face from one of the missiles. And I can assure you it is very poor consolation, after being struck on the head with a tough India-rubber ball, to be asked by one of the players, "What the—do you mean by spoiling our—game?" You must agree with me, Mr. Editor, that such dangerous "ball-practice" as this ought not to be permitted, and that those, like myself, who are daily in the habit of crossing the green, should not be treated as a substitute for skittles by a mixed society of costermongers, roughs and chimney-sweeps.

I believe the parish authorities have no right to exclude any one from the enclosure, or to prevent the sports mentioned, nor should I wish to stop them myself, but they certainly have a right to prevent them from being played so near the paths, and to the annoyance of other people.

I am, Sir, yours very obediently, April 10, 1861, Odd File.[14]

By the 1870s, the many references to rounders in British literature and newspapers made clear that the pastime was predominantly a masculine preserve, although as early as 1853 there were occasional reports of girls taking a turn.[15] The front page of the August 16, 1873, issue of the *Graphic* newspaper displays what I believe is the earliest illustration of men playing rounders. The ball players shown were soldiers of the iconic Forty-Second Highlanders, the famous "Black Watch," all dressed up in regimental tartan and kilts. The accompanying story states: " We have no doubt that most of our male readers have at some time or other taken part in a game of 'rounders' so that they will feel no need of an explanation of it from us. And if the ladies feel curious we must refer them to the gentlemen."[16]

But within three years of this article's publication, "the ladies" were moving in greater numbers to satisfy their curiosity without any help from the gentlemen. Given that women were riding bicycles and playing golf and lawn tennis in Victorian England, it is not surprising that rounders would appeal to them as well. An 1875 article in the *Cardiff Times* described a springtime outing of Sunday school teachers in Wales at which "a spirited game of what we prefer to call 'rustic rounders' was participated in by a not inconsiderable number of ladies, who with their soft and supple hands knocked the hard ball round the field, and ran from post to post to all appearances fully convinced that some great stakes were involved in the game."[17] Two books intended for a readership of "young ladies" were released the following year, and they too advocated a somewhat modified form of the game, advising young women to equip themselves with a battledore or tennis racket and a rubber ball. *The Home Book for Young Ladies* mentions that instead of a racket, "sometimes the ball is struck by hand."[18] This suggests a link to English baseball that was still a popular activity for girls and young women in a number of counties. *The Young Lady's Book* was especially enthusiastic about rounders: "Perhaps this is more properly a boy's game, but it is admirable exercise for a bright fresh morning; and there is no reason why bright young girls in the fresh morning of their lives should not indulge in it; and much less fatigued and languid would they feel after a good game of rounders, than on the morning after a ball, when they have danced till the dawn of day, and the sun peeping into their windows finds their heads on the pillows, trying to sleep off this unhealthy fatigue."[19]

Rounders is better for girls than dancing? Apparently so, because over the next two decades, tens of thousands of English schoolgirls embraced the game with great enthusiasm. Meanwhile, the men kept playing at it as well and began modifying the rules to make the sport more challenging for them than the simpler version that had long been popular with children. Supporters of the sport in Liverpool followed the earlier examples of Bristol and Cardiff and began organizing clubs, the first of which was the Duke of Edinburgh Club founded in 1874. In the 1880s, clubs in Wales, Scotland, and England all coalesced to form local rounders associations. The game became so popular in the Liverpool area that its community supported a weekly newspaper, the *Rounders Reporter and Liverpool Athletic News*. The one issue I was able to locate in the British Library covered the week of May 13,

1885. It reported on the outcomes of dozens of games, furnishing box scores for many of them. It also published long columns of statistics for the leading clubs and posted the schedule for the coming Saturday that listed forty matches, or fixtures, in the Liverpool area alone.

During these years rounders was not immune to the class struggle. A reporter for the *Globe*, a London newspaper that was then associated with the Tories, visited Liverpool and in 1886 filed a report about conflict in the public parks:

> Rounders is becoming immensely popular with Liverpudlians, and with a certain class is threatening the popularity of cricket. Now rounders is only a kind of debased base-ball. It is an inexpensive game, necessitating few preparations, and is decidedly good exercise. People who could not afford to subscribe to a cricket-club could play a game of rounders; and so many have found this out at Liverpool that the parks in the neighbourhood ... have been largely invaded by rounder-players, to the inconvenience of nurses, children, perambulators and the strolling public. Consequently there has lately been a movement to close these places to the votaries of rounders, and the votaries have protested and are prepared to petition and agitate. The grievance is a popular one. Cricket, lawn-tennis and archery are permitted—to the classes; rounders alone is interdicted—to the masses. It is the old complaint revived, and thanks to Mr. Gladstone, we shall see it revived many and many a time. The question is really one of convenience. Parks are for the enjoyment of everyone—masses and classes alike. If the game of rounders is so popular that it causes an inconvenient monopoly of public grounds, than rounders-players, like the Social Democrats, must establish themselves elsewhere. But this is not aristocratic tyranny.[20]

No? Smells like it to me. Why couldn't the cricketers and archers establish themselves elsewhere? In any case, during these years the rounders associations codified new rules for its play. Among other things, these did away with the pentagon-shaped infield that had characterized many versions of rounders for much of the nineteenth century, and replaced it with a diamond configuration. Then, between 1887 and 1892, they enacted some significant additional changes. The short, one-handed bat that had formerly been in use was replaced in some cities by a longer, two-handed implement. The old practice of retiring baserunners by striking them with the ball, which was known as soaking or plugging in North America and as shying or burning in Britain, was eliminated in favor of forcing out or tagging runners at the bases. Then, on April 25, 1892, a brief notice appeared in the *Liverpool Mercury*: "The National Rounders Association having decided to improve on the name rounders by changing the title to that of English baseball, in future all results will appear under this heading."[21] The sport the Liverpool association elected to call "English baseball" in 1892 is what I now refer to as British baseball, but at the time, for their purposes, the label made sense because Liverpool is in England. The following month, the associations in south Wales and Gloucestershire made similar moves, also adopting the name "English baseball."[22] In the case of the Welsh, their acquiescence in having their sport tagged as "English" makes obvious that the nationalist sentiment that would take hold in their country in the twentieth century had not yet gained much traction.

  Why did all these associations change the name of their game to baseball? Almost certainly it wasn't to reconnect with their roots, since by 1892 it was unlikely anyone in Britain knew that the game of rounders was derived originally from an earlier domestic form of baseball.[23] One eminent British sports historian in recent years has implied that the change was influenced by the lasting impact of the Spalding world tour of three years earlier. He suggested that by 1892 the form of rounders played by the associations "was essentially, barring minor rule variations, a similar sport" as American baseball and that the Liverpool rounders group initiated the change to baseball because it was a more "glamorous" name than rounders.[24]

My own findings show something very different. To be blunt, the change was motivated by pretentiousness born of male ego and sexism. The rounders boosters were eager to differentiate their form of the game—which had become a fast and physical sport for men—from the simpler schoolyard version that girls had taken up in ever increasing numbers by the 1890s. A letter from an official with the Liverpool group explained their rationale in unambiguous language: "In view of the prejudice that had always existed against the game of rounders, many considering it, not knowing the rules under which the game was now played, to be something childish, to be played by girls or at a pic-nic, and not fit to be ranked as one of the manly sports, it had been decided by the National Rounders Association to change the name to the English Baseball Association, stress being laid on its being English baseball, so as not to be confounded with the American code."[25] Another supporter of "modern rounders" from that year expressed a similar point of view:

> In the old game but little attention is paid to fielding, the sport being indulged in as a frolic and a vent to exuberant physical activity. The hitting of a player, or the vain attempt to make a target of the flowing skirts of a young girl running round the bases, usually provokes hilarity, and is considered the comedy episode of picnic fun-making. For such a game the modern rounders player would feel the same measure of contempt that a cricketer shows for rounders in general. It is to be regretted that modern rounders suffers by association of name, at least, from its progenitor.[26]

That the rounders organizations chose baseball as the replacement title was likely just a matter of adopting the most obvious and convenient alternative available. And, while happy to appropriate the name, the associations in both Wales and Liverpool made clear they were not at all eager to embrace the American version of the game. Appeals to convert these former rounders organizations to play by American rules were made repeatedly. A mysterious emissary named Mr. Appleton of Cincinnati attended a South Wales Rounders Association meeting in late January 1892 for just that purpose.[27] He ultimately was rebuffed, as were a number of similar entreaties over the next four decades. It seems the former rounders participants in Liverpool and South Wales, now newly dressed as baseball players, were content to play the game just as they had been doing all along.

British baseball—its rules, practices, and culture—had become deeply rooted in the working-class neighborhoods of the cities where it was played. The game filled the need for an enjoyable and accessible summer sport, one that didn't require the time commitment or the expensive white uniforms of cricket. In fact, most teams and leagues allowed players to play baseball in the same jerseys, shorts, and shoes they used for football. Teams were based in factories, churches, schools, pubs, and nearly every other institution of community life. For the past century, the highlight of each season was the "international match" featuring the best players of Wales versus those from England. These contests, which alternated between Liverpool and either Cardiff or Newport, often drew crowds of upward of ten thousand people.

While educating myself about British baseball, I surveyed what those involved in the sport had written about its early history and evolution. It was quickly apparent to me that they had drawn their findings from the realms of legend and folklore, rather than from scholarly investigation. Of course, they are not alone in embracing fables. The Wikipedia article on rounders, along with other websites that mention the game, promote the groundless assertion that Britons have been playing the pastime on village greens since Tudor times. British baseball's historians echo this claim and double down on it by maintaining that evidence of rounders dates back to 1744 when the game was mentioned in *A Little Pretty Pocket-book*.[28] It wasn't, of course, but those who make the assertion dismiss that small inconvenience by protesting that, even though it was called baseball back then, it was really rounders. (My annoyingly scrupulous wife suggests that in leveling this criticism I am being a bit hypocritical, as I make the similar claim that the *englische Base-ball* mentioned by Gutsmuths was, in reality, an early form of rounders. I like to think that, in my case, the evidence backs me up, although as usual, Barbara makes a good point.)

Another assertion that rises even higher on the preposterous scale is one that appears in published histories of British baseball. It reads: "In 1772, John Chadwick, an Exeter journalist and a member of the Gloucester Rounders' Association, emigrated to America [and] introduced the old game there, which over a century later returned to England in its glamourized Yankee form as an American product."[29] Anyone familiar with the early history of American baseball will recognize the name Chadwick, and, yes, he was a journalist born in Exeter. But his name was Henry, not John, and he wasn't born until 1823 when baseball was already being played on the streets of Manhattan. The Gloucester Rounders Association was not formed until 1887, and while American baseball did make its way to Britain in the second half of the nineteenth century, it was not as a reengineered version of rounders.[30] This imaginative Chadwick tale first appeared in print in *The Inside Story of Baseball*, a booklet published in 1962 and written by Ivor Beynon and Bob Evans, two storied names in the history of Welsh baseball. Give them credit for originality. To be fair, though, they were probably just repeating traditional stories about the game's origins that passed down through the decades. Another often repeated axiom about British baseball's roots is that it was invented on the docks of Cardiff by seamen and cargo handlers. This one may have an element of truth, at least to the degree that dock workers in Cardiff and Newport in Wales, as well as their counterparts in Bristol, Liverpool, and other west coast ports, were among the first groupings of adults to play what had previously been a children's game. Without a doubt, it was the working-class populations of those cities that became the pastime's strongest base of support.

Unfortunately, today British baseball is facing extinction. The game was never well suited to be a spectator sport, mainly because its audience had to sit far away from the action. Even then, the vantage point where many spectators placed themselves was part of the playing field, and they often had to scramble to make room for fielders pursuing balls in play. In recent decades, an onslaught of other body blows have threatened the game's viability and diminished its popularity. The first of these, according to Mike Dacey of the Welsh Baseball Union, came in 1986 when the Thatcher government eliminated payments to teachers working after hours to coach students in the sport.[31] That coincided with a government-mandated sell-off of school playing fields to private developers. With few fields left to play on, and with a great reduction in the numbers of players coming out of school programs, British baseball clubs found it progressively difficult to attract new members. And as was true with other amateur and regional pastimes, British baseball was increasingly overwhelmed in the competition for fan loyalty when arrayed against nationally and internationally televised professional sports such as football, rugby, and cricket.

Today there are fewer than twenty clubs remaining in South Wales, most of them in the women's division. The Alexandra Old Boys, an iconic Welsh team that had endured for many decades, was compelled to disband several years ago. In Liverpool, once the stronghold of British baseball, the game has now almost completely disappeared. England and Wales last contested the international match in 2015 because the English side can no longer field a team. Unless something changes, such as a new infusion of funding to rebuild school programs, the sport may vanish altogether. That would be a considerable loss, and for those of us who appreciate the early history of baseball, the departure of this distinctive British variety of the game would deprive us of one more link to the pastime's colorful past.

As for my personal connection to the game, I found myself returning to Wales in June 2007 and finally had the opportunity to observe the game those two women travelers had described to me on the Coast Starlight. I watched games in both the men's and women's divisions and was impressed by the fast paced action. That second journey to Cardiff was part of the same UK visit on which I joined filmmakers of MLB Advanced Media to shoot scenes for the documentary *Base Ball Discovered*. All told, in the space of one week's time, I witnessed games of British baseball, cricket, bat and trap, stool-ball, and rounders, and a youth league American baseball contest as well, quite possibly a spectrum of ball games no one else has ever observed firsthand in such a short span of time. I was lucky to be there and will always relish the memory.

As for the original game of rounders, the one so disdained by the men's associations in the late nineteenth century that they considered its name a stigma, it prospered to a degree those disapproving men could never have imagined. Over the years its rules were updated and standardized, and British schools in the twentieth century adopted it as a core component of their physical education programs. Today millions of students representing the majority of British secondary schools play the game, and although both sexes participate, it is now seen mainly as a game for girls and ranks as the most widely played sport for female students. However, as is the case with British baseball, the future of rounders is threatened. In 2015 the nation's Department of Education removed rounders from the list of eligible sports for the GCSE physical education component, this being the graduation exam required of all secondary students.[32] This act will undoubtedly lead many schools to drop the game from their curricula. I hope that rounders will find a way to avoid the same course of decline that has nearly extinguished its cousin, British baseball.

20

Mottos Are Made to Be Broken

Never, ever, trust a secondary source. These have been my watchwords almost from the moment I first began researching early baseball. The need to adopt such a rigid dictum became evident to me when, in the summer of 2001, I began reviewing what current historians had written about baseball's origins. Virtually all of their accounts relied on "facts" lifted from the writings of earlier historians. Working backward I eventually found that these oft-repeated truisms were often not so true, that there were no actual primary sources to support them. Indeed, I quickly learned that most of what constituted the accepted history of American baseball's beginnings rested upon a jumbled collection of myths, mirages, and misunderstandings, with barely any traces of respectable evidence in sight.

Before proceeding, I must acknowledge the obvious truth that I myself rely on secondary sources all the time, at least for some things. For example, much of the biographical background on characters I mention in this book come from such sources. I also make frequent use of online dictionaries, maps, and other reference websites, including (gasp) Wikipedia, which I find to be a handy place to go when I need to grab an incidental or uncontroversial piece of information.

Those of you who didn't skip over the earlier chapters in this book will recall me describing a couple of instances where secondary sources falsely reported early appearances of the word *baseball*. These came about when writers working more than a century ago came across certain old-fashioned terms in their research—terms such as *prisoner's base* and *stool-ball*—and rather than citing them verbatim in books or articles, decided to replace them with a more familiar word, *baseball*. Presumably they made these swaps under the misguided assumption that such moves would make the terms more understandable to their readers. When later researchers came along and accepted this "baseball" evidence uncritically, the result was further pollution of the historical pool. To avoid the risk of making my own contributions to this problem, I resolved to stick religiously to the motto I stated above. Whenever I find a secondary source that cites an early reference to baseball, I will not treat it as legitimate historical fact unless I am able to locate the primary document in which it first appeared and confirm its accuracy.

Having composed the previous sentence with all the self-righteousness I could muster, I must confess I am now contemplating a violation of my own rule. This is shocking, I know. You may be wondering what could possibly spur me to such reckless behavior. But once I lay out the facts for you, I'm hoping you'll understand my reasons for taking such a drastic step. It all began in the spring of 2016 when I was searching through the excellent *Welsh Newspapers Online* database provided free of charge by the National Library of Wales. Therein I came across a five-part research article that two Cardiff newspapers published in successive weeks in the spring of 1881. The series was entitled "The Old Prison at Cardiff: Jottings from the Prison Records," and what grabbed my attention was a sensational revelation contained in the first of its five segments. While describing conditions for inmates at the prison sixty years earlier, the article's anonymous author divulged that "during the day they were allowed in nice weather to play at baste ball, rounders, or other outdoor amusements in the courtyard at the back of the prison."[1]

Okay, you may ask, what's the big deal? I've already fed you endless citations about baseball and rounders. Why get so excited about another one? Ah, but this was no ordinary reference; the author was reporting on prison conditions from the year 1820. If the account could be verified, it would predate all other known uses of the word *baseball* in Wales by a wide margin. It would also stand as the earliest known appearance of the term *rounders* anywhere. A find like this is the sort of thing that truly tickles me pink and every other shade as well. To give you a better feel for the context of this unexpected gem, here is a longer excerpt:

> The prison life of a debtor at this period was, however, not one of great hardship. Under the old Insolvent Debtors' Act those persons who were able to support themselves fared, if they chose, sumptuously. The windows of the prison enabled them to converse freely with their friends in the street outside. Beer, wine, and spirits were supplied to them from without, and some of the old inhabitants remember a few of the more genial spirits inside holding a bumper to the window, and the debtors inviting their creditors to have a glass. For amusement during the day they were allowed in fine weather to play at baste ball, rounders, or other outdoor amusements in the courtyard at the back of the prison. The new governor, Mr Le Breton, found many irregularities he endeavoured to check, and on some occasions he considered it necessary to stop supplies when the debtors would persist in playing "baste" against his orders, or in refusing to give up the ball when he demanded it.

According to the author, he was able to relate these details of long ago prison life because of an unusual opportunity that fell into his lap. "Through the courtesy of Major Knox, the governor of the county gaol at Cardiff, we have recently examined some of the documents at this place," he wrote. He went on to explain that most of the old records of the prison prior to 1819 were destroyed or otherwise no longer available, and that from the mid-1820s onward preparations were under way to move the "gaol" to a newer location. He added that "the only books available for research are 'The Governor's Journal' and the 'The Visiting Magistrates' Book,' and these are only interesting for the few remaining years during which the old gaol was occupied."

These two documents, covering the administration of Governor Thomas Le Breton for the years 1819 and 1820, became the sole basis for the author's entire five-part series. He quoted them extensively and described the governor's journal as "a book which that officer is supposed to keep with the regularity of a log book at sea. It should contain an entry for every day, even though that entry may be, and frequently is 'nothing extraordinary occurred to-day.' It must not, however, be supposed that the journal contains only extraordinary events. It contains incidents of a very trivial nature." I cite these comments because they explain how this particular prison document came to contain information as insignificant as the types of amusements permitted to inmates in the yard.

You know my motto, and therefore you won't be surprised that almost as soon as I spied this article I was on the hunt for the governor's journal and the visiting magistrates' book. I was certain they had to reside somewhere in the collection of a Welsh institution. I started by searching the online catalog of the most obvious repository, the Glamorgan Archives. They held a number of governors' journals from the prison, but none earlier than 1829. I then searched the catalogs of other likely hosts: the libraries of various universities in Cardiff and elsewhere in Wales, the National Library of Wales, the British Library, the Bodleian Library at Oxford, and the UK's National Archives. No luck. I then enlisted the help of Richard Ireland of Aberystwyth University, a noted expert on the history of Welsh prisons. He kindly agreed to help locate the documents, but ultimately he ran into the same blank wall that I encountered. I was getting very frustrated. It didn't make any sense to me that the documents could just disappear. In 1881, when the anonymous author of the prison series used them as his primary sources, their value as historical documents was apparent to him and also, presumably, to the governor, Major Knox. That was the height of the Victorian era, a time when Britain's sense of itself was at its apex and when social scientists were avidly collecting and preserving the empire's historical records and artifacts. These books would not have been tossed out in the trash.

By December 2016 I was running out of ideas. It was only a few weeks before I was set to depart on one final research trip to the UK before finishing this book. I had planned to visit Cardiff during the visit to examine the prison documents, something that might prove difficult if I was unable to locate them. Desperate, I placed a call to the prison in the unlikely hope that somehow the old papers were still moldering there in a forgotten storeroom. The person who answered was very nice and helpful, but after he connected me with the current governor's assistant I learned that any remaining historic documents had been turned over to the Glamorgan Archives two years earlier. I had a fleeting hope that the two I was looking for had gone to the archives packed in a box full of other stuff but not yet cataloged. A call to the chief archivist there dashed that last remaining possibility.

Yet even upon my departure in January 2017, I still hadn't completely given up the idea of venturing to Cardiff for one last attempt at finding the documents. I didn't really have a plan for how I would go about doing that, but ultimately the voice of reason, and a downturn in my health, dissuaded me. Almost as soon as I landed at Heathrow I came down with a cold, and within days it had settled in my chest. Nevertheless, I trundled on to the various destinations of archives and history centers in England I had intended to visit, sadly accepting that my longed-for diversion to Wales would not be among them.

By now you may be getting a sense of why I am thinking of carving out an exception to my rule about secondary sources. The illusive prison documents may simply no longer exist, or if they do, they could be buried in some private collection where I am unlikely to find them. At the same time, I find the newspaper article describing the documents to be unusually convincing (although I admit my vested interest in trusting its reliability might impact my objectivity). The prison series from 1881 was well written, and the unnamed author appears to have been a serious journalist. It is obvious that the old prison records were still in existence at the time he wrote the piece. Otherwise he would have been called out as a fraud by Governor

Knox, the prison administrator whom the author credited for allow-ing him access to them. But could I trust the accuracy of the author's references to baseball and rounders? If I accept them as authentic, doesn't that disregard the lessons I should have learned from my pre-vious experiences where well-meaning nineteenth-century chroniclers substituted the name *baseball* for older games like prisoners' base? Yes, it does. But for a reason that I can't fully explain—call it a gut feeling—I sense that the author of these articles is credible and that he cited the words describing the prison ball games exactly as he found them in the original documents. I am most confident about this in regard to his citing of baseball, because he referred to it as "baste ball" in his initial mention of the game, and then in his next sentence he doubled down on this spelling by placing quotation marks around the word *baste*. In my opinion it is unlikely he would have done this if he weren't quoting directly. Reasonable people can disagree on the probability of whether the prison governor writing in 1820 actually inscribed the terms *baseball* and *rounders* when composing his jour-nal, but I am inclined to think that he did.

Chest cold and all, I meandered that January by train and bus from London to Aylesbury in Buckinghamshire and then on to Ipswich and Norwich in East Anglia. As with most of my research trips, the findings were slim, but there is always the hope of a big discovery. Aside from the aborted Welsh excursion, there remained one more intriguing lead from a secondary source I intended to check out on this visit, one that would take me to Oxford. Before venturing there, however, I had a date to keep at Windsor Castle. But before you go assuming I had a scheduled audience with the queen, I must disap-point you. My appointment there was with another august body located in the castle, the Royal Archives.

You might remember way back in chapter 2 I regaled you with information about Frederick, Prince of Wales, who evidence shows played baseball at least twice in the 1740s. When planning this latest visit to Britain, it occurred to me that there might be more to discover about the ill-fated prince and his attraction to the pastime. Maybe he left some scorecards lying around his study? Maybe there were some surviving letters of him arranging ball games with his buddy Lord Middlesex? Maybe I was crazy to even think that anything like this was possible? Perhaps so, but it didn't hurt to look. Realizing that any such information would be in the Royal Archives, I investigated what it would take to visit there. Initial inquiries suggested it would be difficult. They didn't let just anyone in the door, much less some American with the wild idea of looking for baseball evidence in the files of a mid-eighteenth-century royal. Nevertheless, I went online and found out how to contact them and what information they needed about my bona fides and the purpose of my visit. I submitted a request and was somewhat surprised when they said yes.

So on a freezing January day I approached Windsor Castle where the archives are housed. First I had to stop at an outside security office so that they could inspect my documentation, ask a few more questions, and issue me a pass. The current administration in Washington could take a few cues from them about extreme vetting. The archive rooms are high up in one of the castle's towers. The staff members were very nice and brought out the few specimens of Frederick's correspondence they had in their files. These included letters he had received, as well as some he had written to others. I was impressed by his penmanship and was also surprised by his strong command of English, as he had lived his first twenty-one years in Hanover.

At one point in the morning I needed to take a loo break, as we all do from time to time. I politely asked for directions to the "gents," but discovered that whenever a visitor has such a need, he or she has to be accompanied on the errand by a staff member. Apparently they don't want absent-minded researchers wandering around the corridors and blundering into the queen's boudoir. So I departed for the WC in the company of a minder who waited outside the door while I took care of business. The same routine applied when it was time for lunch. I took the sandwich I had brought along with me to a little tea room on the archive floor and ate it in the presence of a nice young lady who was keeping an eye on me. We started to talk, and when I began to explain what I was doing there, she assured me she knew all about it and then began to relate some information back to me from my book *Baseball before We Knew It*. Extreme vetting, indeed.

Back in the archive room I was finishing up my search of Frederick's letters while avoiding the worried glances of fellow archive users sitting nearby who must have concluded from my violent coughing that I was going to contaminate them with some dreadful disease. I wasn't overly shocked when I failed to find anything at all in the prince's correspondence about his baseball habit. I did, however, find some juicy letters pertaining to the scandal that erupted in 1737 when Frederick snuck his laboring wife, Augusta, out of Hampton Court Palace in the middle of the night to deprive his parents, with whom he was feuding, of the opportunity to witness the birth of their first grandchild. The act infuriated his parents, George II and Queen Caroline, and also forced poor Augusta to endure a painfully bumpy carriage ride to St. James's Palace as she was about to deliver.

And so I bid a fond farewell to Windsor Castle, though not before trying to take a selfie with one of those guards wearing the tall bearskin hats who never smile or flinch when you make faces at them. (I've since learned that they stopped using bearskin a decade ago as a goodwill gesture to the bears.) Next stop, Oxford, where I had reason to hope I would have better luck corroborating a secondary source than I had with my Welsh misfortune. I was alerted to this reference several months earlier while searching through *British History Online*, a freely available digital library containing more than a thousand texts of primary and secondary sources. Probing for references to baseball, my search produced a hit among the pages of an epic seventeen-volume history of the county of Oxfordshire, part of the mammoth Victoria History of the Counties of England project that has been ongoing since 1899. Specifically, the hit pointed me to an appearance of the word *baseball* in volume 8 of that work, within a section covering the history of a small Oxfordshire town named Watlington. Reading the text of the reference, I saw at once it was a promising one. In discussing the social customs of the town, the compiler of the volume, Mary D. Lobel, cited an earlier work about Watlington written by a man named Badcock. The latter, according to Ms. Lobel, "recommended as early as 1816 that waste ground should be enclosed as a games field for girls to play baseball and other games, for whereas men and boys played cricket, trap ball, and quoits, girls could take exercise only by walking."[2]

This was extraordinary! Somebody was actually looking out for the welfare of girls' sports in 1816. As always, however, my distrust of secondary sources curbed my enthusiasm until its accuracy could be confirmed. The first step in doing this was to locate the original, something I assumed would be straightforward since Ms. Lobel not only provided the document's name but also a shelf mark, "d.d. Par. Watlington (uncat.), Badcock's MS. Hist." Unfortunately, she gave no indication of which institution held the manuscript. Since it was Oxfordshire, my first thought was to contact the Bodleian Library. My assumption was that even if they didn't have the work among their own collections, the librarians there would know where to send me. One of them wrote back to tell me they didn't have it, but she recognized the shelf mark as being a parish record and informed me that all such records since 1984 had been deposited in the Oxfordshire Record Office. I contacted that archive, now operating under the name of the Oxfordshire History Centre, and learned that they did, indeed, have possession of the Badcock manuscript.

I made an appointment to visit, and once arrived in Oxford I found the History Centre to be a short bus ride from town. The full name of the Badcock document is *An Historical & Descriptive Account of Watlington, Oxfordshire, Interspersed with occasional remarks, and concluded with a few reflections arising from a Review of the Subject.* John Badcock, a churchwarden, completed the handwritten manuscript in 1816. After reading through it, I am pleased to confirm that Ms.

Lobel paraphrased its baseball content fairly. I present some longer
excerpts here, notwithstanding that Badcock's prose is a bit convo-
luted in spots, because I find his comments to be as unusual for the
times as they were progressive:

> The rural amusements of the Parishioners are chiefly Cricket,
> Trap-ball, & Quoits among the men & boys. The females of the
> lower classes seldom take any other recreation in the open air
> than that of walking. Whether the writer's opinion may meet
> with ridicule or not, whether he stands solitary in supporting it,
> or whether a few others will coincide with him, he presumes not
> to determine, but he ventures nevertheless to consider it a matter
> of regret that amusements among the youth of both sexes in the
> labouring classes of society are not better provided for, instead
> of there being shown so general a disposition to check them.
> Innocent recreations under due regulations, & within proper
> bounds, are certainly compatible with the most amiable dispo-
> sitions, sobriety & good order, and are what the gay, & active,
> & sportive mind of youth seems to require after school hours
> or other confinement, and what those of riper years cheerfully
> participate in after the toils of the day, and what he considers
> wrong to deny. It is contrary to reason and to common sense to
> expect that the most sober-minded, if wholly restrained from
> a game at cricket, or some other amusement, & the other sex
> from base-ball, or some recreation peculiar to themselves, &
> exclusively their own, would fill up every leisure hour of a fine
> summer's evening better, or perhaps so well, in any other way.
> These healthful sports should, in his opinion, meet with some
> degree of encouragement.

He added:

> Who, upon rational grounds will deny his asserting, that it were
> well, whenever any inclosure of a parish takes place, if the Lord

of the Manor, or other proprietors of land in such parish, were to direct their commissioners to appropriate a piece of the most steril & least valuable ground they could find closely adjoining the town or village for this purpose, or two distinct pieces, at different points, the larger one for the male, & the smaller one for the female youth of the place?[3]

Badcock may not have stood for women's equality, but his arguments that girls should have playing space of their own and the freedom to engage in physical sports stand out as almost radical notions when coming from the pen of an early nineteenth-century church official writing in a rural setting. Badcock himself lived an unsettled life dotted with far more than his fair share of tragedies. He was born in 1776 and was a tanner by profession. He married in 1802 and with his wife had five children. Two died in infancy, two others as teenagers, and the fifth gained a BA from Oxford in 1833 only to follow his siblings in death three years later. His wife had passed away in 1827.[4] Badcock served as churchwarden in Watlington between 1806 and 1820. He was prosecuted for bankruptcy in 1825 and had his house and goods seized and sold before moving his depleted family to a couple of nearby towns.[5] There is nothing known about his rather sad life that explains his modest advocacy for girls, other than that he was a religious man and felt it was only fair that girls, along with boys, deserved the right to play.

So having confirmed the validity of the 1816 reference to baseball, I was able to depart Britain in a happy frame of mind, still coughing like crazy, but finally getting over my disappointing failure to track down the Welsh prison documents. You win some, you lose some.

21

When Games Collide

Not that I'm complaining, mind you, but unearthing the long buried history of English baseball was not without its difficulties. One of those was trying to piece together a picture of the pastime's earliest days in the eighteenth century when I had only a few scattered clues to work with. Yet that phase of my research also had its compensations. It propelled me on several unexpected adventures and graced me with occasional moments of sublime satisfaction. By comparison, my experiences in attempting to unscramble the history of English baseball in its final years proved every bit as challenging but lacked the rewards. Despite the far greater number of references to the pastime that were available to me from the late nineteenth and early twentieth centuries, attempting to arrange them into a rational narrative caused me no end of hesitations and self-doubts. What led to this rougher going was the fact that by the final decades of the Victorian era, English baseball was no longer the only form of the game in Britain; there were now two others. And, as I discovered, distinguishing those multiple forms from each other wasn't always a straightforward exercise.

The least concerning of these was the unheralded third version of the game, the one I call "British baseball." This was the form played in seaport cities on the west coast of the island. That game was relatively easy to differentiate from its namesakes because references to its play were centered in a handful of specific locales, such as Cardiff and Liverpool, where neither English baseball nor the American game had taken root. Posing a far greater challenge to my research was the introduction of American-style baseball into southern England where the original indigenous pastime was still hanging on. Because of this overlap it was sometimes difficult to determine what sort of baseball a newspaper writer might be referring to if they mentioned only the name of the game without providing further clues to its identity.

Contributing to this confusion was the fact that the history of American baseball's arrival in the British Isles is itself incomplete. To be sure, researchers have done excellent work documenting the tours of American professional ballplayers to Britain in 1874 and 1889 and the formation of organized clubs and leagues in the 1890s. Yet their studies failed to address the impact that the American import had upon the wider population. Specifically, they never investigated whether ordinary adults and children in Britain in the late nineteenth century began including American baseball among the pastimes they might play casually at summer outings or other types of informal recreational gatherings. The historians I consulted with acknowledged that they never made it a priority to study the game from that angle, but also added that they couldn't recall seeing signs of British subjects taking any particular interest in the American sport. This was consistent with my own observations, and for many years I proceeded under the assumption that Britons' attraction to the American game during those years was negligible.

Now that's all changed. A disparate collection of tantalizing clues have persuaded me to revise my thinking. I now suspect that informal play of American baseball by Britons in the late nineteenth century was greater than previously supposed. This new hypothesis led to my quandary: how to discern what form of the game was being referenced in dozens of newspaper articles where writers cited the name *baseball*, but offered no other hints to its identity? Of course, while this may be a source of frustration for me, it is my worry, not yours. I expect that you as a reader will be more interested in knowing more about the mysterious clues I alluded to above that have led to my new mind-set. But first, as a prelude, it may be helpful to present some background on the history of American baseball's relationship to Britain.

Even before the revolution of 1776, residents of the British Empire's North American colonies were experimenting with early forms of baseball. Following independence, as Americans ventured abroad, it was inevitable that their emerging methods of ball play would travel with them. One early example of this was reported by a London newspaper in 1809: "On Wednesday a match for 80 guineas, at a game called Ball, was played by Eight American Gentlemen, in a field on the side of the Commercial-road. The novelty of the game attracted the attention of the passing multitude, who departed highly gratified."[1] Other games besides baseball, of course, could have borne the label *Ball* on that occasion, but none seem obvious. Cricket, football, trap-ball, stool-ball, golf, and various games in the hockey family, including bandy, hurling, and shinty, all had a presence in the British Isles in that era, but there is no reason the passing multitude in London that day would have considered any of them a "novelty."

Englishmen also encountered American versions of baseball in far-flung corners of the empire. Researcher Brian Turner found evidence of one such occurrence in a letter written in 1836 by an American China trader named John Murray Forbes who was stationed in the international settlement at Canton: "One day it occurred to me that . . . we might have a game of Ball. . . . Well I had bats and a ball made, and we got up a sort of game; the next day some of the English found their way down to us and we have since had several games: the Balls and bats have improved."[2] Other letters and writings by Forbes make clear that these games were some sort of baseball.

Of course, Britons traveling to Canada in the mid-nineteenth century might well have spotted a baseball game, as the pastime's popularity there, especially in Ontario, rivaled that of its neighbor south of the border. But so might an Englishman visiting the remote Australian penal colony in Tasmania, where an 1855 newspaper reported that men and boys were desecrating the Sabbath by "playing at cricket, base-ball, &c., and making a great noise, and offending the eyes and ears of persons of moral and religious feeling."[3] Indeed, it was in

Australia where British settlers and their descendants took greater interest in the Yankee import than did their contemporaries in other outposts of the empire, excepting Canada. The Melbourne Base Ball Club organized in 1857 and began staging interclub matches among its members, with other clubs following in the ensuing decades.[4] The earliest unambiguous evidence of American baseball in Great Britain itself dates from 1870 when a Scotsman returning from living in the United States formed a club in the Highlands town of Dingwall. That was followed a year later by the first known match played in England, when members of the Sheridan Base Ball Club of Ithaca, Michigan, who were serving as seamen aboard the American frigate USS *Franklin*, organized a game on June 15, 1871, while on shore leave in the town of Gravesend in Kent.[5]

In February 1874, Albert Spalding, then a young pitcher for the Boston Red Stockings club, traveled to England to make arrangements for the inaugural tour of American professional players to Britain that would begin that summer. During that visit, Spalding and another player accompanying him organized a baseball match between two teams made up of cricketers and football players, with one of the Americans joining each side.[6] The game was played on February 24 at the Kennington Oval, a cricket ground in the South London borough of Lambeth. This match appears to have been the first contest of American-style baseball played in England where most of the participants were locals. Several months later during the tour itself, the American professionals staged an exhibition match in the town of Richmond, southeast of London. The game took place on August 8 under rainy conditions at Old Deer Park, the home grounds, then and now, of the Richmond Cricket Club.[7] Mr. Edwin Ash, an officer of that club, was impressed by the American sport; then again, Ash was easily impressed by almost any sport he happened upon, as he was involved in promoting an array of them, from tennis and golf matches, to horse shows and rowing regattas.[8] He had a major hand in organizing Richmond's cricket and rugby clubs and is credited with effecting the formation of the Rugby Football Union, a body that still stands as the sport's governing authority in England.[9]

Ash determined that American baseball had a "fair chance" of becoming popular in Richmond, and he set about organizing additional competitions to take place at Old Deer Park.[10] He scheduled one to follow a cricket match on September 12, 1874, for which he assembled two "scratch nines" of inexperienced local cricketers to do battle.[11] The game's outcome was not reported, but a week later, on September 19, Ash staged another baseball contest, this time matching ten members of his Richmond cricket club against ten other players drawn from the town's sporting community. A local paper reported that seven innings were played that day, with the townsmen besting the cricket club by fourteen runs before darkness descended.[12] Apparently Mr. Ash was thrilled with the outcome of the experiment because he scheduled an additional match between the sides for the following Saturday. Once again, the town team had the better of Mr. Ash's cricket squad, this time winning by eighteen runs.[13] Beyond that third game, however, I was unable to locate any further reports of American baseball in Richmond for many years or any indication that Edwin Ash's enthusiasm for the pastime had any lasting effect.

Nor did the 1874 tour itself succeed in inspiring other Britons to take up the sport. The only possible exceptions are the two baseball clubs that popped up unexpectedly in Leicestershire in 1876 and 1877. There is no evidence, however, that the American exhibition games of two years earlier were the sparks that precipitated the Leicesterites' endeavors. And that was that. No other documented examples of British citizens playing American baseball prior to the spring of 1889 have surfaced. The year of 1889, of course, marked the second foray of professional ballplayers into the country, the final stop of the famous globe-circling, barnstorming tour organized by Albert Spalding, who by then had become a club owner and successful proprietor of a burgeoning sporting goods empire. The 1889 incursion made a far bigger splash than did its predecessor in 1874. And, unlike the first one, its arrival was eagerly awaited by a collection of English businessmen and promoters who harbored ambitious ideas for how to build upon the Americans' visit by creating pathways for their own countrymen to become involved in the game.

The first step toward this goal was an instructional effort that kicked off in July 1889 when a delegation of eight baseball players representing several American universities arrived in Britain. Their objective was to tutor local athletes in the fundamentals of baseball as played in the United States. The college men conducted clinics in the London area, but most of their time was spent in the Midlands and other areas in the country's north. When some of the aforementioned English businessmen gathered later that year to form a small professional league, all four of their newly created clubs would be based in the Midlands as well. In part, this was due to the strength of football clubs in that region, whose organizations played a critical role in fostering the baseball venture and in providing players to fill out its rosters.[14] The new league began play in June 1890, completed its first season despite the midyear withdrawal of one of the teams, and anointed its first champion. But even this limited progress was short-lived, with a host of problems leading to the league's dissolution the following summer.

The debut year of 1890 also saw the creation of a number of amateur baseball clubs in Britain, again concentrated in the Midlands. But these and other undertakings never gained any momentum. Over the course of the 1890s, organized American baseball proceeded in fits and starts in England, with new amateur and professional clubs appearing and disappearing at irregular intervals. In the words of the British baseball historian Joe Gray, who has researched this period extensively: "The post-1890 British baseball scene has been one of oscillating amateur enthusiasm, with troughs of total absence and no spectacular peaks, all punctuated by short-lived experiments in professionalism and semi-professionalism."[15] Still, while Britons undoubtedly were playing American baseball to a far greater degree in the 1890s than ever before, one barrier, by all appearances, remained uncrossed. Although newspapers recounted hundreds of instances of American-style baseball clubs competing against each other in England, none to my knowledge documented a single example of average citizens playing the pastime informally.

Hence my long-held assumption that ordinary Brits rejected the American game. But then one day in 2017, in a eureka moment of clarity, I realized that among my research findings lay a scattered collection of odd facts that when cobbled together appeared to challenge that tidy theory. Looking back, I'm a little chagrined I hadn't made these connections earlier, although in fairness to me, these various clues on the surface seem to be unrelated. First was a newspaper advertisement from 1866 where a purveyor of sports equipment in the town of Luton was offering baseballs for sale. Initially I assumed this fellow must have been selling balls for the original game of English baseball, since there was no evidence the American game had arrived anywhere in Britain by that early date. Yet peddling balls for English baseball was itself a curious undertaking given that I always regarded the older pastime to be such a casual activity that players could put to use any soft ball they had lying around.

Then I made a link between the Luton ad and some similar commercial notices in other English newspapers dating to the time of the first American professional tour in 1874. These were placed by several firms including the venerable John Wisden and Company, known chiefly for publication of its iconic annual cricket "almanack." One advertisement promoting Wisden's full line of sporting equipment informed readers that the company had been "appointed agents for the sale of Base Ball Implements as used by the Base Ball Clubs now in England in all their matches."[16] Another one announced: "Having accepted the agency of the American Base Ball Company, we have now on view a large supply of materials."[17] Why was this English company trying to market baseball equipment in 1874? Was it just a speculative venture to cash in on whatever interest in the game the tour might generate, an effort that fizzled when Britons spurned the Yankee pastime? Or, I wondered, were the Wisden folks and the earlier Luton entrepreneur shrewdly tapping into a previously undiscovered subculture of ordinary Britons who had begun experimenting with American baseball? Additional ads for baseball equipment placed by competing firms appeared in newspapers well into the year 1875 and beyond. Sizing up the implications of these multiple efforts jarred my equilibrium. Contrary to what I thought I knew about that era, it was starting to look as if a small but discernible market for American baseball supplies had taken root in England.

Other clues in my files hinted at a possible American baseball presence in England in the 1870s. One that I couldn't take very seriously came at me from an unexpected direction. In October 2016, while reading the always informative and entertaining blog *Our Game*, which historian John Thorn writes regularly for the Major League Baseball website, I noticed a newspaper report from 1874 that Thorn chose to feature in his column. His subject that day was the 1874 American ballplayers' tour to Britain, although the article he cited was from an American paper, the *Utica Morning Herald and Gazette*. In the paper's August 19 issue, an unsigned piece blared the headline "England's Danger." Here is an excerpt, as quoted by Thorn:

> Those young men who are over in England introducing base ball seem to have taken upon themselves a responsibility far more serious than was at first apparent. So long as Englishmen regarded the game as an American modification of "rounders," long since condemned in England, and condescendingly explained that it was "not to be compared for a moment with cricket, you know," the exhibitions of the American athletes did no harm. But the matter has assumed more dangerous features. Englishmen have actually caught the base ball fever. Clubs are organizing in North England, and American manufacturers are exporting base ball goods to Great Britain.[18]

These are game-changing claims, but is there any truth to them? The Utica writer devoted much of his column to humorous contemplation of the implications for Britain if American baseball were to take hold there. The piece is drolly amusing, which is why Thorn chose to reprint it, but its very lack of seriousness tends to deflate its reliability as evidence. If we are to believe the Utica journalist, American-style baseball clubs were then starting up in the north of England, and equipment was being shipped there for sale. The Wisden ads confirmed the latter point, but there is not an iota of evidence known to me or to any fellow historians that I've consulted that corroborate the claim that clubs were forming in England in 1874 while American ballplayers were still touring. Were such a development under way, it would surely have left traces of itself in the form of newspaper mentions and other documentation, or so I assumed. But as I was beginning to learn, not all of my assumptions could be trusted.

As I was pondering these disturbances to my long held notions, I came across a surprising revelation from the summer of 1875 in an issue of the *Daily Telegraph*, a London newspaper. The paper's "special correspondent" had posted an article describing a visit he made to Aldershot, a locale in northeastern Hampshire that, then and now, was home to a major encampment and training ground of the British army. The journalist provided his readers with an account of what life was like for the militiamen in training there, taking care to praise their fitness and readiness. This was the passage that caught my eye: "They would achieve a march of twenty miles, if called upon, without difficulty; their litheness after a long drill tells you of their strength; they are ready to furbish their arms, boil their camp-kettle, or play at base-ball—a favourite game in camp—after they have been for two or three hours under arms and in constant movement, as though they had done nothing at all during the day, and play was their only employment."[19]

What? English soldiers playing baseball in 1875? And it's their favorite game? This was another head-scratcher. Aldershot rests amid

English baseball's traditional territory in a corner of Hampshire where it snuggles up next to Surrey. Normally, I would have assumed that if any type of baseball was played there in 1875, it would be the home-grown version, especially given the limited evidence of American baseball's presence on English soil at that early date. Yet it seemed curious to me that strapping, highly conditioned English soldiers would adopt as their favorite game a modest form of baseball that required, at the most, only a modicum of physical ability. This was confusing. What sort of baseball were they practicing? I couldn't dismiss the possibility it was the American game.

I went back to my files to pull out other reports of English soldiers engaging in unidentified forms of baseball during that period. In 1884 a newspaper from the Wiltshire town of Swindon described the daily regimen of local militiamen who had traveled to Aldershot to get in some training with regular army troops. "In the evening," the paper's reporter observed, "the men being at liberty, amused themselves with cricket, quoits, base-ball, &c."[20] Additionally, in July 1890, the *Sussex Agricultural Express* reported that volunteer soldiers of the Nos. 1 and 6 batteries of the Brighton Artillery took an excursion to the village of Ringmer in East Sussex. "Upon arrival in Ringmer, arms were piled, and the amateur soldiers engaged in cricket, baseball, &c., or patronised the 'Aunt Sallys,' shooting galleries, and other adjuncts of a rural festivity."[21] Previously I never questioned that the soldiers on these occasions were playing the original English baseball, given their settings in the southern counties where that game had flourished for decades. I now had to reconsider such reflex judgments.

In chapter 10, I described my efforts to collect and analyze demographic statistics of those playing the original English baseball. My findings revealed an unexpected rise in the relative percentage of males participating in the game in the late nineteenth century, especially in the counties of Hampshire and Suffolk. I began wondering whether something was amiss with my methodology, that I might have wrongly categorized some references as examples of the original English game when in reality the players were practicing the American version. To test this possibility, I decided to take a closer look at a sampling of my data, a collection of similar news stories and letters to the editor that appeared on the pages of newspapers in two Hampshire seaport cities, Portsmouth and Southampton. All involved complaints of older boys playing baseball in the streets and spanned the years 1870 to 1900. You may remember that in chapter 18 I quoted one such example from 1879, when an irate citizen wrote to the *Portsmouth Evening News* to protest the "unbearable" danger and "disgusting" language arising from youths playing baseball on public roads. Fourteen years later another unhappy reader submitted a letter to the editor of the same paper, who summarized its contents: "'Fellow Sufferer' writes to emphasise the necessity of official notice being taken of the prevalent annoyance of Portsmouth householders by boys playing baseball in the streets, and breaking windows and committing other damage."[22] This theme was echoed in more than a dozen other letters and news stories, including multiple accounts of police arresting young men for this type of unseemly baseball behavior and bringing them before magistrates to face fines and even imprisonment.

Taken as a whole, these reports raise obvious questions. Could the humble pastime of English baseball, the delight of young children at summer treats and a popular amusement at family-friendly events in the countryside, really be the same game that urban youth in Hampshire were playing in a manner so reckless as to annoy their neighbors and invite punishment? Could the ball used in English baseball, one soft enough that it wouldn't do anything more than sting slightly when striking a runner between bases, be hard enough to injure bystanders and break windows? Something didn't add up, and I had the sneaking suspicion that I was the one responsible for the faulty math.

In the face of this I began asking myself whether I had overlooked some fundamental transformation in Hampshire. This, after all, was a county steeped in the history of indigenous English baseball. From the days of Jane Austen's childhood in the late eighteenth century, and throughout most of the nineteenth century, Hampshire was the locale of nearly fifty references to what I always assumed to be the original version of the game. But did those findings really all point to English baseball? One example I began to question appeared in 1879 in the *Portsmouth Evening News*. In reporting on upgrades being made to a local park, a reporter wrote: "Very great improvements are now being made by the Park Committee in the portion of the ground allotted to the children. The rough stones have all been removed to make room for fine gravel which is now being rolled in. Orders have also been given for fixing some stones to act as bases for the games of rounders and base ball."[23] This raised my suspicions because English baseball always struck me as a pastime needing only a handy, reasonably flat patch of ground, not one requiring a groomed playing field. Then again, if workers were actually readying this Portsmouth playground for children to engage in American-style baseball in 1879, it would run counter to all previous assumptions about the timing of the pastime's importation into that part of the country.

I now felt compelled to cast a doubting eye on every other Hampshire baseball reference from the late nineteenth century. Previously I had categorized them all as English baseball, but now? Aside from the reports of older teenagers causing mayhem playing baseball in the streets, I started noticing that in an unusually high percentage of the accounts the players were described as adults rather than children. This was not the typical demographic ratio, and I wondered if it signaled an unacknowledged shift to the more challenging American form of baseball.

On the other hand, references to baseball in Hampshire during this period continued to indicate that a significant minority of the game's players were women. This doesn't jibe with the notion of a shift to American baseball, as there was no evidence of English females participating in the Yankee import during that era. On July 13, 1889, for example, the *Hampshire Telegraph and Sussex Chronicle* described a countryside outing of some 150 members and friends of the Portsmouth Ladies' Liberal Association. According to the article, "Arrangements had been made to provide the visitors with tea under the shadow of the trees, and a delightful *al fresco* repast preceded the robuster joys of base-ball, cricket, archery, and so on."[24] This resonated with me as the original English baseball. However, only a little more than three months earlier, the same paper published the following astounding commentary in the wake of the recently completed tour of American professional ballplayers:

> With the disappearance of the frosts and the advent of summer days there are preparations in every direction in and about Portsmouth for resorting to the games which are suitable for summer weather, at the head of which still stands the national pastime of cricket, though baseball may come to the front more than it has in past years. Among ladies last year it found many supporters, and with the stimulus which has been given to it by the recent visit of Americans and Canadian colonists to this country there is little doubt that the pastime will be more than ever indulged in.[25]

What could this mean? Is it proof that women, along with everyone else in the Portsmouth area, had converted to American baseball? The writer certainly seems to be equating the game the Americans played on their visit with the one the locals were practicing. Then again, it's entirely possible the writer was simply confused. They may have only noticed that the sport the visitors played, and the one long favored by Portsmouth residents, were both called baseball and inferred that the two were the same pastime. They quite possibly never even witnessed the American professionals demonstrating their sport, since none of their matches were staged any closer to Portsmouth than London, some eighty miles distant.

All of this leaves us with a very muddy playing field, and I'm about to make it muddier. In chapter 16 I acknowledged that players of

English baseball, on occasion, employed a bat in the game. It occurred to me that this might explain some of the phenomena I've described above. Adapting a bat to English baseball would have demanded more athleticism of its players. It would have required a firmer ball that could travel faster and farther when struck, and this, in turn, would have necessitated a larger playing ground. Players trying to field the ball would have needed greater speed and agility to chase it down and throw it back. The availability of a more physical form of English baseball like this might explain why soldiers at Aldershot took it up, or why older boys playing it in the street might be more apt to disturb the tranquility of their neighbors. If some players of English baseball were already using a bat when the second tour of American professionals arrived in the country in 1889, it might account for why one Hampshire journalist so readily equated the pastime played by the visitors with the one the locals had been practicing. Just to be clear, however, that while you may be admiring my cleverness in contriving this new explanation, please be aware I have no actual proof to back it up. Still, the possibility that some casual practitioners of English baseball were using a bat in the late nineteenth century might explain why newspaper writers of the era saw little point in trying to distinguish one type of the game from another.

Meanwhile, local newspapers in those years continued to document baseball's presence at school treats and country picnics in southern England in ways indistinguishable from how they had been covering similar events for the preceding half century. These reports bore the familiar hallmarks of the original, bat-less English baseball. One such example from the *Reading Observer* took note of an 1896 summer outing for children of that city's Carey Sunday School, reporting that "useful prizes were given to the scholars for racing, &c. Others indulged in donkey rides, cricket, football, baseball and other amusements."[26] Similar descriptions kept appearing into the beginning of the twentieth century, including one in a 1902 article about a treat for Sunday school students in Suffolk: "Having met at two o'clock at the

School Room, they marched with flags flying up to Hill Farm, where Mr. Brown placed a newly mown meadow at their service. Swinging, cricket, base-ball, up-and-down, trap and bat, racing, and scrambling were among the pastimes indulged in."[27] Nothing in these reports suggests American baseball or the adoption of a bat; to the contrary, they look and feel like classic settings for the original English game.

So how do we settle this? The British press seems to have had an opinion. One newsman wrote about American baseball in 1883 that "we have never seen it played in England," and "the game is very popular in America, though unknown to English lads."[28] Another writer added, "It would be useless to attempt to acclimatise base ball here."[29] And as late as 1905, a columnist for the *Globe* of London maintained, "We only know baseball by hearsay in this country."[30] Yet they represented the same out-of-touch newspaper establishment whose members were so completely ignorant of the original English baseball being played all around them that when the first tour of American base-ballers arrived in 1874, they could only conjure up rounders for comparison.

Unscrambling the history of baseball in England in the late nineteenth century is no easy matter. Still, I've become convinced that the American version of the game was played to a greater degree during that era than previously documented. Perhaps it, too, merits the label "pastime lost." At the same time, the original English baseball, whether played with or without a bat, had not yet abandoned the playing field, and it has been the murky convergence of these multiple forms of the pastime during the final decades of the Victorian era that has perpetually sent me reaching for the Tylenol. I hope that as new sources of information become available in the future, it will become possible to disentangle their snarled histories once and for all.

22

Pastime Lost

As this book nears its end, you may have noticed that I've tried to emphasize two particular points. It is no coincidence that both relate to the confession I made in my preface, where I admitted committing two notable errors in my previous work, *Baseball before We Knew It*. To refresh your memory, those mistaken claims were (1) that English baseball and the game of rounders were essentially the same pastime, and (2) that use of the name *baseball* as the *nom de jeu* for that pastime faded away by the middle of the nineteenth century. If I have failed to make my revised opinions on these two points eminently clear, then my expository skills are woefully amiss. But, to summarize, I now believe the eighteenth-century game of English baseball lingered on as a popular picnic pastime to the end of the nineteenth century and beyond. There are mounds of data to support this, and I have probably overburdened you with too much of it. Going hand in hand with my case for English baseball's longevity is my corollary contention that it was distinct from rounders. This theory, too, rests upon a pile of evidence, much of which I have heaped upon you in previous chapters as well.

But not all of it. There is one final set of facts that I believe effectively closes the case. In my research I've come across multiple instances in nineteenth-century books and newspapers where the words *baseball* and *rounders* appear side by side within the same phrase or sentence, typically on a list of games played at an outdoor event. These are all situations where it is apparent from context that the authors were referring to the original English version of baseball. Logically, the only reason a writer would itemize the two names individually, but in close proximity, is that he or she meant them to identify different games.

The *Chelmsford Chronicle,* a newspaper in the East Anglian county of Essex, offered one example of this in its issue of August 7, 1874. In its coverage of a picnic for members of two local choirs, the paper reported that "the enjoyments of the party began in earnest, with various sports, such as cricket, rounders, baseball, egg in hat, paper chases, &c., interspersed with songs."[1] It is improbable that the baseball named here was of the American variety, and the same can be said of at least ten similar examples that turned up in my searches. One of those came in a letter sent to the editor of a London newspaper and published in 1887. The writer was complaining that new rules imposed by the local governing authority of Wandsworth Common, a large park in south London, would severely limit children's access to that traditional ball-playing venue. He wrote: "Rounders, base ball, bat and trap, games as old as cricket, will be forbidden under irksome regulations and rules by which thousands of children will be deprived of that pure innocent pleasure which these games afford."[2] There can be no mistaking that the writer had the original English baseball in mind, as no right-minded Englishman would suggest that the upstart game of American baseball was as old as cricket.

Nor can there be any question that it was the indigenous form of baseball that a group of English mothers opted to play at a function in August 1894. They were all volunteer supervisors of the Girls' Friendly Society chapter in Hannington, a village in Hampshire, and were attending a celebration in their honor hosted by the local rector. A day earlier, the same clergyman had sponsored a separate event for girls in the society, at which "races, rounders, tug-of-war, and other sports were vigourously engaged in." On the following day, at the mothers-only gathering, the women "entered with the greatest zeal into some of the old games of their childhood—base ball, oranges-and-lemons, &c., and enjoyed them even more than their little ones had the day before."[3]

At the very beginning of this book I quoted a passage from an essay written in 1908 by thirteen-year-old Alice West, a Sussex schoolgirl, who named baseball and rounders among the usual games enjoyed by girls at her school. What to young Alice was an innocent and incidental observation is now, more than a century later, an important waymark in the history of English baseball. It documents that, even at that late date, English children in isolated pockets of the country were still playing and enjoying the humble original game. It was also one of the last hurrahs of the pastime, as references documenting its continued play fall off sharply after 1908. Local communities in Sussex, Hampshire, and Suffolk seem to have held on to the game the longest, with scattered instances of its presence persisting in those counties until almost 1920. There is even a later possible example, from the year 1924, when a Suffolk newspaper published the following report of a holiday outing taken by a group of temperance cadets from the town of Hadleigh: "During the evening, amusements of various kinds, viz., cricket, skipping, base ball, and racing for money, were freely indulged in, the hunting for hidden treasures causing much fun."[4] This brief notice resembles many hundreds of English baseball reports that came before it, but if those Hadleigh cadets were indeed playing the original form of the game in 1924, it was an extreme outlier.

Thus did English baseball quietly fade into the realm of the extinct and forgotten. Ultimately, the pastime succumbed to a variety of factors that also eroded the popularity, or led to the complete disappearance, of many other traditional English folk games. A contributing circumstance was the consolidation and standardization of games played and taught in the nation's schools, something that followed upon the restructuring of British education brought on by the passage of the Balfour Act in 1902. This had the effect of limiting the number of pastimes familiar to youngsters and thus reducing their choices at summer gatherings. One of those that remained on the list of favored games was rounders, and its widespread play and acceptance by schoolchildren, particularly by girls, probably had more to do with the demise of English baseball than anything else.

Still, English baseball had had a great run, lasting nearly a full two centuries from its beginnings sometime in the early 1700s until its fade-out in the early 1900s. Yet for all its longevity, Britons have lost all memory of the game's existence. Why they have forgotten it is not easily answered. One contributing factor may be that none of its participants ever organized clubs or associations, or codified rules, the types of actions that might have left documentary records behind for researchers to stumble upon. Moreover, English baseball was never in its day viewed as anything more than a simple amusement, not the sort of thing that those who chronicled the social and cultural trends of its era would have noted. It was seen for long stretches of its existence as a girls' game, a tag that guaranteed its relegation to a rung in the social hierarchy many echelons below the activities associated with boys. Even the better-known pastime of rounders, played mainly by boys and men for nearly a century before evolving into a girls' game, never gained much societal respect. It amazes me that, to this day, no one has ever written a history of rounders, despite the fact that tens of millions of Britons now alive have played it at some point in their lives. Contrast this to the thousands of books devoted to the history of cricket.

Notwithstanding my cogitations in the previous chapter about whether American baseball eclipsed English baseball in the twilight of its years, there can be no argument that the original game staked out a proud and colorful history. Following its trail has been a joyful adventure for me, driven on by my sense of wonderment that a game so long lasting and so interesting (at least to me) could vanish so totally from its nation's cultural memory. I make no allegation that English baseball holds anything more than a negligible ranking in the hierarchy of sports and games. Its only claims to fame rest on it being the immediate ancestor of American baseball and rounders and on the enjoyment it brought to English citizens of every age, gender, occupation, and social class at untold outdoor gatherings for many generations. Whether this is enough to justify my obsession with the game I leave for you to decide, but at the least it provided a diversion to keep me busy for more than a decade. I'm sure I could have found something else to do, perhaps something more significant, but the pursuit of English baseball brought me great satisfaction, not to mention the contentment of having a field of research all to myself. But with *Baseball before We Knew It* and now this book, I think I have squeezed as much out of English baseball as possible. It looks like I'll now have to find another quaint and forgotten English amusement to research. Dipping for eels comes to mind.

Notes

INTRODUCTION

1. *Sussex Agricultural Express* (Lewes), February 8, 1908, 70.

1. A LITTLE PRETTY DEBUT

1. The mythical tale that Abner Doubleday, a nineteenth-century American military hero, invented baseball in Cooperstown, New York, in 1839 was widely believed to be true for many decades before historians proved it to be nonsense.
2. Maxted, "Newbery, John."
3. Those who have written about Newbery have supposed his move to London from Reading occurred at the end of 1743, but a real estate notice in the *London Evening Post* of September 8, 1743, indicates that he had already set up shop in London by that date.
4. Henderson, "Baseball and Rounders," 305.
5. *A Little Pretty Pocket-book,* [38].
6. Welsh, *Bookseller of the Last Century,* 33, 293.
7. *Daily Gazeteer* (London), May 18, 1744, 1.
8. *Manchester Mercury,* September 20, 1757, 3.
9. *Daily Advertiser* (London), June 27, 1744, 1.
10. *Reading Mercury,* July 16, 1744, 3. The writer's allusion to "a suitable moral or rule of life subjoined" referred to a short, additional verse that Newbery attached to each of the games depicted in *Pocket-book.* The one on the baseball page reads as follows: "Moral. Thus *Britons* for Lucre / Fly over Main; / But, with Pleasure transported, / Return back again."

2. THE SPORTING PRINCE

1. Kilburn, "Frederick Lewis."
2. The contrast between the two brothers is well illustrated by their respective roles and attitudes toward the Jacobite rebellion of 1745–46. William, Duke of Cumberland, led the Hanoverian military forces that overran the

Jacobites at Carlisle Castle and then routed Charles Stuart's army of Highlanders at the Battle of Culloden in 1746. His brutal nature was evidenced
when he ordered his men to slaughter any of the opposing clansmen who
lay wounded or were otherwise unable to escape the battlefield. Frederick,
meanwhile, far from supporting the military campaign, instead staged a
mock siege of Carlisle Castle at a social gathering at his house as a way of
ridiculing his brother's successes in Scotland. Frederick also made a point
of visiting Flora MacDonald after her release from the Tower of London.
She was the young Highland woman who gained celebrity status when
William had her arrested for helping Charles Stuart (aka Bonnie Prince
Charlie) make his escape from Scotland. Frederick was far more sympa-
thetic toward her. When he asked Flora why she assisted a rebel who was
trying to overthrow his father's throne, she replied, according to her biographer, that "she would have done the same thing for him had she found
him in like distress." Macgregor, *Life of Flora Macdonald*, 116.

3. Kilburn, "Frederick Lewis."

4. Underdown, *Start of Play*, 63.

5. Browning, "Hervey, John."

6. Kilburn, "Vane, Anne."

7. Kilburn, "Hervey, Mary."

8. Lady Hervey to Rev. Edmund Morris [copy], November 14, 1748, HFA,
ref. #941/48/1–2,

9. The April 14, 1969, issue of *Sports Illustrated* magazine includes a cover
article by journalist Harold Peterson in which he claimed that Alexander
Cartwright, a member of the original New York Knickerbocker Base Ball
Club, was the true inventor of baseball. The piece was entitled "Baseball's
Johnny Appleseed," and it suggested that Cartwright implanted baseball
all across the United States during his journey from New York to California in the gold rush year of 1849. In reality, Cartwright made only minor
contributions as a baseball pioneer, and most of the claims made on his
behalf, including those appearing on his plaque in the National Baseball
Hall of Fame, are unfounded. Several historians in recent years have produced ample evidence discrediting the Cartwright myth, including Monica Nucciarone in her 2009 biography.

10. MS Book Wm Hervey, HFA, ref. #941/5/8/1.

11. *Letters of Mary Lepel*, 140.

12. *Old Whig* (London), July 10, 1735, 4.

13. *General Evening Post* (London), July 29–31, 1735, 1.

14. *Whitehall Evening Post* (London), September 14–16, 1749, 3.

15. *Whitehall Evening Post*, September 19–21, 1749, 3. My search process that produced this find was both circuitous and fortuitous. I had been taking advantage of a free trial of one of the many online genealogy sites and had entered the phrase *bass ball* as one of several search arguments I was trying out. Results from these searches come back as lists of text snippets that ostensibly contain the word or phrase you are looking for. Most of these are useless for various reasons, including, in the case of old newspapers, being badly garbled because of the poor quality of the original source. One such result gave me pause. It was dated September 23, 1849, and, though garbled, appeared to signal the presence of the word *bass ball*. I've seen other uses of that spelling of baseball even later than 1849, but there was something about this one, perhaps the mention of the Prince of Wales, that hinted to me that something was not right. I tried to pull up the entire newspaper page, but was unable to because of a malfunction with the website or the underlying database. I took note of the newspaper producing the hit, the *Remembrancer*, and quickly learned it no longer was in publication in 1849. At that point I went to the British Library's database of eighteenth-century newspapers and located the *Remembrancer* for September 23, 1749, one hundred years earlier. Paging through the columns, I spotted the notice of the prince's baseball game, and that was my eureka moment. Checking other London papers issued during that week, I spotted the same report in a *Whitehall Evening Post* issue of three days earlier. All of this was serendipity because when entering the term *bass ball* directly into the British Library's search engine, as I have done many times, I failed to find the term in either of the 1749 papers.

16. John Rocque, "Topographical Map of the County of Surrey," SHC, M/477/2.

17. BBC News, "Baseball: Prince of Wales Played 'First' Game in Surrey," June 10, 2013, http://www.bbc.com/news/uk-england-22840004bbc.com; Martin Robinson, "The Birthplace of Baseball Was in Britain!" *Daily Mail,* June 12, 2013, http://www.dailymail.co.uk/news/article-2340053/u-s-baseball-expert-proves-baseball-played-England-royalty.html.

18. *London Advertiser and Literary Gazette*, March 18, 1751, 2.

19. *London Evening Post*, March 19–21, 1751, 1.

20. *London Advertiser*, March 21, 1751, 2.

21. *London Advertiser*, March 26, 1751, 2.

22. The original subject of the epitaph allegedly was Edward Hoblyn, a disreputable lawyer from Cornwall. According to a nineteenth-century journal article, the following verse appeared on Hoblyn's grave: "Here lies Ned. I am glad he is dead. If there must be another, I wish 'twere his brother, And for the good of the Nation His whole relation." "Vicissitudes of an Epitaph," *New England Historical and Genealogical Register* 11 (January 1857): 67.

3. TWO WEEKS, TWO DISCOVERIES

1. Details on Kidgell come from Nigel Aston's article in the *Oxford Dictionary of National Biography*.
2. *Middlesex Journal or Chronicle of Liberty*, May 13, 1769, 2.
3. *London Chronicle*, May 8–10, 1764, 1.
4. Cash, *John Wilkes*, 202.
5. "Art. XIX. *The Card*," *Monthly Review* 12 (February 1755): 117. Apparently Newbery was waiting until after Christmas 1754 to publish *The Card*. *Whitehall Evening Post*, December 21, 1754, 2.
6. Bat and trap is the modern descendant of the game trap-ball, an English pastime played with bat and ball that may have been one of baseball's ancestors.
7. William Bray diary, SHC, Z/493. High resolution copy; original has disappeared.

4. WORD PERFECT

1. Bandy was a form of hockey originally played in fields, but from the early nineteenth century onward it was played on ice. It differs from ice hockey in that it uses a ball rather than a puck.
2. *Oxford Journal*, April 25, 1767, 4.

5. WILD GEESE AND RED HERRINGS

1. Henderson, *Ball, Bat, and Bishop*, 132.
2. Woodruff, "Origin of Cricket," 51.
3. Swinnock, *Life and Death*, 40.
4. "The History of Baseball," May 2, 2013, http://baseballsquare.com:80 /the-history-of-baseball/. The site has been discontinued, but it can be retrieved by using the Internet Archive Wayback Machine to view a snapshot of baseballsquare.com taken May 18, 2013.
5. "Local Gleanings," *Mancheste Courier and Lancashire General Advertiser*, April 21, 1876, 6.

6. [Lowe], *Diary*, 5.

7. Pomeroy, *Women*, 61.

8. Chapman. *Whole Works*, 89.

9. Jed Thorn to author, January 11, 2011.

10. Sources differ on the identities of the four student authors of the *Trifler*. It is agreed they were under twenty years of age and seniors at Saint Peter's College, Westminster, but one source, Nathan Drake's *Essays*, 408, named them as "Mr. Oliphant and Mr. Allen" (who moved on to Trinity College, Cambridge), and "the Hon. W. Aston and Mr. Taunton" (who moved on to Christ Church, Oxford). A second source, C. S. Northrup's *Bibliography of Thomas Gray*, 130, named them as "Mr. Aston, later Lord Aston, Mr. Upton, Mr. Slade and Mr. Taunton." This source claimed the information was conveyed in a MS note in the British Museum copy of the *Trifler*.

11. Touchstone, *Trifler*, 371, 373.

12. Touchstone, *Trifler*, 374. A jarvey is a coach driver.

13. *London Daily News*, June 25, 1878, 4. In cricket, a trial ball is a practice ball delivered by a new bowler beginning his spell. The MCC is the Marylebone Cricket Club, recognized since the eighteenth century as the sole authority on the game's rules.

6. BALL, BAT, AND BEYOND

1. Monica Nucciarone's superbly researched 2009 biography, *Alexander Cartwright: The Life behind the Baseball Legend*, removes any doubt that Cartwright played anything more than a minor role in the founding of modern baseball. Her findings, along with those of John Thorn and others, show conclusively that he is undeserving of the accomplishments credited to him on his plaque in the Baseball Hall of Fame.

2. Peterson, *Man Who Invented Baseball*, 37–40.

3. Gutsmuths, *Spiele zur Uebung und Erholung*, xiii. I've not been able to locate the word *freystäten* in any German-English dictionary, nor do I remotely qualify as a linguist, but it seems apparent that the author intended it to signify "free place" or "free station," i.e., "base."

4. Beloe, *Incidents*, 94.

5. "Westminster School," *Oracle and Public Advertiser* (London), January 14, 1797, 2.

6. *Youthful Sports*, unpaginated.

7. "Intelligence," *Monthly Repository*, 500

8. [Clarke], *Boy's Own Book*, 20. The first and second editions of this work were both issued in 1828, but it was only in the second that rounders made its appearance.

9. Carver, *Book of Sports*, 37–38.

10. See, e.g., *Pennsylvania Gazette*, December 11, 1750, 2, and *New-York Mercury*, August 30, 1762, 3.

11. *Proceedings*, 71, 61.

12. Peterson, *Man Who Invented Baseball*, 37.

13. Joachim Ott, Thuringian University and Jena State Library, email to author, November 11, 2004.

14. Salzmann, *Elements*, 107.

15. Godwin, *Memoirs*, 66–67

16. I had a strange experience in London one day that involved Mary Wollstonecraft. In January 2012 I was combing through the British Library's collections of prints and engravings when I came across an eighteenth-century image of a playing field for trap-ball. The field was located on the grounds of St. Pancras Old Church, and it occurred to me that I passed that very church on my daily walk to the library from my friends' home in Camden Town where I was staying. I determined to stop by the church on my return walk that day to see if I could locate where the ball field had been situated. I made some rough sketches of the print in my notebook so I could orient myself to the field's position relative to the church building. That afternoon the light was already fading as I made my way to the church. Railway lines leading into St. Pancras station and King's Cross had long since encroached upon portions of the former eighteenth-century churchyard, and much of the surviving grounds were now covered by graves. As I meandered about, with my vision alternating between the church building and my sketches, I failed to pay close heed to where I was walking. Suddenly, my foot struck something hard and I temporarily lost my balance. No harm done, but when I righted myself I took notice of what I had stumbled upon. To my amazement it was the corner of a large tombstone engraved with the words "Mary Wollstonecraft Godwin Author of A Vindication of the rights of Woman born 27th April 1750 Died 10th September 1797." Completely by coincidence, I literally tripped over her grave. I later learned that Ms. Wollstonecraft's remains were no longer under the tombstone because years after her death her grandson, Percy Florence Shelley, arranged for them to be disinterred and reburied

in the Shelley family tomb in Bournemouth, per his mother's wishes. This grave-digging and transference of body parts—already a bit ghoulish—seems even more ominous when you consider it was Mary Shelley, Mary Wollstonecraft's daughter, who was the instigator.

17. Professor Dr. Willi Schröder to author, April 5, 2005; also, John Burland to author, February 3, 2013. Mr. Burland acted as intermediary between me and Dr. Leonhard Friedrich, providing translated answers of questions that had been put to Dr. Friedrich.

18. Burland to author, January 17, 2013, forwarding comments of Friedrich.

19. Gutsmuths to university friend Herr Geh. Regierungsrat G. Kramer, June 7, 1791, in *Festschrift*, 146. Translation provided in Burland to author, February 3, 2013.

20. Gutsmuths to Kramer, June 21, 1791, in *Festschrift*, 146. Translation provided to author by William C. Hicklin, March 14, 2016.

21. Knight, "Glover, Julia."

7. AUSTEN'S AURA

1. Austen, *Northanger Abbey*, 7. *Northanger Abbey* and *Persuasion* were published together as a four-volume set in December 1817, although 1818 appears on their title pages. *Northanger Abbey* formed the first two volumes.

2. The 2007 film *Becoming Jane*, starring Anne Hathaway, includes a scene showing Jane playing baseball with some friends, but the filmmakers erred by picturing her with a bat in hand.

3. Tomalin, *Jane Austen*, 27–28.

4. *Hampshire Chronicle* (Winchester), July 21, 1817, 4.

5. [Cooke], *Battleridge*, 2.

6. Mrs. Cooke was the daughter of Theophilus Leigh, who served as master of Balliol College, Oxford, for an astounding term of fifty-nine years. At birth, Mrs. Cooke and Mrs. Austen were both named Cassandra Leigh.

7. Austen-Leigh and Austen-Leigh, *Jane Austen*, 19.

8. Tomalin, *Jane Austen*, 148–49.

9. "Novels," 238.

10. Byrne, *Real Jane Austen*, 84–85.

8. SCIENCE AND LETTERS

1. Steve Riese, email to SABR_L, September 30, 2004.

2. This is the correct title and subtitle, and 1806 is the correct year of publication. Most authors who refer to *Conversations on Chymistry* cite an alternate subtitle, *Intended More Especially for the Female Sex*, and a publication year of 1805. These are incorrect and derive from the entry for Mrs. Marcet in the *Oxford Dictionary of National Biography*, which has been the source of erroneous data about the book since the nineteenth century.

3. Marcet, *Conversations*, 13.

4. Morse, "Marcet, Jane."

5. Maria Edgeworth to Jane Haldimand Marcet, February 24, 1818, in Häusermann, *Genevese*, 90.

6. Austen, *Northanger Abbey*, 63.

7. Maria Edgeworth to Sneyd and Harriet Edgeworth, n.d. [1816], in Butler, *Maria Edgeworth*, 445.

8. McCormack, "Edgeworth, Maria."

9. L'Estrange, *Life of Mary Russell Mitford*, 4.

10. Austen-Leigh, *Memoir*, 14.

11. Garrett, "Mitford, Mary Russell."

12. Mitford, *Our Village*, 2:71–72.

13. Mitford, *Our Village*, 2:28.

14. Mitford, *Our Village*, 3:4.

15. Mitford, *Belford Regis*, 1:136.

16. Mitford, *Belford Regis*, 1:136–37.

17. Swanton, *Barclay's World of Cricket*, 582.

18. Mary Russell Mitford to Sir William Elford, April 3, 1815, in L'Estrange, *Life of Mary Russell Mitford*, 235.

9. LADIES FIRST

1. "Game at Skittles," 267.

2. Appleton, *Early Education*, 384.

3. Seccombe, "Moor, Edward."

4. Moor, *Suffolk Words*, 238.

5. [E.H.P.], *Geraldine Murray*, 212–13.

6. "Sights of Books," 617.

7. [A.M.H.], "Gipsey Girl," 423.

8. "Diary for Month of July," 117. A beadle is a local church or court officer; chuck-farthing is a gambling game that involves pitching coins into a hole.

9. "Female Gymnastics," *Times* (London), January 29, 1828, 2.
10. "Review of New Books," 183. Ladies' Toilet is a game where each of multiple players sitting on chairs represents an item used for dressing a lady, such as a comb or a scarf. Play proceeds with a designated "lady's maid" calling out one of these items, or the word *toilet*, after which one or all of the players scramble around in a manner reminiscent of musical chairs.
11. Bartrip, "Newnham, William."
12. Newnham, *Principles*, 123.
13. Lake, *British Newspapers*, 213.

10. THE NUMBERS GAME

1. *Reading Mercury and Oxford Gazette*, May, 17, 1830, 1.
2. *Reading Mercury and Oxford Gazette*, May 23, 1831, 2.
3. *Bucks Gazette*, August 27, 1831, 4; *Cambridge Chronicle and Journal*, September 7, 1821, 1.
4. Strutt, *Glig-gamena*, 327–28.
5. Strutt, *Glig-gamena*, 328.
6. Radford, "Women's Foot-Races," 51–52.
7. *Windsor and Eton Express*, August 12, 1826, 4.
8. *Windsor and Eton Express,* November 9, 1901, 5. A trade bill dated August 7, 1826, announced the festival and listed the competitions. It was reprinted in this 1901 issue of the *Windsor and Eton Express.* Its authenticity is well supported by the fact that the same newspaper covered the event seventy-five years earlier.
9. In this book I will refer to these two tours frequently. The first, in 1874, involved players from two American professional clubs, the Boston Red Stockings and the Philadelphia Athletics. In July and August they played a series of exhibition matches in England and Ireland. They also participated in a number of cricket matches against British and Irish opponents. The second tour took place in March 1889. It was the final stop in a five-month, barnstorming world tour of American professional baseball players organized by sporting goods magnate Albert Spalding. The players included members of Spalding's Chicago White Stockings club along with a number of star players from other clubs. The visitors played exhibition matches throughout England as well as in Scotland and Ireland.
10. *Bucks Herald*, August 26, 1899, 6.

11. A CLASS ACT

1. Young, *Literary Recreations*, 291.
2. Barber-Lomax, "Delabere, Pritchett Blaine," 135.
3. Blaine, *Encyclopædia*, 131.
4. "Railway Rambles," 412.
5. *Norfolk News* (Norwich), December 11, 1847, 4.
6. *Norfolk Chronicle and Norwich Gazette*, August 2, 1851, 4.
7. *Northern Star and National Trades Journal* (Leeds), May 25, 1850, 1.
8. *Reading Mercury*, July 1, 1854, 4.
9. *Windsor and Eton Express*, September 11, 1858, 3.
10. *Morning Post,* August 18, 1858, 5, and many other papers.
11. Longford, "Victoria, Princess."
12. Longford, "Victoria, Princess."
13. *Reading Mercury*, August 13, 1859, 5.
14. *West Middlesex Herald* (Staines, Surrey), August 25, 1855, 15.
15. *Windsor and Eton Express*, July 25, 1857, 4.
16. *Windsor and Eton Express*, August 26, 1865, 3; *South Bucks Free Press and South Oxfordshire Gazette*, June 30, 1865, 2.
17. *Hampshire Chronicle* (Winchester), July 11, 1857, 4; July 3, 1858, 5; and July 16, 1859, 3.
18. *Hampshire Chronicle*, July 16, 1859, 3.

12. LITERARY ALLUSIONS

1. Various sources have attributed her death to Addison's disease or Hodgkin's lymphoma.
2. Laughton, "Austen, Sir Francis William."
3. Klippert, *Englishwoman in California*, 7.
4. Klippert, *Englishwoman in California*, 12–14.
5. Deborah Yaffe, "The Watsons in Winter: Catherine Hubback," January 9, 2014, http://www.deborahyaffe.com/blog/4586114521/The-Watsons-in-Winter-Catherine-Hubback/7176157.
6. Hubback, *Younger Sister*, 166.
7. Hubback, *Younger Sister*, front matter.
8. Klippert, *Englishwoman in California*, 31.
9. Yaffe, "Watsons."
10. "Miscellaneous Notices," 142.

11. [Old Merry], "Along Fleet Street," 245.

12. Dickens, *Posthumous Papers*, 514.

13. [Keddie], *Lady Jean's Vagaries*, 142.

14. Orr, *Life and Letters*, 15.

15. Ouida, *Cecil Castlemaine's Gage*, 351.

16. Huntington, *Memories*, 258.

17. *Sara la Juive* [Sara the Jewess] is an 1838 three-act play by Hippolyte Deschamps and Émile Fontaine. It centers on the anguish of a young Jewish woman over whether to abandon her religion and marry a Christian lover, but who ultimately decides to wed someone of her own faith. It is not clear to me why the author of "Polling" chose to cite it in his poem. Perhaps it was being performed in London at the time and served as a handy stand-in for playgoing.

18. "Polling," *Fun*, April 14, 1880, 147.

19. "The Death of the Duke," *Coventry Evening Telegram*, January 20, 1892, 3.

20. *Diss Express*, September 2, 1898, 5.

21. *Ipswich Journal*, August 26, 1884, 2.

22. *Ipswich Journal*, December 9, 1893, 5.

13. GLORIFIED ROUNDERS OF ANTIQUITY

1. See, e.g., *Bedfordshire Mercury* (Bedford), August 8, 1874, 6, or *Leicester Chronicle*, August 8, 1874, 6.

2. See, e.g., *Morning Post* (London), August 4, 1874, 6.

3. See, e.g., *London Evening Standard*, August 4, 1874, 6, or *Northampton Mercury*, August 8, 1874, 5.

4. *London Daily News*, August 11, 1874, 2.

5. *Western Daily Mercury* (Plymouth), August 25, 1874, 3.

6. *Taunton Courier and Western Advertiser*, August 26, 1874, 5; and *Southern Reporter* (Selkirk, Scotland), August 13, 1874, 2.

7. *Graphic* (London), August 22, 1874, 26.

8. *Times* (London), August 13, 1874, 10.

9. *Daily News* (London), August 13, 1874, 3.

10. *Hull Packet and East Riding Times*, September 7, 1883, 6.

11. *Cornishman* (Penzance), June 17, 1886, 7.

12. *South London Chronicle*, March 29, 1873, 2.

13. *Kent & Sussex Courier* (Royal Tunbridge Wells), November 25, 1892, 6.

14. Nichols, *Literary Remains*, 310–11.

15. Dulcken, *Illustrated History*, 386.

16. Monk, *History of Burford*, 20.

17. In 1974 Wallingford was transferred to Oxfordshire for purposes of administration.

18. Allnatt, *Rambles*, 45.

19. *Punch* (London), August 29, 1874, 86.

20. See, e.g., *Leicester Chronicle*, March 11, 1876, 10, and April 8, 1876, 10.

21. *Daily News*, November 20, 1874, 5.

14. SUMMERTIME TREAT

1. *Berkshire Chronicle* (Reading), September 30, 1843, 3.

2. *Bucks Herald* (Aylesbury), August 18, 1860, 6.

3. *Bucks Herald*, August 25, 1860, 5.

4. *Reading Mercury*, August 3, 1850, 2.

5. *Bucks Herald*, September 13, 1879, 7.

6. *Bucks Herald*, August 3, 1889, 7.

7. *Framlingham Weekly News*, September 8, 1866, 1. Kissing in the ring, or kiss-in-the-ring, was a mildly titillating game played widely at nineteenth-century English children's parties and sometimes by adults as well. Its rules varied from county to county, but generally involved one person moving around a ring of seated players and dropping a handkerchief near one of them who then tries to run around the ring to avoid being kissed (or slows down to allow oneself to be kissed). Its roots date back hundreds of years to medieval courting rituals and was earlier known by such names as "drop the handkerchief" or "drop glove."

8. *Bristol Mercury and Daily Post*, August 26, 1878, 6.

9. *Hull Packet*, July 7, 1882, 7.

10. *Grantham Journal*, July 18, 1891, 8.

11. *Grantham Journal*, May 18, 1895, 3.

12. Durham is the only English county where the word *county* precedes the proper name in common usage. This practice is, of course, common in Ireland.

13. *Northern Echo* (Darlington, Durham), August 30, 1889, 3.

14. *Morpeth Herald* (Northumberland), March 31, 1894, 3.

15. *Southern Reporter* (Selkirk, Scotland), September 11, 1879, 3.

16. *Aberdeen Weekly Journal*, September 6, 1890, 6.

17. *Inverness Courier*, September 25, 1894, 5.

18. Joe Gray, "New Findings Upturn Previous Beliefs on Baseball's Intro to the UK," *Baseball GB*, June 17, 2013, http://www.baseballgb.co.uk/?p=16856.

15. PEOPLE'S PASTIME

1. *Sussex Agricultural Express* (Lewes), April 18, 1857, 5.
2. *Luton Times and Advertiser*, July 11, 1857, 5.
3. *Bucks Herald* (Aylesbury), August 29, 1857, 6.
4. *Kentish Gazette* (Canterbury), May 4, 1858, 6.
5. *Norfolk Chronicle* (Norwich), July 2, 1859, 5.
6. Supplement to the *Suffolk Chronicle; or Ipswich General Advertiser & County Express*, June 7, 1862, 1.
7. *Buckingham Advertiser and Free Press*, June 20, 1885, 4.
8. *Suffolk Chronicle; or Ipswich General Advertiser & County Express*, August 2, 1862, 9.
9. *Suffolk Chronicle; or Ipswich General Advertiser & County Express*, August 20, 1864, 5.
10. *Brighton Gazette*, July 26, 1866, 6. Izaak Walton was author of the classic seventeenth-century fishing work, *The Compleat Angler*.
11. *Brighton Gazette*, August 25, 1864, 7.
12. *West Surrey Times* (Guildford), October 3, 1863, 3. Aunt Sally is a traditional game whereupon players attempt to knock a model of an old lady's head off a platform by throwing sticks at it. A modified version is still played today in some pubs in the south of England.
13. *Bury Free Press*, July 21, 1866, 11.
14. *Ipswich Journal*, August 13, 1870, 5.
15. Baby boomers will recall that "Ferry Cross the Mersey" was a 1965 hit recording of the Liverpool singing group Gerry and the Pacemakers, reaching the top ten on the pop charts in both the United Kingdom and the United States.
16. *Liverpool Mercury*, June 16, 1885, 6.
17. "A Picnic for Lunatics," *Hampshire Telegraph and Sussex Chronicle* (Portsmouth), August 4, 1888, 6. Coconut shying was a traditional English game played at fairs. Contestants threw balls at coconuts balanced on poles, with the object being to knock them off and win prizes. It was related to the game Aunt Sally. The old music hall song "I've Got a Lovely Bunch of Coconuts" celebrates coconut shying.

16. RULES DON'T APPLY

1. Clark's *Jolly Games* is undated, but its year of release, 1875, can be estimated by newspaper advertisements.
2. Clark, *Jolly Games*, 110.
3. Clark, *Jolly Games*, 247–48.
4. [Clarke], *The Boy's Own Book*, 20. Three American books that provided the earliest descriptions of American baseball, *The Book of Sports* (1834), *The Boy's Book of Sports* (1835), and *The Boy's and Girl's Book of Sports* (1835), also copied and adapted the rounders text from *The Boy's Own Book*.
5. Ward, *Base-ball*, 19.
6. *Punch*, August 29, 1874, 86.
7. *York Herald,* August 18, 1874, 8.
8. *Derbyshire Times and Chesterfield Herald*, October 6, 1883, 8.
9. "Royal Academy," 163.
10. *Reading Mercury*, November 3, 1855, 4.
11. Dafforne, "British Artists," 134.
12. *Blouin Art Sales Index*, lot 53, Sotheby's, March 23, 1981, https://www.blouinartsalesindex.com/auction/William-Knight-93351.ai?93351&page=9, and https://www.blouinartsalesindex.com/auctions/-119131/-1854.
13. The seller advised that the painting was photographed "when passing through the London Art Trade circa 1980." Fine Art Photo Library to author, January 28, 2018.
14. Leprince, *Les Jeux*, 57.
15. *Western Gazette* (Yeovil, Somerset), April 28, 1882, 8.
16. *South Wales Daily News* (Cardiff), August 28, 1885, 4. A hagioscope is an opening in an interior church wall that allows worshippers sitting behind the wall to still see the altar.
17. *Western Times* (Exeter, Devon), February 26, 1886, 2.
18. *Luton Times and Advertiser*, May 26, 1866, 2.

17. THE OLD BA' GAME

1. *Manchester Guardian*, July 31, 1874, 5.
2. *Lichfield Mercury*, January 4, 1924, 6.
3. Bennett, *Anna of the Five Towns*, 5.
4. See, e.g., *Sheffield & Rotherham Independent*, September 28, 1874, 4.

5. Addy, *Glossary*, 176.

6. See, e.g., *Leeds Mercury*, August 9, 1879, 1 (for pise-ball), and *Barnsley Chronicle*, September 10, 1881, 8 (for pies-ball).

7. *Newcastle Daily Chronicle*, June 25, 1863, 2.

8. Ross, "Pize-ball," 63, 68.

9. "Bredoyne House and Burnside Farm," *Aberdeen Weekly Journal*, April 13, 1878, 3.

10. *Aberdeen Press and Journal*, September 21, 1946, 2.

11. *Banffshire Advertiser*, April 6, 1967, 7.

12. Penny, *Traditions of Perth*, 116–17.

13. Maclagan, *Games and Diversions*, 22–24.

14. MacGregor, *Pastimes and Players*, 1.

15. *Glasgow Evening Post*, June 10, 1886, 1.

16. *Shields Daily News*, August 31, 1891, 1.

17. *Dundee Courier*, March 26, 1935, 6 (same as rounders); *Dundee Courier*, October 11, 1888, 3 (different than rounders).

18. *Dundee Evening Telegraph*, April 29, 1939, 5; and June 9, 1939, 5.

19. *Dundee Courier*, April 11, 1939, 3.

20. Neill, *Carroty Broon*, 136.

21. *Arbroath Herald*, July 24, 1908, 6.

22. *Dundee Evening Telegraph*, March 24, 1914, 1 (violent sport); *Dundee Courier*, July 10, 1899, 6 (ladies); *Dundee Evening Post*, February 19, 1902, 2 (manly).

23. *Dundee Evening Telegraph*, July 8, 1930, 6.

24. Tate, *History of the Borough*, 437.

25. *La soule* was a game in the hockey family, although some historians have linked it to baseball's ancestry.

26. *Freeman's Journal and Daily Commercial Advertiser* (Dublin), March 26, 1889, 7.

27. Howard Burman, "Irish Rounders (Burman's Report)," *Protoball*, March 2013, http://protoball.org/Irish_Rounders_(Burman%27s_Report).

28. Patterson, *Glossary*, 108.

29. *Cork Examiner*, April 10, 1863, 3.

30. *Freeman's Journal*, September 21, 1881, 7.

31. See, e.g., *Dublin Daily Express*, December 5, 1881, 2.

32. *Waterford Standard*, March 28, 1888, 3.

33. *Waterford Standard*, March 28, 1888, 3.

18. STRANGE DIVERSIONS

1. *Hastings and St. Leonards News*, June 6, 1856, 3.

2. *Rebecca Nathan*, 81.

3. The earliest stroke-bias description I've found appears in a British travel book from 1700. It reads as follows: "The Kentish Men have a peculiar Exercise, especially in the Eastern Parts, which is no where else used in any other Country I believe but their own, 'tis called *Stroke-Biass*, and the manner of it is thus; In the Summer time one or two Parishes convening make choice of twenty, and sometimes more, of the best Runners which they can cull out in their Precincts, who send a Challenge to an equal number of Racers within the Liberties of two other Parishes, to meet them at a set day upon some neighbouring Plain, which Challenge, if accepted, they repair to the Place appointed, whither also the Country resort in great numbers to behold the Match, where, having stripped themselves at the Goal to their Shirts and Drawers, they begin the Course, every one having in his Eye a particular Man at which he aims, but after several traverses and courses on both sides, that side whose Legs are the nimblest to gain the first seven strokes from their Antagonists, carry the Day, and win the Prize: Nor is this Game only appropriated to the Men, but in some Places the Maids have their set Matches too, and are as vigorous and active to obtain a Victory: And on a Plain near *Chilham* there is an annual Tie, as they call it, fixed in May for two young Men and two young Maids of the adjoining Hundreds to make a Trial of Skill, which can course the nimblest for a certain *Stadium* of Forty Rods, and the Person of both Sexes, whose Heels are the nimblest, is rewarded with Ten Pound each, there being a Yearly Pension setled for that Diversion." Brome, *Travels*, 264–65.

4. "Upon Sticks," 434.

5. Wright, *English Dialect Dictionary*, 143.

6. *Brighton Gazette*, June 22, 1865, 5.

7. *Leicester Chronicle*, August 12, 1882, 7.

8. *Leicester Chronicle*, August 19, 1882, 6.

9. See, e.g., a game report, including a line score, in the *Leicester Chronicle*, April 8, 1876, 10.

10. Sawyer, "Sussex Folklore," 242.

11. There is one other reference that may have some bearing on the brace-ball question. An author writing in the December 1855 issue of a monthly Amer-

ican publication, *Burritt's Citizen of the World*, compared the holidays, or "joy-days," of New England to those of "old England." In it he wrote the following passage: "I do not know how old 'I Spy the Wolf,' or 'Hide and Seek,' or 'Leap-Frog,' or 'Prison-Brace,' or 'Bass-Ball' is; but I am inclined to think that the little flaxen-haired Saxon boys knew and played these games in England, a thousand years before America was discovered." Aside from this being a wonderfully early suggestion from an American source that baseball originated in England, this sentence also adds new spice to the brace-ball stew. All at once the author uses the word *brace* as a substitute for *base* in the game of prisoner's base, yet in the same moment he uses *bass* as an alternative for *base* in baseball. How can you not love this stuff?

12. *Illustrated Sporting and Dramatic* News (London), July 13, 1878, 411.

13. *Weston-super-Mare Gazette and General Advertiser*, September 17, 1879, 4.

14. *Morning Post* (London), August 22, 1874, 1.

15. *Northampton Mercury*, July 7, 1883, 7.

16. *Illustrated Sporting and Dramatic News*, November 28, 1908, 14.

17. *Portsmouth Evening News*, May 15, 1879, 3.

18. *Hull Daily Mail*, August 12, 1902, 2.

19. Thompson, *Dr. Salter*, 19. Though born and raised in Sussex, Dr. Salter spent the last seventy of his ninety-two years in Essex. He was described as a "medical man, freemason, sportsman, sporting-dog breeder, and horticulturist." He began keeping diaries at the age of eight and continued doing so without significant interruption until his final days. It is fortunate that they were transcribed and that Thompson included many of the entries in his 1933 biography, because the doctor's original handwritten manuscripts were destroyed in a World War II bombing raid. Though being an avid cricketer, it seems that Dr. Salter was happy to engage in a social game of baseball when in mixed company.

20. *Norwich Mercury*, June 19, 1858, 6.

19. THE THIRD BASEBALL

1. "Three Years at Cambridge," 463.

2. Dickens to Forster, September 23, 1849, in Forster, *Life of Charles Dickens*, 404–5. Forster appears to have destroyed the original letter from Dickens, along with as many as one thousand others. Thanks to Bill Humber for alerting me to this reference.

3. *Glasgow Herald*, June 1, 1855, 5.

4. *Bell's Life and Sporting Chronicle* (London), May 9, 1858, 7.

5. *Western Daily Press* (Bristol), August 3, 1864, 2.

6. *Western Daily Press*, May 24, 1865, 3.

7. *Western Daily Press,* October 22, 1866, 2.

8. *Western Daily Press*, August 24, 1867, 3.

9. *Western Daily Press*, August 3, 1870, 3. The two clubs were Kingswood and Warmley.

10. *Western Mail* (Cardiff), July 7, 1869, 4.

11. *Western Mail*, April 18, 1870, 4.

12. Reported in the *Western Mail*, April 18, May 3, May 17, and May 23, 1870. In the *Cardiff Times* on April 23, May 7, May 21, and May 28, 1870.

13. *North Devon Journal* (Barnstaple), April 14, 1836, 4.

14. *Marylebone Mercury* (London), April 13, 1861, 2.

15. Newland, *Confirmation*, 249. Reverend Newland describes an experimental coed school: "In school at Westbourne I generally examine boys and girls together, and I find that this always produces a greater degree of attention and emulation, each being ashamed to lose credit in the eyes of the other. In the playground they have full permission to play together, if they like (which is much the best security we possess against their wandering away together); but they very seldom do play together, because boys' amusements and girls' amusements are of a different character, and if, as happens at rare intervals, I do see a dozen boys and girls going down a slide together in the winter, or engaged in a game of rounders in summer, I believe both parties are improved by their temporary coalition."

16. *Graphic* (London), August 16, 1873, 1–2.

17. *Cardiff Times*, May 22, 1875, 5.

18. Valentine, *Home Book*, 4.

19. Mackarness, *Young Lady's Book*, 459.

20. *Globe* (London), July 20, 1886, 1.

21. *Liverpool Mercury*, April 25, 1892, 7.

22. *Western Mail,* May 24, 1892, 7; *Gloucester Citizen,* May 30, 1892, 4.

23. The secretary of the Liverpool Rounders Association made a curious comment about the history of rounders in a letter sent to the editors of several newspapers in western English cities for the purpose of attracting and spreading interest in the game. While referring to rounders as "an old school game," he said it was "newly governed and ruled by laws as to bowl-

ing, batting, &c., as in cricket, these laws mainly founded on a very popular American game called base ball." *Sheffield Independent*, June 5, 1883, 8.

24. Johnes, "'Poor Man's Cricket,'" 154.

25. *Western Mail,* May 24, 1892, 7.

26. Walker, *Rounders*, 10.

27. *Western Mail*, February 1, 1892, 7.

28. Beynon, *Inside Story*, 3.

29. Beynon, *Inside Story*, 3.

30. *Gloucester Journal*, July 2, 1887, 5.

31. Mike Dacey to author, April 13, 2017.

32. Jonathan Petre, *Daily Mail*, "The Bounders! They've Axed Rounders from the GCSE Curriculum in 'Sexist' Move Furious Critics Say Could Sound Death Knell for Game in Our Schools," January 31, 2015, http://www .dailymail.co.uk/news/article-2934799/The-bounders-ve-axed-rounders -gcse-curriculum-sexist-furious-critics-say-sound-death-knell-game -schools.html.

20. MOTTOS ARE MADE TO BE BROKEN

1. *Cardiff Times and South Wales Weekly News*, May 7, 1881, 5; *South Wales Daily News*, May 7, 1881, 2. The five-part prison series was published simultaneously in both newspapers.

2. Lobel, "Parishes: Watlington."

3. Badcock, *Historical & Descriptive Account,* OHC, 66–67.

4. Badcock, *Making of a Regency Village*, 128–29.

5. *Oxford University and City Herald*, August 20, 1825, 1.

21. WHEN GAMES COLLIDE

1. *Public Ledger and Daily Advertiser* (London), June 23, 1809, 2.

2. Forbes, *Letters*, 25, quoted in Turner, "Cogswell's Bat," 65–66.

3. *Colonial Times* (Hobart, Van Diemen's Land [Tasmania]) September 22, 1855, 3.

4. *Bell's Life in Victoria, and Sporting Chronicle*, March 7, 1857, 4, quoted in John Thorn's blog, *Our Game*, May 3, 2014, https://ourgame.mlblogs.com /australian-baseball-a-brief-history-54e1cadfddb1.

5. *Gravesend Reporter, North Kent and South Essex Advertiser*, June 17, 1871, 4.

6. Albert Spalding to Harry Wright, February 27, 1874, in "Baseball Cards," Robert Edwards Auctions. An article in the March 15, 1874, issue of the *Philadelphia Sunday Republic* also described the game and included a line score.

7. *Illustrated Sporting and Dramatic News* (London), August 15, 1874, 10.

8. *Surrey Comet* (Kingston), February 11, 1893, 6.

9. *Sporting Life* (London), February 8, 1893, 6.

10. *Surrey Comet*, September 26, 1874, 6.

11. *Surrey Advertiser* (Guildford), September 19, 1874, 3.

12. *Surrey Comet*, September 26, 1874, 6.

13. *Sportsman* (London), October 1, 1874. 4.

14. Gray, *What about the Villa?*14–15, 17–18. Joe Gray's book provides an excellent and detailed accounting of American baseball's history in Great Britain in the aftermath of the 1889 tour.

15. Gray, *What about the Villa?* 165.

16. *Sporting Life* (London), August 19, 1874, 1.

17. *Sporting Life*, July 29, 1874, 1. The American Base Ball Company was a small manufacturing and retail operation based in Salem, Massachusetts. I have not found any indication they produced anything other than baseballs.

18. "England's Danger," *Utica Morning Herald and Gazette*, August 19, 1874, 2, quoted in John Thorn's blog *Our Game*, October 20, 2016, https://ourgame.mlblogs.com/englands-danger-the-1874-tour-8c1ce52634f0.

19. *Daily Telegraph* (London), June 21, 1875, 5.

20. *Swindon Advertiser and North Wilts Chronicle*, August 16, 1884, 8.

21. *Sussex Agricultural Express*, July 15, 1890, 3.

22. *Portsmouth Evening News*, April 13, 1893, 3.

23. *Portsmouth Evening News*, May 13, 1879, 2.

24. *Hampshire Telegraph and Sussex Chronicle* (Portsmouth), July 13, 1889, 6.

25. *Hampshire Telegraph and Sussex Chronicle*, March 30, 1889, 2.

26. *Reading Observer*, July 1, 1896, 5.

27. *Framlingham Weekly News* (Suffolk), July 19, 1902, 4.

28. *Boston Guardian* (Lincolnshire), September 8, 1883, 2.

29. *Horsham Advertiser* (West Sussex), August 21, 1886, 2.

30. *Globe* (London), December 15, 1905, 8.

22. PASTIME LOST

1. *Chelmsford Chronicle* (Essex), August 7, 1874, 2.

2. *Daily News* (London), March 28, 1887, 3.

3. *Hants and Berks Gazette and Middlesex and Surrey Journal* (Basingstoke), August 4, 1894, 6.

4. *Bury Free Press*, August 30, 1924, 9.

Bibliography

ARCHIVES

HFA. Hervey Family Archives, Ickworth. Suffolk Record Office, Bury St. Edmunds.

OHC. Oxfordshire History Centre, Oxford.
Badcock, John. *An Historical & Descriptive Account of Watlington, Oxfordshire.* Watlington: 1816. PAR279/9/MS/1.

SHC. Surrey History Centre, Woking.

PUBLISHED WORKS

Addy, Sidney Oldall. *A Glossary of Words Used in the Neighbourhood of Sheffield.* London: Trübner, 1888.

Allnatt, William. *Rambles in the Neighbourhood of Wallingford.* Wallingford, Berkshire: S. Bradford, 1873.

[A.M.H.] "The Gipsey Girl." *The Amulet; or, Christian and Literary Remembrancer.* London: W. Baynes & Son, 1828.

Appleton, Miss [Elizabeth]. *Early Education; or, The Management of Children Considered with a View to Their Future Character.* 2nd ed. London: G. and W. B. Whittaker, 1821.

"Art. XIX. The Card." *Monthly Review or Literary Journal* 12 (February 1755): 117–21.

Aston, Nigel. "Kidgell, John (bap. 1722, d. c. 1780), Church of England clergyman and political writer." *Oxford Dictionary of National Biography.* March 11, 2018. http://www.oxforddnb.com/view/10.1093/ref:odnb/9780198614128.001.0001/odnb-9780198614128-e-15519.

Austen, Jane. *Northanger Abbey: and Persuasion.* Vol. 1. London: John Murray, 1818.

Austen-Leigh, James Edward. *A Memoir of Jane Austen.* 2nd ed. London: Richard Bentley and Son, 1871.

Austen-Leigh, William, and Richard Arthur Austen-Leigh. *Jane Austen, Her Life and Letters: A Family Record.* 2nd ed. New York: E. F. Dutton, 1914.

Badcock, John. *The Making of a Regency Village: Origin, History, and Description of Summertown in 1832.* From the original manuscript in the parish chest, edited by Christopher Hicks; with an introduction and an essay on the author by Ruth Fasnacht. Oxford: St. Michael's, 1983.

Barber-Lomax, J. W. "Delabere Pritchett Blaine: A Biographical Note." *Journal of Small Animal Practice* 2, no. 1–4 (February 1961): 135–36.

Bartrip, P. W. J. "Newnham, William (1790–1865), General Medical Practitioner." *Oxford Dictionary of National Biography.* March 13, 2018. http://www.oxforddnb.com/view/10.1093/ref:odnb/9780198614128.001.0001/odnb-9780198614128-e-20030.

"Baseball Cards, Memorabilia & Americana." Catalog. Robert Edwards Auctions, spring 2004.

Beloe, William. *Incidents of Youthful Life; or, the True History of William Langley.* London: R. Faulder, 1790.

Bennett, Arnold. *Anna of the Five Towns.* London: Chatto & Windus, 1902.

Beynon, Ivor, and Bob Evans. *The Inside Story of Baseball.* Cardiff: 1962.

Blaine, Delabere P. *An Encyclopædia of Rural Sports.* London: Longman, Orme, Brown, Green and Longmans, 1840.

The Boy's and Girl's Book of Sports. Providence: Cory and Daniels, 1835.

The Boy's Book of Sports. New Haven: S. Babcock, 1835.

Brome, James. *Travels over England, Scotland, and Wales.* London: Abel Roper, 1700.

Browning, Reed. "Hervey, John, second Baron Hervey of Ickworth (1696–1743), courtier and writer." *Oxford Dictionary of National Biography.* March 11, 2018. http://www.oxforddnb.com/view/10.1093/ref:odnb/9780198614128.001.0001/odnb-9780198614128-e-13116.

Butler, Marilyn. *Maria Edgeworth: A Literary Biography.* Oxford: Clarendon Press, 1972.

Byrne, Paula. *The Real Jane Austen: A Life in Small Things.* New York: Harper Collins, 2013.

Carver, Robin. *The Book of Sports.* Boston: Lilly, Wait, Colman and Holden, 1834.

Cash, Arthur. *John Wilkes, the Scandalous Father of Civil Liberty.* New Haven: Yale University Press, 2006.

Chapman, George. *The Whole Works of Homer: Prince of Poets in His Iliads, and Odysses.* London: Nathaniell Butler, 1616.

Clark, Georgiana C. *Jolly Games for Happy Homes.* London: Dean & Son, c. 1875.

[Clarke, William]. *The Boy's Own Book: A Complete Encyclopedia of All the Diversions, Athletic, Scientific, and Recreative, of Boyhood and Youth.* 2nd. ed. London: Vizetelly, Branston, 1828.

[Cooke, Cassandra]. *Battleridge: An Historical Tale Founded on Facts.* 2 vols. London: G. Cawthorn, 1799.

Dafforne, James. "British Artists: Their Style and Character. No. LXV.— William Henry Knight." *Art-Journal*, July 1, 1863, 133–35.

"Diary for the Month of July." *London Magazine*, 3rd ser., 2, no. 5 (August 1828): 110–22.

Dickens, Charles. *The Posthumous Papers of the Pickwick Club.* London: Chapman & Hall, 1837.

A Dictionary of the Scottish Language. Edinburgh: James Sawers, 1818.

Drake, Nathan. *Essays Biographical, Critical, and Historical Illustrative of the Rambler, Adventurer, and Idler.* Vol. 2. London: W. Suttaby, 1810.

Dulcken, Henry William. *The Illustrated History of England from the Earliest Times to 1887.* London: Ward, Lock, 1888.

[E.H.P., late Miss M'Leod]. *Geraldine Murray: A Tale of Fashionable Life.* Vol. 3. London: A. K. Newman, 1826.

Festschrift zur Hundertjährigen Jubelfeier der Erziehungsanstalt Schnepfenthal. Schnepfenthal [Gotha, Germany], 1884.

Forbes, John Murray, and Sarah Forbes Hughes, eds. *Letters (supplementary) of John Murray Hughes.* Boston: George. H. Ellis, 1905. Quoted in Brian Turner, "Cogswell's Bat," *Base Ball* 4, no. 1 (Spring 2010): 59–71.

Forster, John. *The Life of Charles Dickens.* Vol. 2. London: Chapman and Hall, 1873.

"A Game at Skittles." In *The Plain Englishman*, vol. 2. London: Hatchard and Son, 1821.

Garrett, Martin. "Mitford, Mary Russell (1787–1855), playwright and writer." *Oxford Dictionary of National Biography.* March 12, 2018. http://www .oxforddnb.com/view/10.1093/ref:odnb/9780198614128.001.0001/odnb -9780198614128-e-18859.

Godwin, William. *Memoirs of the Author of a Vindication of the Rights of Woman.* 2nd ed. London: J. Johnson, 1798.

Gray, Joe. *What about the Villa? Forgotten Figures from Britain's Pro Baseball League of 1890.* Ross-on-Wye, Hertfordshire: Fineleaf, 2010.

Gutsmuths, Johann Christoph Friedrich. *Spiele zur Uebung und Erholung des Körpers und Geistes für die Jugend, ihre Erzieher und alle Freunde Unschuldiger Jugendfreuden.* Schnepfenthal [Duchy of Saxe-Gotha], 1796.

Häusermann, H. A. *The Genevese Background*. London: Routledge & Kegan Paul, 1952.

Henderson, Robert W. *Ball, Bat, and Bishop*. New York: Rockport Press, 1947.

———. "Baseball and Rounders." *Bulletin of the New York Public Library* 43, no. 4 (April 1939): 303–14.

———. "How Baseball Began." *Bulletin of the New York Public Library* 41, no. 4 (April 1937): 287–91.

Hubback, Mrs. [Catherine Anne]. *The Younger Sister*. Vol. 1. London: Thomas Cautley Newby. 1850.

Huntington, Henry G. *Memories, Personages, People, Places*. London: Constable, 1911.

"Intelligence.–Parliamentary: New Churches' Bill." *Monthly Repository of Theology and General Literature* 29, no. 224 (August 1824): 449–512.

Johnes, Martin. "'Poor Man's Cricket': Baseball, Class and Community in South Wales c. 1880–1950." *International Journal of the History of Sport* 17, no. 4 (March 2000): 153–66.

[Keddie, Henrietta]. *Jane Austen and Her Works*. London: Cassell, Petter and Galpin, 1880.

———. *Lady Jean's Vagaries*. London: Richard Bentley and Son, 1894.

[Kidgell, John]. *The Card*. Vol. 1. London: J. Newbery, 1755.

Kilburn, Matthew. "Frederick Lewis, prince of Wales (1707–1751)." *Oxford Dictionary of National Biography*. March 11, 2018. http://www.oxforddnb.com/view/10.1093/ref:odnb/9780198614128.001.0001/odnb-9780198614128-e-10140.

———. "Hervey [née Lepell], Mary, Lady Hervey of Ickworth (1699/1700–1768), courtier." *Oxford Dictionary of National Biography*. March 11, 2018. http://www.oxforddnb.com/view/10.1093/ref:odnb/9780198614128.001.0001/odnb-9780198614128-e-13118.

———. "Vane, Anne (d. 1736), royal mistress." *Oxford Dictionary of National Biography*. March 11, 2018. http://www.oxforddnb.com/view/10.1093/ref:odnb/9780198614128.001.0001/odnb-9780198614128-e-28083.

Klippert, Zoë. *An Englishwoman in California: The Letters of Catherine Hubback, 1871–76*. Oxford: Bodleian Library, 2010.

Knight, Joseph. "Glover [née Betterton or Butterton], Julia (1779/1781–1850), actress." *Oxford Dictionary of National Biography*. March 12, 2018. http://www.oxforddnb.com/view/10.1093/ref:odnb/9780198614128.001.0001/odnb-9780198614128-e-10829.

Lake, Brian. *British Newspapers: A History and Guide*. London: Sheppard Press, 1984.

Laughton, J. K. "Austen, Sir Francis William (1774–1865), naval officer." *Oxford Dictionary of National Biography*. March 13, 2018. http://www .oxforddnb.com/view/10.1093/ref:odnb/9780198614128.001.0001/odnb -9780198614128-e-903.

Leprince, Xavier. *Les Jeux des jeunes garçon*. 4th ed. Paris: Chez Nepveu, Libraire, c. 1815.

L'Estrange, Rev. A. G. *The Life of Mary Russell Mitford*. Vol. 1. London: Richard Bentley, 1870.

Letters of Mary Lepel, Lady Hervey. London: John Murray, 1821.

A Little Pretty Pocket-book, Intended for the Instruction and Amusement of Little Master Tommy and Pretty Miss Polly. 10th ed. London: John Newbery, 1760.

Lobel, Mary D., ed. "Parishes: Watlington." *A History of the County of Oxford: Volume 8, Lewknor and Pyrton Hundreds*. In *British History Online*, 210–52. London: Oxford University Press, 1964. http://www.british-history.ac .uk/vch/oxon/vol8/pp210–252.

Longford, Elizabeth. "Victoria, Princess [Princess Victoria of Saxe-Coburg-Saalfeld], duchess of Kent (1786–1861), mother of Queen Victoria." *Oxford Dictionary of National Biography*. March 13, 2018. http://www .oxforddnb.com/view/10.1093/ref:odnb/9780198614128.001.0001/odnb -9780198614128-e-28273.

[Lowe, Roger]. *The Diary of R. Lowe of Ashton-in-Makerfield, Lancashire 1663–1678, Re-printed from the Leigh Chronicle*. Leigh, Lancashire: 1877.

Macgregor, Alexander. *The Life of Flora Macdonald*. 2nd ed. Inverness: A. and W. Mackenzie, 1882.

MacGregor, Robert. *Pastimes and Players*. London: Chatto and Windus, 1881.

Mackarness, Mrs. Henry. *The Young Lady's Book*. London: George Routledge and Sons, 1876.

Maclagan, Robert Craig. *The Games and Diversions of Argyleshire*. London: David Nutt, 1901.

Marcet, Mrs. [Jane Haldimand]. *Conversations on Natural Philosophy*. London: Longman, Rees, Orme and Brown, 1819.

Maxted, Ian. "Newbery, John (bap. 1713, d. 1767), publisher." *Oxford Dictionary of National Biography*. March 14, 2018. http://www.oxforddnb.com /view/10.1093/ref:odnb/9780198614128.001.0001/odnb-9780198614128 -e-19978.

McCormack, W. J. "Edgeworth, Maria (1768–1849), novelist and education-ist." *Oxford Dictionary of National Biography.* March 12, 2018. http://www.oxforddnb.com/view/10.1093/ref:odnb/9780198614128.001.0001/odnb-9780198614128-e-8476.

"Miscellaneous Notices." *New Monthly Magazine and Humorist* 89 (May 1850): 142.

Mitford, Mary Russell. *Belford Regis.* Vol. 1. London: Richard Bentley, 1835.

———. *Our Village.* 5 vols. London: Geo. B. Whittaker, 1824–32.

Monk, W. J. *History of Burford.* Burford, Oxfordshire: C. W. Swatman, 1891.

Moor, Edward. *Suffolk Words and Phrases.* Woodbridge, Suffolk: J. Loder for R. Hunter, 1823.

Morse, Elizabeth J. "Marcet, Jane Haldimand (1769–1858), writer on sci-ence and political economy." *Oxford Dictionary of National Biography.* March 12, 2018. http://www.oxforddnb.com/view/10.1093/ref:odnb/9780198614128.001.0001/odnb-9780198614128-e-18029.

Neill, Alexander. *Carroty Broon.* London: Jenkins, 1921.

Newland, Henry. *Confirmation and First Communion.* London: Joseph Mas-ters, 1853.

Newnham, William. *Principles of Physical, Intellectual, Moral, and Religious Education.* Vol. 1. London: J. Hatcher and Sons, 1827.

Nichols, John Gough. *The Literary Remains of King Edward the Sixth.* Lon-don: J. B. Nichols and Sons, 1857.

Northrup, C. S. *Bibliography of Thomas Gray.* New Haven: Yale University Press, 1917.

"Novels." *Critical Review; or, Annals of Literature* 27 (October 1799): 238–40.

Nucciarone, Monica. *Alexander Cartwright: The Life behind the Baseball Leg-end.* Lincoln: University of Nebraska Press, 2009.

[Old Merry]. "Along Fleet Street." *Merry & Wise: An Illustrated Monthly Magazine for Young People* 2 (April 1871): 244–50.

Orr, Mrs. [Alexandra Sutherland]. *Life and Letters of Robert Browning.* Lon-don: Smith, Elder, 1891.

Ouida. [Maria Louise Ramé]. *Cecil Castlemaine's Gage and Other Novelettes.* Toronto: Belford Brothers, 1877.

Patterson, William Hugh. *A Glossary of Words in Use in the Counties of Antrim and Down.* London: Trübner, 1888.

Penny, George. *Traditions of Perth.* Perth, Scotland: Dewar, Sidey, Morison, Peat, and Drummond, 1836.

Peterson, Harold. *The Man Who Invented Baseball.* New York: Charles Scribner's Sons, 1973.

Pomeroy, Sarah. *Women in Hellinistic Egypt.* New York: Schocken Books, 1984.

The Proceedings of a general court-martial, held at Cambridge, on Tuesday the twentieth of January; and continued by several adjournments to Wednesday the 25th of February, 1778: upon the trial of Colonel David Henley. Boston: J. Gill, 1778.

Radford, Peter F. "Women's Foot-Races in the Eighteenth and Nineteenth Centuries: A Popular and Widespread Practice." *Canadian Journal of History of Sport* 25, no. 1 (May 2004): 50–61.

"Railway Rambles." *Penny Magazine* 10 (October 23, 1841): 412–14.

"Review of New Books." *London Literary Gazette, and Journal of Belles Lettres*, no. 531 (March 24, 1827): 177–86.

Rebecca Nathan; or, a Daughter of Israel. London: James Burrill, 1844.

Ross, Alan S. C. "Pize-ball." *Proceedings of the Leeds Philosophical and Literary Society* 13, pt. 2 (1968): 55–77.

"The Royal Academy. Exhibition, 1854." *Art-Journal* 16 (June 1, 1854): 157–72.

Salzmann, Rev. Christian Gotthilf. *Elements of Morality for the Use of Children.* Vol. 1. London: J. Johnson, 1790.

Sawyer, Frederick Ernest. "Sussex Folklore and Customs Connected with the Seasons." *Sussex Archaeological Collections, Relating to the History and Antiquity of the County* 33 (1883): 237–60.

Seccombe, Thomas. "Moor, Edward (1771–1848), writer on Hindu mythology." *Oxford Dictionary of National Biography.* March 13, 2018. http://www.oxforddnb.com/view/10.1093/ref:odnb/9780198614128.001.0001/odnb-9780198614128-e-19089.

"Sights of Books." *London Literary Gazette, and Journal of Belles Lettres*, no. 506 (September 30, 1826): 616–17.

[Society of Gentlemen]. *A General Dictionary of the English Language.* London: J. and R. Fuller, 1768.

Strutt, Joseph. *Glig-gamena Angel-deod; or, The Sports and Pastimes of the People of England.* 2nd ed. London: Printed by T. Bensley, for White and Co. [and 7 more], 1810.

Swanton, E. W. *Barclay's World of Cricket.* 2nd ed. London: Wm. Collins and Sons, 1980.

Swinnock, George. *The Life and Death of Mr. Tho. Wilson, Minister of Maidstone in the County of Kent.* London, 1672.

Tate, George. *The History of the Borough, Castle, and Barony of Alnwick.* Vol. 1. Alnwick, Northumberland: Henry Hunter Blair, 1866.

Thompson, J. O. *Dr. Salter of Tolleshunt D'Arcy in the County of Essex.* London: John Lane, Bodley Head, 1933.

"Three Years at Cambridge." *Monthly Magazine; or, British Register*, n.s., 7, no. 41 (May 1829): 463–73.

Tomalin, Claire. *Jane Austen: A Life.* New York: Alfred A. Knopf, 1997.

Touchstone, Timothy [pseud.]. *Trifler*, no. 29 (December 13, 1788): 371–80.

Tucker, George Holbert. *Jane Austen the Woman: Some Biographical Insights.* Basingstoke, Hampshire: Palgrave Macmillan, 1994.

Underdown, David. *Start of Play: Cricket and Culture in Eighteenth-Century England.* London: Alan Lane/Penguin Press, 2000.

"Upon Sticks." *Belgravia: A London Magazine*, 3rd ser., 7 (September 1875): 433–36.

Valentine, Laura. *The Home Book for Young Ladies.* London: Frederick Warne, 1876.

Walker, J. M. *Rounders, Quoits, Bowls, Skittles, and Curling.* London: George Bell & Sons, 1892.

Ward, John Montgomery. *Base-ball: How to Become a Player.* Philadelphia: Athletic, 1888.

Welsh, Charles. *A Bookseller of the Last Century.* New York: Griffith, Farran, Okeden & Welsh, 1885.

Woodruff, C. H. "The Origin of Cricket." *Baily's Magazine of Sports and Pastimes* 76, no. 497 (July 1901): 50–54.

Wright, Joseph, ed. *The English Dialect Dictionary.* Vol. 1. London: Henry Frowde, 1898.

Young, Rev. J. *Literary Recreations; or, Scenes from Real Life.* London: Whittaker, 1833.

Youthful Sports. London: Darton and Harvey, 1801.

Index

Page numbers in italic indicate illustrations; page numbers with "t" indicate tables